INDIAN TREATY-MAKING POLICY IN THE
UNITED STATES AND CANADA, 1867–1877

Indian Treaty-Making Policy in the United States and Canada, 1867–1877

Jill St. Germain

University of Nebraska Press

Lincoln and London

© 2001 by the University of Nebraska Press
All rights reserved
Manufactured in the United States of America
⊗
First Nebraska paperback printing: 2004

Library of Congress Cataloging-in-Publication Data
St. Germain, Jill, 1962–
Indian treaty-making policy in the United States
and Canada, 1867–1877 / Jill St. Germain.
p. cm.
Includes bibliographical references and index.
ISBN 0-8032-4282-4 (cloth : alk. paper)
1. Indians of North Amercia – Treaties – History.
2. Treaty-making power – United States – History.
3. Treaty-making power – Canada-History.   I. Title.
KF8205.S714   2001
323.1 197073—dc21
00-060786

ISBN 0-8032-9323-2 (paper: alk. paper)

To Kerry Abel and Peter King

Contents

Illustrations

Maps

Tables

Acknowledgments

Writing is a solitary task and the author alone bears responsibility for the organization, construction, and expression of all that follows, including any flaws or failings attributable to oversight, error, or resistance to good advice. The will to persist in such an endeavor, however, and the endless refinement of the product are sustained by the interest and inspiration of many.

Del Muise first suggested to me the idea of a comparative study of Indian treaty policy as a way to combine my research interests in Canadian, American, and Native history. Later, when I was procrastinating on revisions, he threatened to break my legs if I did not soon submit the manuscript to a publisher. I did.

Ruth Pritchard, Virginia Elwood, Lise Hughes, and Carol Hartry read early drafts of this book just because I had written it. They responded with enthusiasm and delight even beyond that expected from friends and relatives. I am especially indebted to Ruth Pritchard—thanks for being there in 1999. Sonya Lipsett-Rivera and Rod Phillips offered me the benefit of their experience in publishing. Carter Elwood, not only read the manuscript with an exacting editorial eye but also cheerfully chauffeured me across the Prairies in search of relevant historical sites, despite the fact that he would rather have been in the mountains—any mountains. Others who read the manuscript and offered helpful suggestions include Dominique Marshall, Peter King, Roger Nichols, Margaret Connell-Szasz, and an anonymous reader for the University of Nebraska Press. Kevin Brock made the copyediting process a pleasurable one, and the text is all the better for his contributions.

I relied heavily on the services of the staff of the Interlibrary Loans office at Carleton University Library, and they found everything I needed. Frances Montgomery helped me dust off the microfiche of the *Congressional Globe* and supplied answers about government documents. Joan White solved a few technical problems for me and let me use her typewriter. I exploited the resources of the National Archives of Canada and found in the National Library a wonderful collection of United States government documents. The Ottawa Public Library periodicals department offered me easy access to pristine editions of the *Canadian Illustrated News* and enthusiastic support for my work. At Athabasca University, Judith Hughes provided me with a number of important articles.

I came to the study of Canadian history belatedly and through the unlikely medium of television. I am, therefore, indebted to Gordon Tootoosis, whose brilliant portrayal of Canada's most compelling villain on CBC's "North of 60" fired my interest in this nation's history in a way no book or teacher ever had.

Kerry Abel supervised my thesis in Canadian Studies on which this book is based, though I have profited from our association in many ways well beyond this project. She has celebrated my discovery of Canadian history with an enthusiasm equal to my own. Peter King has long nurtured my passion for American history, and I have long admired his insatiable quest for knowledge. This book is dedicated to them.

Introduction

In the Speech from the Throne delivered in early February 1877, the usually parsimonious government of Prime Minister Alexander Mackenzie defended a recently negotiated Indian treaty despite provisions that were admittedly "of a somewhat onerous and exceptional nature." Although the terms of Treaty 6 would require considerable monetary expense, the government asserted, "the Canadian policy is nevertheless the cheapest, ultimately, if we compare the results with those of other countries." Canada's approach was "above all a humane, just and Christian policy." In case the point still eluded the parliamentary audience, a more explicit statement of justification was offered for the extraordinary expenses Canadian Indian treaty policy entailed: "Notwithstanding the deplorable war waged between the Indian tribes of the United States territories, and the Government of that country during the last year, no difficulty had arisen with the Canadian tribes living in the immediate vicinity of the scene of hostilities."[1] The implication that a large expenditure of funds was more desirable than a vicious plains war was an effective ploy, and the Mackenzie government can hardly be faulted for invoking the shadow of the American disaster at the Little Bighorn in June 1876 to counter accusations of extravagance.

But there was more to the government's imagery than the rationalization of a budgetary matter, although in the financially straitened circumstances of the 1870s a concern for economy was not unimportant. The comparison to the American experience satisfied a variety of constituencies, but more importantly it marked the beginning of one of the most deep-seated myths of the Canadian self-image. In historian J. R. Miller's words, this speech "nicely captured both the frugality of the Mackenzie government and Canadians' smugness about their Indian policy."[2] Canadians promoted their Indian policy as an intentionally benevolent one—"humane, just and Christian" by design. By implication, the American approach was none of these things. This attitude neatly dovetailed with the affirmation that Canada's Indian policy was deliberate, and it credited the Dominion government with specific decisions that accounted for the differences between the Canadian and American frontiers. In other words, Canada obviously made the wiser choices.

These blunt assertions of the superiority and distinctiveness of Canadian Indian policy have long haunted discussions of Indian relations in Canada and the United States. On the whole, historians—Canadian and American—have rejected these conclusions based on nineteenth-century observations, but little effort has been expended to prove the case. In 1965 Wilcomb Washburn, puzzled by the paradox of similarities in the two nations' Indian relations and yet their vastly different results, asked, "Was Canadian Indian policy more efficient, more moral, more beneficial than American Indian policy?"[3] He urged his colleagues to pursue the question, but without much success.

Although there have been few serious comparative studies of Indian policy, opinions on the subject abound. In a book on the American Indian frontier, Robert Utley refuted the notion of any superiority in Canadian policy, observing that Canada's single violent outburst, the 1885 Northwest Rebellion, was "explained less by enlightened Canadian policies than by the vastness of the land in relation to the Indian and white population."[4] He agreed with nineteenth-century U.S. secretary of the interior Carl Schurz that when Canada experienced the emigration and railroad pressures the United States faced, then "Canadians, too, would have their day of reckoning."[5] Robert Wooster, in a study of the U.S. Army and Indian policy in the post–Civil War West, identified a whole series of factors for the absence of conflict in Canada, among them emigration, geographical barriers, and economic considerations, as well as the presence of the Northwest Mounted Police and the Métis population.[6] Acknowledging the discrepancy between Canada and the United States in the extent of violence with Indians, Christine Bolt observed that "demography and history were still on the side of the Canadians."[7] Canadian historians have not significantly challenged these explanations. J. R. Miller also invoked economic concerns and a sparse population as important elements and added that Canadian history had impressed the attitude that "Indians were not ferocious and implacable enemies but cooperative people with whom it was possible to do business."[8] For Olive Dickason economics prevailed since "Canada was not in a financial position to repeat the costly frontier wars of the United States."[9]

Such opinions are suggestive as to why differences existed between the Canadian and American experiences, but they are neither conclusive nor adequate. There is no denying that emigration, for instance, or the lack of it in Canada, was an important element in violence and Indian relations. But emigration and contact did not have to lead to bloodshed, as later Canadian experience demonstrates. As well, the suggestion that the 1885 Northwest Rebellion mirrored any of the explosions on the American Great Plains would be an exaggeration of that event and the role of Canadian Indians in it.

The other glaring difference between Canadian and American Indian policy in the West, then and now, has been the land question. A cursory glance at a map of reserve holdings in both nations today reveals that all Canadian Indian reserves combined constitute less than one-half of the Navajo reservation in Arizona alone.[10] This situation derives directly from Indian treaty policy in the post–Civil War/post-Confederation era, apparently from policies that many historians assert to be the same or similar. Yet external factors such as demography, economics, and geography fail to explain this land discrepancy.

To emphasize elements such as geography or emigration is to suggest that the contact between the races made conflict inevitable. It was, in this view, only the absence of emigrants in Canada, or the vast distances there, that precluded violence. This interpretation echoes the long-discarded views of historians like George F. G. Stanley, who posited a battle between "civilized" and "savage" to explain the development of western Canada.[11] It also overlooks the active role of the participants—white and Indian—in the shaping of subsequent events.

These problems and discrepancies are more satisfactorily addressed in a study explicitly devoted to a comparison of Canadian and American Indian policy. Indian treaties serve as an appropriate focus for such a comparison, as they were the primary instruments of Indian relations in both British North America and the United States from the eighteenth century. These documents also provided the framework in which Indian relations in the West, in both Canada and the United States, were pursued during the 1860s and 1870s.

Treaties lend themselves well to comparison and, therefore, to a focused exploration of Canadian and American Indian policy. In the 1860s the United States clashed with Indians in Idaho, Oregon, New Mexico, Arizona, and Texas but, as Robert Utley has observed, "developments in these far-off places did not much affect debates on Indian policy. Easterners seemed only dimly aware of hostilities beyond the Great Plains. Ever since [the] Sand Creek [massacre], relations with the Plains Indians had almost alone shaped public opinion and government policy." [12] At Medicine Lodge Creek in October 1867 and at Fort Laramie in April and May 1868, the United States concluded a series of important treaties with the peoples of the southern and northern plains, and in doing so set Indian policy for the nation.[13] Canada negotiated the seven Numbered Treaties with the Indians of the West, from Lake Superior to the Rockies, between 1871 and 1877. Like the American documents, these agreements set the stage for Canadian Indian policy in the West. The Treaties of Medicine Lodge and Fort Laramie and the Numbered Treaties are geographically and chronologically compatible. But they also embodied reserve and civilization programs, the central features of both Canadian and American Indian policy, thus making them ideal subjects for a comparative study.

This book, in focusing on a comparison of Canadian and American treaty policy in the West between 1867 and 1877, addresses a number of issues not adequately served by strictly national studies. A comparative approach clearly illustrates the common features of Indian policy in the two countries. It also facilitates the identification of critical differences in policy development that help explain the discrepancies in experience and results, especially the frequency of violence and the size of reserve land holdings. Perhaps more importantly, a comparative examination of treaty policy places the players at center stage, dislodging those contributing factors of emigration, geography, and economy (among others) that have long distracted interested commentators. By concentrating on the actors, the decisions they made, and the directions they chose to take, it is possible to avoid the lure of inevitability, which so often shadows discussions of Indian relations.

The subject of this book is a comparison of government policy. Emphasis is placed on the reasons why the governments embarked on treaty-making ventures in the 1860s and 1870s, how they conducted those negotiations, and what terms resulted. Clearly this is but one side of a process that involved not only white negotiators but also active and influential Indian participants. The decision to deal only with the government side is deliberate, in large part because comparative treatments of Canadian and American Indian policy are as yet few and far between. In *Indians in the United States and Canada*, Roger Nichols has provided an overall framework in which to pursue comparative studies of Indian policy, and others have made isolated contributions, but comparative history in general remains a frontier.[14] One of the difficulties in pursuing such a study is the necessity of digesting the history of two nations at once. This task is complicated, in the case of Indian relations, by the different directions taken by scholars in each country. American historians have focused on the development of Indian policy in specific periods and on the major forces in that policy, particularly the U.S. Army and Christian humanitarian reformers.[15] Less attention has been paid to the treaties, the only comprehensive title being Francis Prucha's *American Indian Treaties*. Studies of the Treaties of Medicine Lodge and Fort Laramie are not common.[16] In Canada, attention has been divided between investigations of Indian policy in the West and examinations of treaty making and implementation.[17] Canadian historians have been less preoccupied with the major influences on Indian policy, and there is little to compare to American treatment of institutional players.[18] Because the material addresses different issues in each country, there are any number of gaps to be filled even in a study of government policy alone.

This is not to minimize or dismiss the other half of the picture. In Canada and the United States, Indians were willing and active participants in treaty negotiations, and Indian interests and pressures shaped the process and the terms in both countries. Indian perspectives and actions were as complex and important as those of the white governments involved. A proper understanding of them, a task deemed outside the scope of this undertaking, would require as thorough a knowledge of the several Indian nations represented at the treaty councils as of the Canadian and American governments themselves. Until both sides of the process have been examined and combined, however, the picture will remain incomplete. Nevertheless, aboriginal perspectives have not been ignored—Indian input is acknowledged and detailed where it sheds light on government policies and approaches.[19] The secondary role given to the Indians herein reflects only the needs of this study, not the real influence of Indians in the process.

This work is intended as an initial foray into a sparsely populated field, that of comparative analysis of Canadian and American Indian policy. In juxtaposing the treaty-making policies of the two nations in 1867–68 and the 1870s, I have responded to Wilcomb Washburn's call to determine where and how Canada and the United States differed in the application of their treaty policy and to assess their efforts. This study also challenges the assertions made by the Canadian government in 1877 of the superiority and distinctiveness of Canada's policy, raising doubts about which nation may more legitimately claim to have adopted a policy that was "humane, just and Christian."

INDIAN TREATY-MAKING POLICY IN THE
UNITED STATES AND CANADA, 1867–1877

1 Treaty-Making Precedents and Progress

The Royal Proclamation of 1763, issued in the wake of the Seven Years War (1755–63) by a harried British government, represented the foundation on which the practice of Indian treaty making in both the American republic and, a century later, the Dominion of Canada rested. Although certain aspects of this document became core to treaty-making practices in both nations, common history did not guarantee a parallel course in the development of Indian policy.

The proclamation reserved the right to negotiate for land title exclusively to the Crown and also insisted that such negotiations be open, public affairs with as broad a representation of the Indians involved as possible.[1] British concerns, as manifested in this document, were entirely pragmatic. Colonial relations with the various Indian tribes and nations in the trans-Appalachian frontier were fractious and problematic, a situation that had only exacerbated the fragile strategic position of Britain during the late war. Anxious to placate Indians whom it could not possibly control or defeat, Britain offered at least tacit recognition of Indian possessory rights in unceded territory. The restrictive provisions on the extinguishment of that land title, on the other hand, were aimed more directly at the Americans in an attempt to minimize colonial opportunities to cheat the Indians, thereby reducing the potential for friction and, not incidentally, British frontier expenses.[2] The proclamation offended American sensibilities, particularly those of western land speculators, among them men such as Benjamin Franklin and George Washington, who would soon gain fame for their revolutionary exploits.

A further provision in the proclamation disseminated colonial dissatisfaction somewhat more broadly. The establishment of the Proclamation Line, a north-south boundary approximating the crest of the Appalachian Mountains, restricted colonial expansion to the eastern slopes of that range. Again the British were concerned with practical matters. Colonial American infiltration of western territories had resulted in the conflict that sparked the Seven Years War, and Britain almost lost the ensuing contest once it spilled over onto the international stage. Almost bankrupt, unable to afford a frontier military presence that could enforce peace with the Indians and good behavior among the colonists, and exasperated by American refusal to provide either manpower or financial contributions for the upkeep of imperial troops, Britain opted for an exclusionary policy instead.[3]

Although the measure was one of expediency, never meant to provide a permanent solution to either the westward expansion of the colonies or the "Indian problem," Americans took exception to the proclamation.[4] It obstructed the play of both free enterprise in the form of land speculation and the 'natural' impulses of expansion and settlement. As long as British authority remained intact, Americans could only grumble under the restrictions. When that authority was ousted little more than a decade later, the American course, which continued to be dictated in part by the tenets of the 1763 proclamation, brought a number of adjustments to the policy.

The Quebec Act of 1774, another measure of British expediency aimed at resolving the problems of administration in Quebec and the western territories, only exacerbated American resentment. Chafing under perceived injustice and the punitive measures imposed in the wake of the Boston Tea Party in December 1773, Americans understood more ominous things of the Quebec Act that, by unfortunate coincidence, came down at the same time. Designated one of the Intolerable Acts, the Quebec Act was a direct cause of the American Revolutionary War, which erupted the following year. The offensive element was the extension of the jurisdiction of the colony of Quebec to the Old Northwest, the territory beyond the Appalachians that Britain had won in 1763 and into which Americans sought to expand. The change in jurisdiction brought with it the dual pariahs of French civil law and Roman Catholicism. These, along with the appointed council that governed the colony, were interpreted by Americans, whose sensitivity to infringements on their legal rights and political freedoms was already at a fever pitch, as confirmation of a conspiracy to enslave them all.[5] The fact that British troops relieved of their responsibilities in the West were garrisoned in Boston, a violation of the British tradition of no standing army in peacetime, did not help matters. British concerns, as manifested in both the Royal Proclamation of 1763 and the Quebec Act of 1774, and American reactions to these documents illuminate the future course of Indian policy and Indian treaty making in the two nations that would come to occupy the North American continent.

Britain was consistent in a policy of expediency and economy. These elements, along with an admirable capacity for delaying actions not of immediate benefit to the central government, were the hallmarks of the nascent British administration. The policy initiatives for the trans-Appalachian West during this decade contain the origins and precedents of the approach and policy adopted by the Dominion of Canada a century later, when that nation was confronted by the problems of its own West in the abruptly acquired and vast unknown of the Northwest Territory.

National weakness and pecuniary considerations in the early days of independence dictated that the United States make no abrupt changes in Indian policy. National security indicated a conciliatory and cautious approach to the several powerful Indian nations in adjacent regions, and Americans turned to the practices enunciated in the proclamation for lack of an alternative, not out of newfound commitment to principles they had rejected in the revolutionary struggle. Jurisdiction over the extinguishment of Indian title was vested in the federal government to resolve a constitutional states' rights issue, not to impede speculation.[6] As a practical means to an end, the United States also retained the policy tool of treaty making, which had flourished in the decade prior to 1775 as a means to establish the exact contours of the Proclamation Line. Independence from Britain meant, however, independence from this artificially imposed barrier as well. After 1783, Americans were free to act on their own views in these matters. The superiority of the settler's claim to that of the Indian had only the pragmatic considerations of personal security to keep it in check, and the new national government proved reluctant to impose any restrictions other than reserving to itself the right to make formal arrangements with the Indians over title to the land. This selective application of British policy in the expanding American West would have lethal consequences, not only for individuals on the western frontier, but eventually for Indian treaty making itself.

Until the War of 1812, both Britain and the United States had good reason to continue the practice of making treaties with various North American Indian nations, namely their rivalry with one another on the continent. In the aftermath of the American Revolutionary War, Britain felt obliged to resettle both American Loyalists and Indian allies, largely the Six Nations, driven from the newly formed United States. Plans to establish Loyalists in Quebec, another measure of expediency designed to alleviate a British dilemma in that colony, failed to gain momentum and, while significant numbers of these refugees went to Nova Scotia, many turned to lands north of Lake Ontario and along the St. Lawrence in what would become in 1791 the colony of Upper Canada. Six Nations refugees also sought lands in these areas. To accommodate them, Britain initiated the first of a series of land cession treaties with the indigenous population there. This move was thought to have some strategic advantage, for former allies and disgruntled expatriates might be expected to serve as a buffer against the new and unpredictable nation to the south.

Britain posed a potentially greater threat to its former colonies on the Atlantic seaboard. Although bound by the Treaty of Paris (1783) to remove themselves from the Old Northwest, which they had formally relinquished to the United States, the British continued to occupy the territory until a second agreement, Jay's Treaty, in 1795, compelled their departure. The Americans, wary of British motives as well as of Indian allegiance, could not rest easy in their own Indian relations even then. As long as the two countries remained at odds, there was a role for Indian nations to play as military allies. Diplomatic and commercial clashes arising out of the Napoleonic Wars continued to strain relations between the two English-speaking nations. American suspicions of British-Indian conspiracies became reality when these antagonisms mushroomed into the War of 1812, and the Indian confederacy forged under the leadership of Tecumseh arrayed itself on the British side.

But even in this moment when the worst fears of Americans were realized, when Britain found common ground with Indian compatriots, and Indian nations brokered the balance of power in yet another European contest on North American soil, the relationship between Indian and non-Indian was changing. In the wake of the war, the British and Americans patched up their differences with an alarming ease and, while a deep distrust of Britain remained in some quarters, fears of another direct assault on American nationhood largely subsided. The British, too, relaxed their concerns for the security of British North America, or perhaps merely lost interest in colonial misadventures there. Inured to the habit of treating Indians as either potential allies or a force to be reckoned with, both nations only slowly came to the realization that the strategic significance of Indians in their administrative operations was in decline.

This revelation came to the Americans in a gradual recognition of their own growing strength, both in general terms and vis-à-vis Indians in particular. It was exemplified in the 1810s and 1820s in the career of Indian-fighting general, later president, Andrew Jackson. Significantly, both a greater interest in the future of Indians within American territory and questions about the validity of the still youthful treaty system began in this era. As was usually the case when the matter intruded on official British consciousness, it coalesced on the issue of economics. Unlike the United States, however, British policymakers saw no reason to question the practice of treaty making even as they implemented a change in the direction of Indian policy.

Administrative responsibility for Indian affairs followed a parallel, if unsynchronized, course in the United States and British North America. The U.S. Constitution stipulated Indian affairs as a federal responsibility. Control of treaty making and commercial relations was divided between the president and Congress, but responsibility for day-to-day administration lay, from the founding of the Republic, with the secretary of war. A similar situation prevailed in British North America, where England directed Indian affairs until 1860 and responsibility resided in the secretary of state for war and the colonies. When military exigencies faded in importance, the appropriateness of military authorities for the management of Indian affairs diminished.

Britain moved first in transferring responsibility out of the hands of military officers, making the shift to civilian control within the same department in 1830. At the same time, Britain inaugurated a policy of "civilization" toward the Indians. Both changes applied only to those Indians under direct British jurisdiction and excluded the peoples in Rupert's Land, who remained in British eyes the responsibility of a commercial corporation, the Hudson's Bay Company, which administered this vast western territory.

As always in matters of Indian relations, Britain's policy initiatives were spawned by economic considerations. In 1818 Britain unloaded the cost of land cessions in Upper Canada onto the colonial government there, prompting a shift from lump-sum payments to annuities, which better accorded with the straitened state of colonial coffers.[7] Maintaining diplomatic relations with Indians involved an annual distribution of presents, an expense from which the penny-pinching imperial government wished to rid itself. Eager for a solution, British officials embraced a civilization policy with assimilation as a long-term goal and suggested an immediate alteration in the nature of the annual gifts, according to which "ammunition was to be replaced gradually by decreasing grants of cash."[8]

This impulse to shed what the British increasingly perceived as an economic liability characterized their approach to Indian affairs for the next forty years. In 1860 Britain relinquished authority for Indian affairs to the Canadian colonies and in 1867 divested itself entirely of responsibility, saddling the new Dominion with the burden. The status that Britain thereby invested in both the Dominion of Canada and Indian relations is indicated by the fact that the imperial government retained control of what it deemed the more significant administrative jurisdictions of external affairs and defense. Canada was not yet prepared to handle matters involving international obligation, and Indian affairs were clearly not included in this category. In 1869 Britain exercised its last official duty to Indians in North America during the negotiations for the acquisition of Rupert's Land, exacting from Canada a promise to abide by the time-honored principles of the Proclamation of 1763 in its dealings with the Indians of that region, who came thereby, for the first time, under the jurisdiction of parliamentary government.[9]

Canada, operating under the precedent of recent British administrative practice and having no military option in any case, assigned Indian affairs to the secretary of state for the provinces. It was under this authority that Canada negotiated its first treaties, concluded with Indians in the Red River region of the lately purchased Northwest Territory in 1871. A slight administrative adjustment in 1873 brought forth the Department of the Interior, to which Indian affairs were promptly transferred. The Office of Indian Affairs, a small branch in the large department devoted to, among other things, the administration of Crown lands, oversaw the day-to-day needs of Indian matters throughout Canada as well as supervising the implementation and administration of the Numbered Treaties with the Indians in the Canadian West. Well into the 1870s Canada's Indian affairs operated in an almost schizophrenic manner. In eastern Canada, where treaty making for the purpose of extinguishing land title no longer had practical applications, a policy of "assimilation through civilization" was in progress. In western Canada, where land control was the fundamental concern, treaty making was the first order of business and civilization merited little, if any, official attention. Canada, like Britain before it, sought to avoid problems rather than confront them and blithely followed the path dictated by economy and expediency, and characterized by official indifference.

Different motivations marked the development of American Indian policy. Like the British, the United States after the War of 1812 lost interest in the strategic value or threat of aboriginal nations. Although Indians continued to menace individual Americans and their aspirations, they no longer counted as a real danger to national existence. But Americans could not just ignore the Indians. They were actively seizing lands from these people and needed a justification for doing so. Civilization was an easy answer. The idea of "civilizing" the Indians as a national policy had emerged at the turn of the century in the musings of President Thomas Jefferson, and in 1819 the concept found more concrete expression in the establishment of a ten-thousand-dollar "civilization fund" dedicated to uplifting the "savages." [10]

In contrast to Britain, however, the United States could not simply shift from one policy to another. A major element in the American context, almost entirely absent in British North America, was an exploding population base. Complicating matters even more, Americans were individually, at a state level, and nationally unrestrained expansionists. The nineteenth century saw manifestations of each of these as would-be settlers expanded to fill the continent, as states sought to expel Indian populations from reservations within their borders, and as the nation itself swallowed whole territories that had once existed under the jurisdiction of European nations as diverse as Spain, France, Russia, and Britain. Operating under this mentality, there was no possibility of the leisurely piecemeal land surrenders obtained in Canada under British authority between 1815 and 1850. In the United States, settlers did not wait for the government to clear title to the land. They just took it.

Enjoying a growing spirit of national self-confidence—buoyed by Andrew Jackson's victories against the Creeks at Horseshoe Bend and the British at New Orleans in 1814 as well as his successful seizure of Florida from the Spanish in 1819—Americans were rapidly losing regard for the Indians, who from before the dawn of the Republic had existed in their midst. Reform organizations promoted "civilization" of the tribes, but pragmatism dictated the settlement of the land controversy first, and "removal" was the preferred solution.

Because the expediency that drove Indian policy in Britain, and later Canada, was largely economic, attitudes toward treaty making in which land acquisition was the primary purpose were not directly premised on the relative strength of the parties involved. Britain wanted to disentangle itself from financial obligations to the Indians and to escape new commitments. Avoiding conflict was an integral aspect of this concern, and the British pursued a policy designed to achieve their ends and keep the peace. Because of these priorities, Britain had no need to flex its military muscles. This was not the case in the United States. That nation had only reluctantly embraced the colonial precedents of British Indian policy, and once the exigencies that had forced that approach—military weakness in the early national period—had dissipated, strength was everything. Americans were less concerned with the expense than with an assertion of power and authority. With the realization that it was no longer necessary for national survival to placate Indian demands, interest in doing so began to decline.

American opinion on treaties diverged abruptly into two streams of thought. Attachment to legal niceties based on colonial precedent and national tradition, given voice in the Supreme Court judgments of Chief Justice John Marshall in 1823, 1831, and 1832, ran headlong into the conviction of "might makes right," which prevailed in practice.[11] Although Marshall argued against the constitutionality of forceful relocation in a case brought by the Cherokee Nation, Indians—north and south—were removed from their homes east of the Mississippi River to what was designated the permanent Indian Territory in the trans-Mississippi West. National habit and the Supreme Court required that the land surrenders preceding this removal be accomplished by treaty, and President Jackson acceded in form if not in spirit. The treaties of removal accorded technically with the traditional principles of treaty-making practice, but undeniable elements of coercion, an explicit and ruthless application of the technique of "divide and conquer," and in many cases a simple matter of *fait accompli* land possession, cast a pall on the legitimacy of the proceedings, leading many to question the legitimacy of the treaty-making process itself. American contempt was already apparent in the cynical commentary of the governor of Georgia: "Treaties were expedients by which ignorant, intractable, and savage people were induced without bloodshed to yield up what civilized people had the right to possess by virtue of that command of the Creator delivered to man upon his formation— be fruitful, multiply, and replenish the earth, and subdue it."[12]

To coordinate the conclusion of removal treaties and then to implement their terms, the Office of Indian Affairs was created in 1824. Although its personnel were civilians, the office and the commissioner remained under the administrative authority of the secretary of war. Removal was in the best of circumstances an unpleasant affair, and the army was the only force in the United States capable of managing the round-ups, policing, and enforcement involved in what were in some cases thousand-mile treks across the continent.

Throughout the removal process the incipient commitment to the "civilization" of the Indians had not faded. It was, in fact, used as a justification for the policy, with President Jackson himself arguing that Indians should be allowed to advance to a "civilized" state in isolation, away from the vices of white society to which they would be vulnerable until so-called civilization took hold.[13] Once removal had been carried out, neither the government nor the Indian reform movement forgot its duty, continuing to finance the civilization fund and other missionary endeavors in the Indian Territory.[14]

Even in this, however, the Americans could not manage the uncomplicated transition Britain had implemented to the north. British missionary efforts and civilization measures among the Indians operated in an environment largely free from outside distraction. In the United States, the reform movement had other concerns, and until the abolition of slavery, that issue absorbed the bulk of the energy of the tidal wave of evangelical reform that swept the nation during the antebellum period. Concern for Indians, along with interest in women's rights, temperance, prison reform, and a vast number of other causes, did not cease to exist, but they all played a poor second fiddle to the antislavery campaign. For the moment at least, Indians were secure behind the "permanent" barrier of the Mississippi.

The complications of and resistance engendered by removal were not resolved until the 1840s, by which time the U.S. government realized the absurdity of military responsibility for the essentially civilian tasks required of the Office of Indian Affairs. In 1849 that office was transferred to the newly created Department of the Interior, a catch-all cabinet post, the conglomerate responsibilities of which included the disposition of the public domain. Finally, American Indian affairs had ended up in the U.S. equivalent of the civilian hands in which Britain had placed authority nineteen years earlier.

Circumstances once more overtook the Americans, reinforcing the fundamental premises of national strength, individual aspirations, and the limits of governmental authority where individual freedom was concerned. Between 1845 and 1848 the United States grew by more than half. Texas was admitted to the Union in 1845, and the settlement of the northwest boundary dispute brought the Oregon Country under U.S. jurisdiction in 1846. The peace of Guadalupe-Hidalgo in 1848, yielding up the lands of Arizona, New Mexico, Utah, California, and parts of what would become Colorado and Wyoming, along with the 1854 Gadsden Purchase completed the continental landscape of the United States. Despite the expansion of American authority over tens of thousands of new Indian peoples, the transfer to civilian authority went ahead. This was not, in the very immediate circumstances of 1849, necessarily a contradiction in policy, because the assumption prevailed for part of the year at least that the trans-Mississippi Indian frontier would remain inviolate except for a trickle of emigrants to Oregon. Even the flood of cross-country traffic in the summer of 1849, occasioned by the discovery of gold at Sutter's Mill in California in January 1848, did not immediately dash the illusion. Emigrants poured west, but they were headed for the Far West and had little time for what was considered, at first glance, territory unsuitable for white habitation and christened "the Great American Desert." There was some application for traditional Indian policy practices in the negotiation of rights of transit along the Oregon and California Trails, but the American government had little inkling as yet of the inadequacy of the Department of the Interior's civilian administration for the Indian challenge that lay ahead.

In British North America during the early nineteenth century, Indians had become an economic burden in the government's eyes. Anxious to divest themselves of this problem, British administrators embraced a long-term policy of civilization for the Indians under their immediate authority, gradually shifting responsibility to the North American colonies under the guise of expanded colonial self-administration. The treaty-making process continued unabated, however, and even broadened in scope with the Robinson Huron and Superior Treaties of 1850. For the first time large tracts of land beyond the immediate needs of Upper Canadian settlement were surrendered by the Indians involved, and the policy of setting aside "reserves" of land from territory just ceded rather than purchasing land elsewhere was inaugurated. The pace of expansion and colonization in British North America permitted treaty making and civilization measures to coexist. Because Britain and later the colonial legislature sought to secure land title before settlement pressures forced their hand and had the luxury to do so, the treaty-making process remained largely unquestioned, successfully serving the government's purposes.

This was not so in the United States, where treaty making and civilization efforts were subsumed by more demanding national developments. A growing crisis over the "national sin" of slavery marginalized ideas of the "civilization" of the Indians. It was instead the ever-growing, ever-expanding population that recognized the Pacific Ocean as its only limit and identified the Indians as a natural obstacle, akin to the Rocky Mountains, that directed the course of U.S. Indian treaty making in the antebellum era. The practice did not cease, and in fact, between 1848 and 1867 the United States signed more than one hundred treaties with various Indian parties. But it was increasingly a legal formality effected by the federal government, often in the wake of dust churned up by settlers anxious to take advantage of new lands and later by railroad interests that made a connection to California, admitted to statehood in 1850, a priority.

National realities soon intruded on the casual decision to transfer Indian affairs from military to civilian control. The acquisition of the West and the stream of white emigrants thundering across the plains raised the potential for renewed conflict between white and Indian. Until the 1860s, while the Plains Indians faced intrusion on their lands and disruption of their game, they generally encountered white settlement only at trading posts and military forts. Still, incidents occurred and the realization dawned on officialdom that the military had an important and growing role in Indian relations in the West. As long as relations remained peaceful, which they did, surprisingly, except for Texas, until the late 1850s, the potential jurisdictional conflict was in abeyance. When serious disturbances began to erupt, fueled by Indian responses to the same arrogant and obnoxious attitudes toward them that had characterized American settlers from colonial days, the administrative conflict became overt. In British North America, Indian affairs were a burden to be shed. In the United States it was a much fought-for responsibility. This conflict, as much as the violence that precipitated it, impeded and obstructed what was to become in the post–Civil War years a gripping national reform impulse that made a priority of the "civilization" of the Indians.[15] British and later Canadian Indian policy was a more compartmentalized affair, where treaty making and civilization were seen as equally legitimate and useful practices, depending on the circumstances. This was not possible in the United States, where both policies were practiced simultaneously and increasingly at odds with each other. This friction, exacerbated by a bitter jurisdictional dispute originating in very real military conflict, eroded the already questionable practice of treaty making.

Britain and Canada could afford the treaty process. Focused on the acquisition of land title, untroubled by complications of overwhelming power, unrestrained expansion, and military conflict, treaty making continued to serve a purpose, and to serve it successfully. In the United States the formal practice of treaty making, bolstered by the Marshall decisions, remained an integral element of Indian relations but was increasingly problematic. The national government may have been committed, by tradition and the perceived restrictions of the Constitution, to treaty making, but the average American on the western frontier had passed it by.[16] To remain effective instruments, treaties had to do something tangible, as they still did in British North America. Given the violence that erupted on the American frontier in the 1860s, an obvious role for treaty making was at hand in the negotiation of peace settlements. Thus, unlike the situation in Canada, where the process entered the age of national expansion virtually intact in purpose to its original formulation in the Proclamation of 1763, to survive as an institution in the United States treaty making had to change functions. It also had to work.

2 Treaty-Making Problems

In 1867 the Dominion of Canada was born in Confederation and the United States initiated the final round of Indian treaty making in its history. Within four years, Canada too would embark on treaty negotiations, the most ambitious ever undertaken in British North American Indian relations. Ironically, the treaties negotiated by the Americans in 1867 and 1868 were instrumental in the demise of the treaty system in the United States in 1871, the year Canada concluded the first of the Numbered Treaties. As the American Republic was discarding the tool that had been a central component in its Indian relations for almost a century, the Dominion was inaugurating its own Indian policy by embracing that same form of diplomacy in the Prairie West. Closer scrutiny dispels the irony, however, for the two processes were by then very different in purpose if not in format. It was not that Canada was behind in the theory of treaty making, although the practice in British North America had not, in fact, changed as dramatically in a century. It was more a matter that in the 1870s Canadians still perceived a utility for treaties, whereas in the United States a consensus had been reached that treaties, as a means to deal with Indians, had outlived their usefulness.

The American system of making treaties with Indians disintegrated, in the most literal explanation of events, as a result of a power struggle between the Senate and the House of Representatives. But the conflict was not just about power — or was perhaps only incidentally so — for the resolution of the struggle in 1871 left the Senate's treaty authority virtually untouched. The compromise solution accepted by both houses of Congress simply removed *Indians* from executive treaty-making powers. After the passage of House Bill 2615, the 1871 Indian appropriations legislation to which the compromise was attached, Indians ceased to be parties with whom the United States could legitimately make treaties. Arrangements between the two parties were henceforth known as "agreements" and subject to general congressional approval rather than the exclusive domain of the executive.

The controversy was one, therefore, not so much of treaties, but of Indian treaties. The system foundered only technically on the issue of who made the treaties. In truth, the troublesome element of the quarrel was that of the legitimacy of the practice as it applied to Indians. Questions started to surface as American national power began to assert itself, notably during the presidency of Andrew Jackson, but serious challenges were the hallmark of the 1860s. They culminated in the ratification and appropriation debates of the 1867–68 treaties, which were likely the most legitimately sponsored and well-founded Indian treaties in American history. The resulting furor brought down the treaty system nonetheless.

The vitriolic debates that ended in 1871 really began in 1865 over the ratification of treaties negotiated in that year with many of the same plains people who would be the focus of the Great Peace Commission of 1867–68. This first round in the debate established a climate of opinion that, even before the commission was created, boded ill for the future of its work.

The legitimacy of making Indian treaties was broached in many ways, but questions generally coalesced around three areas of concern: the attitudes and behavior of the executive branch—that is, the president and the Senate in "executive session"—in carrying out their constitutionally appointed duties; the competence and status of the Indians involved; and the actual procedures of treaty making on the ground in the West.

The Constitution was the source of legitimacy for treaty-making powers, but it was really very brief on the subject and not particularly explicit where Indians were concerned. Article 2, section 2, asserted that "He [the president] shall have Power, by and with the Consent of the Senate, to make Treaties, provided two-thirds of the Senators present concur." It was understood, rather than clearly stated, that Indians constituted a body with whom treaties could be made. Congressional understanding of that status relied on a second item in the Constitution. Article 1, section 8, described the powers of Congress, among them responsibility "To regulate Commerce with foreign Nations, and among the several States, and with the Indian Tribes." This appeared to place the Indians in a special category, perhaps comparable to that of foreign nations. Although the connection was not explicit, reference to constitutional principles impeded significant changes to official Indian status so long as policymakers interpreted these terms in this way, despite growing dissatisfaction with the practical implications.

Constitutional authority directed that the president play a major role in treaty making, but in practice where Indians were concerned this seldom happened. In the first hundred years of the republic's history, perhaps three presidents—George Washington, Andrew Jackson, and Ulysses S. Grant—took an active interest in the task.[1] Few others gave the matter more than a passing thought. Presidential disinterest might have been offset had the other branch of authority, the Senate in executive session, exercised its powers under Article 2, section 2. But in an indication of the languid attitude of officialdom toward Indian issues, the Senate chose, by and large, to abdicate that authority. "Advice and consent" dwindled to consent alone.[2] It was a frequent allegation by members of Congress after the Civil War that Indian treaties inevitably came up for ratification during the summer, making the closed-door councils required of executive session unbearable to senators sensitive to Washington heat waves, with the result that treaties were ratified with only a mere handful of the hardier senators present to pay attention.[3] This was hardly an appropriate attitude toward a procedure ostensibly as weighty as a treaty with a foreign nation. A doubt began to form. Perhaps the Senate was merely negligent, but it was also possible that such behavior was a pointed indication that Indian treaties did *not* carry the same significance as did other documents of a similar nature. More than one member of Congress denounced as "a farce" the practice of concluding an arrangement with the Indians "and bringing that treaty in here to be ratified as a high negotiation with a foreign Power."[4]

But the "farcical" nature of this treaty-making process extended beyond questionable ratification processes. Authority may have resided with the president and the Senate, but presidents never engaged in such negotiations and senators did only rarely. The secretary of war or of the interior might play a direct role if the negotiations took place in Washington, as they sometimes did, but lesser officials usually bore the brunt of such work. The commissioner of Indian Affairs shared the chore with Indian agents and superintendents, military officers, territorial governors, and others who were simply political appointees. Literally anyone could be assigned to the task. In early days the president might have made such appointments, but even this fell to lesser hands as time passed.[5] When Indian affairs were of little consequence to the nation and the treaty-making function insignificant, such patterns went unquestioned. But with the expansion of the role of treaties in the 1860s coupled with the increasingly sizable price tag that accompanied this broadening of function, criticism began to mount.

Once attention was focused on the practice, other elements also came under scrutiny, in particular the second party to treaties, the Indians. When in 1867 Congress contemplated the prospect of a conclusive treaty-making venture with the Plains Indians, two facts did not escape the notice of interested observers. The first was that there had already been two rounds of treaty talks with these peoples since the decade began, in 1861 and again in 1865–66. The other inescapable truth was that the United States had been involved in almost constant and increasingly bloody conflict with the very same peoples for much of this period. This led some members of Congress to question the effectiveness of treaty making as well as to speculate on why the Indians kept coming back to the bargaining table. To the cynical mind, it was the generosity of American presents and terms that drew them. "Peace lasts while your provisions last," Sen. William Stewart declared. "When the provisions run out, in order to get more the Indians commence murdering."[6] Disdain for such a result was not limited to Congress. Gen. John Pope, departmental commander of the Division of the Missouri, which oversaw much of the Plains Indian territory, confirmed misgivings about the effectiveness of Indian treaties. "No country ever yet preserved the peace, either with foreign or domestic enemies, by paying them for keeping it," he said.[7]

One of the major weaknesses of the treaty system was that even its supporters often found themselves in agreement with critics on the failings of the process, if not on the solution to its problems. This was apparent in the widespread consensus on the "inevitable" fate of the Indian population. The conviction prevailed that Indians were a dying race, and this could hardly be denied when it was a central conclusion of investigatory commissions sent to examine Indian conditions in the West in the 1860s.[8] Those who could not be convinced that treaty making had always been a mistake might waver over its relevance in the 1860s, when it was a constantly reiterated "fact" that Indians were not long for this world. This assumption also raised questions about the legitimacy of the process. Sen. James McDougall disputed any responsibility to treat with Indians at all, suggesting instead that the United States simply "let them die out by a law established by a greater Master than confines himself to this sphere."[9] This inevitable result of the collision of "civilization" and "savagery" was echoed throughout Congress. Sen. John Sherman, whose famous brother, Gen. William T. Sherman, presided over the army in the West during the immediate post–Civil War years, intimated that it might be the will of "Divine Providence."[10] There was a distinct implication in these sentiments that any attempt to counter the "natural" impact of such a collision by, among other things, treaties to alleviate the situation, was unwarranted interference.[11] Even Indian advocates agreed. Sen. James Doolittle described them as "a feeble people . . . , a dying people; they will soon pass away, and nothing will remain of the Indian tribes but the beautiful names which they gave to our rivers and our towns." For Doolittle, treaties with such people were also inconsequential, but he supported the practice as a last favor, a deathbed concession.[12] Supporters of the treaty system could, in their way, be almost as devastating as detractors.

These difficulties with and doubts about the Indian partners to treaties were compounded by an emphatic disgust with what were alleged to be standard operating procedures. Castigating the process in 1870 in the midst of an appropriations debate wherein the treaties of 1867 and 1868 were the sticking point, one senator described a procedure he well knew did not apply to those treaties: "We have got to catch him [the Indian] first, put a hat on him, clothe him, give him a little whisky, and then we make a treaty! That is the way we treat with Indians."[13] The pervasiveness of this image, or at least of the willingness of members of Congress to employ it, is apparent in the repetition of the essence of it on many pages of the *Congressional Globe*.[14] Aggravated by one of his colleague's persistent invocations of the illustration, Sen. Alexander Ramsey, who claimed to have been present at some treaty negotiations, tried to set the record straight, but few opponents of treaty making could resist the picture.[15] Despite the questionable accuracy of this portrait, the propaganda effect remained a powerful factor in interpretations of Indian negotiations.

Less inflammatory but still troubling and perhaps more accurate accusations about the procedures of treaty making cast further shadows on the practice. Some members of Congress wondered about the representativeness of those Indians who signed treaties, thereby calling into question the legitimacy of the Indian authority involved. There was reason for concern here. The treaties of 1865 with the Sioux, though declared an American diplomatic triumph by their optimistic chief U.S. negotiator, had in reality been signed by Indians known, uncharitably, as the "stay-around-the-fort" types.[16]

Another complaint of wary members of Congress was that Indians were not the real partners to the treaties in any case. The effective players, it was asserted, were "a few white men who have got among them who want some goods and who use the Indians for their purposes."[17] This accusation also had some merit, and there were instances in American treaty making where annuities were simply paid over to the traders to whom the Indians were indebted. (In Canada the government refused absolutely to be responsible for Indian debts and left it to Indians themselves to resolve the claims of traders against them.)[18]

Concerns about the legitimacy of the treaty-making process contributed directly to the deterioration of the system in the United States, but treaties were also the innocent victims of a serious jurisdictional dispute. The problem was a struggle between the Interior Department, which had control over Indian affairs, and the War Department, which wanted it. The "transfer issue," as it was referred to through the dozen years it existed as a factor in U.S. Indian policy, did not constitute as overt an assault on treaty making as did questions of legitimacy, but it played a role in the overall depreciation of the system by employing it as a pawn in the struggle for control.

If land administration had been the only worry of the national government in the American West, then Interior's domination might have gone unchecked. But the rising tide of warfare created an indispensable role for the military, which was employed to make peace and enforce it. This purpose collided with the Interior Department's own expanding cause in the West—the "civilization" of the Indians. This calling was every bit as immediate and as serious as the army's goal. Emigration, which caused the conflicts the army was required to defuse, also threatened the very survival of the Indians. The threat of extinction was perceived, by reformers in the Interior Department and their supporters in Congress, to have only one solution—civilization—and that became the major concern of the department in its consideration of the peoples of the plains.[19] It soon became clear, however, at least to these advocates that the Indians were threatened not only by extinction but perhaps also by a concerted policy of extermination, a program in which the U.S. Army on the plains was held to be one of the culprits.[20] The battle for exclusive jurisdiction was joined.

Treaty making became a weapon in the struggle. The Interior Department embraced treaties as a tool of civilization, claimed it was largely army violations of existing treaties that caused wars, and denounced military officers as "exterminationists." Support for this position came in part from documents like the Doolittle Report, the result of a joint congressional investigation of conditions on the plains, and the Sully-Sanborn Commission investigating the causes of the Indian hostilities of 1865. It was noted in the latter report that but for army aggression on the plains in the winter and spring of 1866–67, the Indians would have asked for peace.[21] Army personnel, it was pointed out, were trained for war and were hardly appropriate forces to carry out the civilization work for which treaties set the stage.[22] It could also be noted that, with reference to Indians, "extermination" sometimes seemed to be General Sherman's favorite word, although it would also have been unfair to label the general as an advocate of it.[23] More telling evidence of military brutality was the 1864 massacre by members of the Colorado militia of a Cheyenne band in winter camp at Sand Creek. Although the troops involved were volunteer militia on a term enlistment and not regular-army men, critics did not differentiate. Events of this nature occurred often enough in the next decade to kill every bill introduced in Congress to return Indian affairs to the jurisdiction of the War Department.

That department was not without its own ammunition in the battle. Its most effective critiques of Interior's administration were charges of corruption in the Indian service, where accountability was nonexistent and fortunes were regularly made by members of a staff in constant turnover.[24] The questionable benefits of such a system for either the government or the Indians were frequently raised. While there was a possibility that transfer might be achieved, the War Department and its congressional supporters sang the praises and advantages of having army officers, bound by both the honor of their reputation and a chain of responsibility armed with court-martial authority, as more honest and respectable candidates for Indian agents.[25] However, the prospect of a losing battle turned the War Department against the whole process. Corruption and charges of an "Indian ring" were significant factors in the decline of support, both popular and congressional, for the treaty-making system. But accusations, in some cases well founded, of the brutality of the army and its role in precipitating conflict were equally devastating. It was, in the words of one disgruntled senator, "a question of whether the Indians are to be governed by force, by fraud, or both."[26] The solution that gained increasing empathy in several quarters was to abolish the process altogether.

The other serious criticism arising from the War-Interior conflict emerged from conflicting priorities. Few military men disputed the view that civilization was the only way to prevent the extinction of the Indians.[27] They did, however, question the possibility of striving for "civilization" while Indians remained potential aggressors. By 1867 the Interior Department was sponsoring a policy of "conquer with kindness," while the War Department was clearly convinced that the appropriate approach was "conquer, *then* kindness." The army's position on this earned its officers a reputation as exterminationists. Army officers and their supporters effectively turned that charge back on their accusers, arguing that filling the Indians' minds with false attitudes about their status, primarily through the treaty process—wherein they were treated as equals, offered bribes for good behavior, and not infrequently armed and with the latest model rifles at that—led directly to the massacres not only of innocent whites but of the Indians as well.[28] The impact of these assaults on the treaty-making practice was not immediately apparent but contributed in the long run to the dismantling of the system. Unable to reconcile the conflicting goals of war and "civilization," Americans eventually just abandoned the process.

The combined impact of specific questions of the legitimacy of Indian treaty negotiations and the disillusionment encouraged by administrative infighting at both legislative and executive levels of government placed an overwhelming burden of expectation on the next major treaty-making venture, the talks carried out under the auspices of the Great Peace Commission of 1867–68. To continue as a viable element of U.S. Indian policy, the system had to undergo a transformation of function from the simple land transfers of its original purpose, now largely irrelevant except as a legal formality, to the means of achieving not only peace on the plains but also the civilization of the region's aboriginal inhabitants. The treaties of 1867–68 were to be the test case for the effectiveness of these new goals.

The treaty-making problems endemic to the American system were entirely absent from the Canadian context. There were no troubling jurisdictional wrangles nor was there a tremor of doubt about either the legitimacy or function of treaties. Canada simply did not experience in any comparable form the waves of internal emigrants that engulfed the United States in every decade of its western expansion. The absence of that pressure meant that many of the snarls encountered by the United States in its takeover of the Plains West never raised their ugly heads in

Canada. The result, in retrospect, gives the casual observer the impression of a planned, orderly advance into the Canadian West marshaled by an astute, far-sighted government in stark contrast to the frenzied free-for-all south of the forty-ninth parallel. In reality, the absence of conflict in Canada allowed for a somewhat haphazard expansion under vague, indifferent, and distinctly myopic governments. In these circumstances there was much latitude for error and second attempts, if not necessarily correction.

If "manifest destiny" unleashed hordes of unrestrained emigrants on a distinctly militant and potentially hostile Indian population in the American West, then Canada's "national policy" was its opposite in almost every respect. These processes, primarily labels imposed for organizational purposes, are not rightly comparable, but they do embody the spirit of expansion that each nation took to the plains. While the U.S. government fretted about the population explosion in its West, Canada avidly sought a population migration in order to advance the colonization of its own western territory. Canada could afford a policy on the subject. The only West Canadians were rushing into in 1870 was the American one. Canada's potential colonists for the Northwest Territory were still in Europe waiting to be recruited. The governmental impulses and dreams of the great Canadian nationalists came together loosely in what would be known as the "national policy." This called for a railroad across the new nation, though unlike the Kansas–Central Pacific line its purpose was to take settlers west, not to catch up to them. Canada's pace in arrangements for this dream was affected by elements beyond its control. The threat of American encroachment on the proposed colony lent an element of urgency to the purchase of Rupert's Land in 1869. Indian demands for recognition of their rights and a settlement of the land question prompted the Dominion government to inaugurate the treaty-making system in the new nation. Illegal American trading practices in the foothills and on the plains of southern Alberta advanced the schedule of the dispatch of the Northwest Mounted Police to that region. Even so, these pressures were hardly comparable to the forces weighing on American territorial expansion. The Canadian timetable was telescoped somewhat by external pressures, but there was still sufficient breathing space to maintain a linear order of progression. That, at least, was how it happened, even if it was not planned so exactly.

In Canada there was no reason to question the legitimacy of the treaty system. It had served its purpose so well in central Canada that it had no dissatisfied detractors. It might have occurred to Canadian parliamentarians to examine the process for its applicability in the new context of the Northwest, especially as, in practice, the land treated for came in vastly greater swathes than had been the case in the rest of the country. But there was some suggestive precedent even for that in the Robinson Treaties of 1850.[29]

The structure of a parliamentary system obviated some of the power struggles that arose in the United States. The Proclamation of 1763, never rejected in Canada as it was by revolution in the United States, remained a constitution-level document of the new Dominion. Its terms had explicitly excluded the Northwest Territory, but in negotiating for control of the region in 1869, Canada had committed itself to the principle that "the claims of the Indian Tribes to compensation for lands required for the purpose of settlement, would be considered and settled in conformity with the equitable principles which have uniformly governed the Crown in its dealings with the Aborigines."[30] The proclamation, and Canada's subsequent acquiescence to the principles enunciated therein, may have involved tacit recognition of the Indians of Canada as "nations," but there was no explicit statement of status to complicate parliamentary considerations of treaty making in Canada, at least not in the nineteenth century. The single and very innocuous reference to Indians in the British North America Act, designating "Indians, and Lands reserved for the Indians" a federal responsibility, inspired nothing like the agonized debates in the U.S. Congress over interpretation of the Constitution.[31]

The British North America Act was also mercifully silent on the division of powers within the federal government, a separation simply not possible in a parliamentary system in the same way it was under congressional rule. Canada's power divisions lay along federal/provincial lines, and so long as the public lands of the Northwest remained in federal hands, which they did until the Natural Resources Transfer Act of 1930, this was not a point of contention.

Responsibility for treaty making resided with the prime minister, who in practice with regard to Indian treaties made all decisions in consultation with his cabinet. Constitutionally, it was the Privy Council with which the prime minister consulted, but this body rarely if ever formally met, although cabinet decisions and directives were issued in its name. Of particular importance to Indian treaties was the secretary of state for the provinces, or later the minister of the interior, under whose administrative jurisdiction Indian affairs lay. This cozy coterie of men appointed the treaty commissioners, usually men with whom they were acquainted, and recommended the results for approval to the governor general, again a familiar face. Treaties did encounter some parliamentary inspection, although ratification rested with the governor general. Like the Privy Council, the governor general's role was more a formal than real hurdle, although his approval was necessary to legitimize a government act and it was at least theoretically possible that he might withhold that permission. Parliament had to appropriate the funds for the negotiation and implementation of the treaties, but if more than a cursory acknowledgment of these expenses was ever made, it is not apparent from the records of the House of Commons. The excessive and acrimonious debates on Indian treaty making in the United States, almost all of which occurred in discussions of Indian appropriations bills, were nonexistent in Canada. Executive action raised no questions or qualms about the legitimacy of treaty making in the Dominion.

The legal void on the status of Indians, at least where it touched on treaties, eliminated the problems stirred in the United States over the equation of Indian tribes to foreign nations. In practice Canada regarded Indian status, in this situation only, as a category defined a century later as *sui generis*, unique. It was therefore beyond the thought of anyone remotely concerned with the process to question the legitimacy of Indian treaties in comparison to other treaties. In fact, Indian treaties were the only kinds of treaties that the Dominion was legally empowered to conduct on its own authority, as foreign relations remained the purview of the imperial government until the Statute of Westminster in 1931 surrendered all remaining governmental authority to Canada. By implication, unlike the legal quagmire created by the ambiguities of the American Constitution and Chief Justice Marshall's decisions, Indian treaties in Canada did *not* have a status equal to those with foreign nations.

The second level of jurisdictional dispute that embroiled the United States also found no equivalent in Canada. The civilian authority of the Ministry of State or Interior had no competition for administration of Indian affairs. The absence of settler pressure in the Northwest Territory created no role for an army to play. A militia existed and was sent west to repress the Red River Rebellion of 1869–70, but it could in no way compare in either size or importance with the U.S. Army, which in 1865 had emerged victorious and powerful from a major war. Britain had an army and was technically responsible for Dominion security but played only a minimal and reluctant role in suppressing the rebellion. In the wake of that conflict, the military presence in the West was reduced, not enlarged, much to the chagrin of the resident lieutenant governor.[32]

The absence of an army in Canada brought forth other solutions to potential conflict in the territory. Again Canadians had a circumstantial advantage over the Americans. Unlike the United States, where the army had been the first force of law and order, Canada had the legacy of the Hudson's Bay Company on which to rely. The company had been charged with keeping the peace in the region, and while its rule may have been haphazard, informal, and arbitrary, it had existed, and the ground rules for expected behavior were known to Indian and emigrant alike.[33] Canada replaced this authority with a small hybrid force, the Northwest Mounted Police. In contrast to the U.S. Army, reduced to a punitive role by circumstances, the Northwest Mounted Police were there to prevent conflict, not eradicate it.

By the time the police made their way west in 1874, the government had already initiated treaty making with the Plains Indians, but the process in no way impeded police responsibilities. Conflict between the two forces, police and treaty commissioners, therefore did not arise. The Northwest Mounted Police found a part in the procedure similar to that played by the U.S. Army in terms of security and ceremonialism, as well as in the role of commissioner in one instance. But the lethargy of the Canadian government in implementing the treaties, and the lack of emigration to force the issue, ensured that the police had no enforcement role until somewhat later, and so there were no grounds for the conflict that had arisen in the United States between civilian and military jurisdiction on the plains.

Neither did Canada confront the pressing ultimatum of civilization or extinction bearing down on humanitarian policymakers in the United States. What perceptions there were of Indians dying off focused on other causes, primarily alcohol and disease.[34] These were accepted as byproducts of the clash between "civilization" and "savagery," but Canada's appreciation of these elements was compartmentalized. In central Canada, where a policy of civilization was in full force by the 1870s, the deputy superintendent of Indian affairs could point to statistical evidence that the aboriginal population of the region was actually on the rise in contrast to commonly held opinion.[35] Disease and liquor were factors of more concern in the West, where there was no attempt before 1880, quite deliberately after the treaties had been concluded, to impose civilization.

In the United States treaties were transformed into tools of civilization, as well as of peace, in order to remain viable instruments. As far as the Canadian government was concerned, however, there was no need to alter the function of treaties since they still served their purpose of extinguishing land title.

The procedures that accompanied treaty making also escaped criticism in Canada. Perhaps this came about in part because of a remarkable lack of public interest in the proceedings. In the 1870s little attention was given to Indian affairs in the press beyond local coverage.[36] Then, as now, the bulk of the Canadian population lived outside the Northwest Territory and did not much care, apparently, what happened there. Parliamentary debate on the issue was almost nonexistent.

Had a critical eye been leveled at the process, however, the accusations made against treaty making in the United States would not have applied anyway. For the seven Numbered Treaties negotiated in the 1870s, significant public figures were appointed as chief commissioners, and the Privy Council exercised its authority to name these men. There could be no charges of dereliction of duty or of not taking the procedure seriously. Neither was the status of the Indians questioned. There were no qualms about the chiefs and headmen selected to represent their peoples at the treaty meetings because great care was taken to ensure their authority as the first order of business, the legacy of an ongoing controversy over the Indian signatories of the 1817 Selkirk Treaty at Red River.[37] Finally, the process itself was a formal affair in Canada, and the pomp and circumstance surrounding an Indian treaty negotiation could hardly have been exceeded by the formality associated with any other treaties. The process was held in the name of the queen, and she was explicitly identified in the treaties as the partner with whom the Indians were concluding an agreement. In short, there were no grounds on which to challenge the legitimacy of the system within Canada, at least from the white point of view.

Canadians thus experienced none of the jurisdictional bickering at either the executive or legislative level that gave rise to and shaped the challenges to the legitimacy of the system in the United States. Even if malcontents had closely scrutinized the Canadian procedures, they would have found little to which they could object. Canada had remained true to the original function of treaty making and retained the formalities that had attended the process from the beginning. In that role, treaty making continued to serve the ends of the government in advancing the national policy. So rigidly did Canada adhere to this definition that it resisted attempts, sponsored by the Indians themselves, to broaden the function treaties were to serve.

Canada therefore embarked on a round of treaty negotiations in the 1870s full of confidence in the very process that the Americans were dismissing as an irrelevant failure. But Canada's treaty-making procedures were not wracked with the dissension in practice and multiplicity of functions imposed on the fragile American system. In Canada treaty making remained pristine. If any changes were to be made—and in the development of the Numbered Treaties they were—they would be made in the field, not in the Privy Council or the cabinet and certainly not in Parliament.

3   The Context of Treaty Making

The nature of the treaty-making process in the United States and Canada was mirrored in the negotiations themselves. An American peace commission, on the highest official authority, ventured forth in 1867 and 1868 to make peace in the Plains West but also to inaugurate a new way of life for the Indians involved, whether they wanted it or not. In Canada an erratic piecemeal approach focused single-mindedly on land acquisition, conceding only grudgingly to a broadening of the terms it proposed and always at the insistence of its active and interested treaty partners, the aboriginal inhabitants of the Prairie West.

In 1867 the United States was convinced that it was on the brink of a general Indian war on the plains.[1] There were only two solutions to what had become an intolerable situation—total war or peace. Neither was a satisfactory option, for both had been put to the test as recently as 1865 and found wanting. The course of violence on the American Plains in the previous decade had been sporadic, but by the 1860s the trend was intensifying. The single greatest Indian uprising in American history occurred in 1862, not on the plains but in Minnesota, when the Santee Sioux, a people under treaty with the United States, murdered more than eight hundred white settlers. But the repercussions of this event reverberated across the northern plains. The pursuit of the Santee perpetrators brought the western Sioux peoples into their first sustained contact with the U.S. Army, and conflict ensued. This development only exacerbated Indian-white tensions with the Sioux. In 1851, at the first Treaty of Fort Laramie, these peoples had accorded the United States a right of way through their territory to facilitate emigration to California and Oregon in return for annuity payments. Tranquility was broken at mid-decade in a dispute over a stray Mormon cow, but order was quickly restored after Gen. William S. Harney's victory over the Sioux at Ash Hollow in 1855. Then, at the end of the decade, silver mines were opened in Montana and the most direct route to them was cut directly through Sioux territory. The beginning of the American Civil War in 1861 did little to diminish either new settler traffic on the plains generally or the rush to the mines. The Sioux were antagonized. In the aftermath of the Minnesota massacre, clashes between the army and various Sioux peoples were frequent, and by 1865 the departmental commander of the Missouri, Gen. John Pope, was authorizing the third major campaign against the Sioux that he had ordered in three years.

Far to the south on the Texas border, a century-old conflict between Texans and the Kiowas, Comanches, and Kiowa-Apaches continued at its usual pace in somewhat less dramatic form than events on the northern plains, though always steady. Clashes between these peoples and the emigrant settlers of the Lone Star State continued unabated, treaty or no treaty, until the Red River War of 1874 forced the expulsion of the Indians from Texas and imposed confinement on the reservations they had been assigned under the 1867 Medicine Lodge Treaties. The participation of these peoples in a "general" war in 1865 was a tenuous accusation at best, but from the standpoint of politicians in Washington it was difficult to differentiate between a specific war and a long-term border conflict.

The catalyst to a major war with the Indians at mid-decade, however, came from the central plains. The Cheyenne and Arapaho peoples, occupying a belt of land that included most of Colorado, faced the combined onslaught of prospectors pouring into the Colorado mines and the projected transcontinental railroad, plotted on a route that ran right through the Smoky Hills, a premier Indian hunting-ground. Denver, at the crossroads, became a boomtown in the 1860s. The pressures of contact, most acute in Colorado, brought the most severe conflict as white settlers and miners ran roughshod over Indian rights and claims, provoking Indian retaliation. Distressed by what he perceived to be "an alliance of the Cheyenne and a part of the Arapahoe tribes, with the Camanche [sic], Kiowa, and Apache Indians of the south, and the great family of Sioux Indians of the north plains," Colorado governor John Evans authorized the formation of citizen militia units "to kill and destroy as enemies of the country, wherever they may be found, all such hostile Indians."[2] A Colorado militia unit under an expiring term limit and out for blood, in combination with an officer ambitious for political office and armed with the official sanction of the governor's orders, descended on a Cheyenne village on November 29, 1864. What they did there was so vicious, brutal, and savage that the events at Sand Creek remained a symbol of military barbarity under which the army labored for decades to come.[3] The most immediate impact of the Sand Creek Massacre was to inaugurate the general war that western whites had so feared as the Cheyenne survivors actively enlisted the support of other plains nations in exacting vengeance.[4] The consequences of Sand Creek went further, however, than immediate military complications. Although the treaty negotiations of 1867–68 were one round away in 1865, an understanding of some aspects of this event sheds light on the motivations for peace in 1867 as well as on the terms that eventually resulted.

The first reaction to Sand Creek was of necessity a military one, as Indian "outrages" multiplied across the plains. While there may have been some understanding in army circles of the provocation Indians felt, the military was not the appropriate instrument to effect amelioration. Its role was to bring peace at any price, and the summer campaigns of 1865 were meant to do just that. But the army faced insurmountable odds that year. Though victorious in the Civil War and unchallenged as the supreme power on the plains, the U.S. Army suddenly encountered massive manpower shortages as Civil War enlistments, in what was primarily a volunteer force, ran out. With the nation finally free of the internecine struggle that ended in April 1865, thousands of potential emigrants and railroad financiers turned West, and the revelation dawned on many that war on the Great Plains was impeding financial gain. The governor of Dakota Territory, watching people fleeing the region because of the threat posed by the hostile Sioux, pleaded for peace.[5] In Colorado it was the railroad speculators, anxious to embark on the transcontinental railroad link delayed by the Civil War and Indian conflicts, who brought pressure on the government to negotiate.[6] These forces of unbridled self-interest coincided with both a dispirited and abrupt collapse of military initiative in the West and the emergence of a particularly vital and growing tide of humanitarian interest in Indian reform to make peace the operative word in 1865.

The military came to grief on two fronts. In the field, the massive campaign of 1865 ended in abysmal failure. In Washington, Congress, embarking on the first rounds of a bitter debate on Reconstruction that would culminate two years later in impeachment proceedings against Pres. Andrew Johnson, might not even have noticed except for the price tag that accompanied these disasters. The 1865 campaign purportedly cost twenty million dollars.[7] Expenditures at these levels inspired the commonly uttered criticism of both military authority over Indian affairs and the option of war as a viable solution that it was "cheaper to feed them than fight them."[8] Some congressmen, exhibiting a gift for hyperbole, would extend this truism by commenting that putting every Indian up in a first-class eastern hotel would be cheaper.[9]

Such pragmatic, self-absorbed, and pecuniary motives inspired a solution that accorded completely in 1865 with the burgeoning interest in the Indian reform movement, itself bursting with energy as a result of Sand Creek (and not uninfluenced by the parallel drive to "raise up" liberated Black slaves).[10] Congress was not entirely devoid of humanitarian sentiment, and the Senate in particular harbored a number of compassionate men. These senators spearheaded the movement for peace, spurred by a populace in the Northeast awash with sympathy for the Indian. One result was a spate of investigatory commissions appointed to examine the details of the Sand Creek Massacre as well as two general reports on the state of affairs on the plains.[11]

Working in conjunction with the Congressional investigators were peace commissions. One, under the direction of Dakota governor Newton Edmunds, who was anxious to bring people and prosperity to his territory, set out to make peace with the Sioux.[12] The Doolittle Commission, created to investigate conditions of Indians in the West, reconstituted itself in one of those questionable practices of irregular treaty making into another peace commission to the central and southern plains.[13] Between them they concluded an array of brief treaties, in October at Fort Sully in Dakota Territory and on the Little Arkansas River in Kansas. These agreements were directed toward making peace between whites and Indians, establishing nonviolent arbitration procedures for inter-Indian conflict, and drawing general boundaries for "reservations," which were very loosely defined.

Both sets of accords were of the sort that gave treaty making a bad name. General Pope, still licking his wounds after the military debacles he had masterminded in 1865, declared, "I do not consider the treaties, lately made with the Sioux, Cheyennes, Arapahoes, Kiowas, and Comanches worth the paper they are written on," and he was right.[14] The commission under Governor Edmunds in Dakota secured assurances of peace from a variety of Sioux peoples but managed to avoid signing up any of the bands that were actually "hostile."[15] The southern commission also neglected to win the support of leaders of the Cheyenne "Dog Soldiers," another hostile force.[16] The attempt to restrict these peoples to specific, although extensive, territories also came to naught. The fact that a sizable chunk of the designated areas lay in Texas, which had retained control of its public lands upon entering the Union in 1845 and refused to make them available for federal Indian reservations, made the Treaty of the Little Arkansas inoperable from the beginning.[17] In addition, both treaty commissions incorporated annuities of such exceptional extravagance and engaged to pay them for terms of such unprecedented length that the normally somnambulant ratification procedures in the Senate erupted in the first of many acrimonious debates on the legitimacy of the process at a time when Congress was mired in Reconstruction woes. These treaties were ratified, but the battle was only postponed.

As General Pope had warned, these "farcical" treaty-making ventures were all for naught, and in 1866 the plains threatened to disintegrate into war once again. In June, in recognition of the importance of making peace with the real "hostiles," another treaty commission summoned the true Sioux belligerents, among them Red Cloud of the Oglala Sioux, to Fort Laramie. The ostensible object, reflecting official American awareness of the need to acquire legitimate Indian land cession before territories could legally be claimed, was to gain Sioux acceptance of American use and fortification of the Bozeman Trail. This was the road leading through Sioux territory to the Montana mines and the primary bone of contention. The arrival of an army command in the midst of negotiations, with the announced purpose of fortifying the Bozeman Trail with or without Sioux permission, abruptly ended the talks and initiated the two-year contest known as Red Cloud's War. This conflict coexisted until December of that year with what were the usual sporadic outbursts of violence elsewhere in the region. Then another critical episode, comparable to Sand Creek in ferocity and atrocity, though this time at American expense, brought the cycle of events in the Plains West full circle and set the stage for the treaty-making commission of 1867–68.

On December 21, 1866, a truly arrogant and vastly overconfident army captain named William Fetterman led eighty men out of Fort Phil Kearny on the Bozeman Trail, violated explicit orders, and died with his entire command in a battle against an overwhelming Sioux force under the leadership of Red Cloud. It was the greatest American military disaster in the history of Plains Indian warfare and would remain so until 1876, when another U.S. military defeat, strikingly similar in detail although on a larger scale, occurred at the Little Bighorn. By January 1867 Washington was once more awash with reports of a general Indian war on the plains, this time against exultant rather than vengeful Indians.[18] The southern Plains Indians had no new reason to engage in hostility. They were encouraged, however, by the apparent Sioux victory to intensify their own expressions of dissatisfaction with relentless settler pressures on land and game and the continued disregard for their rights as well as their lives. Conflict there escalated too.

The Fetterman Massacre inspired a number of investigative commissions, but the military found no solace in the scrutiny that now turned with renewed zeal on the situation in the West. The harbinger was the long-awaited report of the Doolittle Commission, ordered in March 1865 and published in January 1867. The report included, among other things, the results of a detailed questionnaire circulated among military men, traders, Indian affairs agents and superintendents, and others in the West deemed knowledgeable on Indian conditions.[19] The findings were damning. The long litany of violence on the plains was traced in every instance to white hands, often those of the military, but primarily of ordinary people, the pioneers. The precipitous population decline of the Indians was ascertained as a fact, and the causes were identified as war, disease, alcohol, and the disintegrating basis of Indian life through the diminution of game animals and the decimation of the buffalo in particular. Indians were found to have had due cause for the hostilities they had perpetrated, and they emerged clearly as victims of unrestrained, licentious white expansion.[20] A military investigation of the Fetterman Massacre could not exonerate its own service, attributing the continuing violence to military actions.[21]

The humanitarians—Northeastern public opinion and the press, missionary and reform organizations, and committed congressional representatives—demanded redress.[22] Although the military was unable to marshal steam for a comprehensive campaign such as it had managed in 1865, neither did it sit idly by while Congress made plans and easterners fumed. But continued exertions to control the waves of violence flooding the plains only strengthened the hands of the peacemakers. In April 1867 Gen. Winfield Scott Hancock, commanding a punitive expedition on the central plains, sacked and burned a Cheyenne village. Retaliation resulted, but in Congress sympathy came down hard in favor of the victimized Indians, and the errant general faced rigorous interrogation on the legitimacy of his actions.[23] The event only hardened congressional intent in favor of a thoroughgoing and final peace settlement on the Great Plains to bring this "national disgrace" to an end. The proposed solution was the Great Peace Commission, enacted by a joint resolution of Congress and made law on July 20, 1867.

The conviction by many that the continuous tumult on the plains constituted a national disgrace was not unimportant in the development of American Indian policy in general and treaty making in particular. From its earliest days the American Republic labored under the Puritan vision of itself as "a city upon a hill."[24] Born to serve as an example to the world, the United States suffered real and troubling pangs of conscience when it failed to live up to its own expectations and perceptions of what was right. An undercurrent of opinion held that the Indian wars were a punishment for the "national sin" of American treatment of Indians. In Congress, Sen. Willard Warner reminded his colleagues of this: "There is a wide-spread conviction in the country that our treatment of the Indians amounts to a national disgrace and a national crime second only to that of our treatment of the colored race, and that we are suffering, and will suffer, the like penalty which we suffered in that case if we do not deal with them upon principles of humanity."[25] A similar conviction had seized reformers in the pre–Civil War years regarding the subject of slavery. Many Northern reformers had come to the antislavery cause certain that unless this "national sin" was eradicated, the whole country would be eternally damned. In this framework, the bloodletting of the Civil War had been just punishment for an erring nation. The desire to avoid not only the sin itself but also another round of Divine fury impelled Indian reformers to campaign vigorously for a just solution to the "Indian problem."[26] In Congress, Rep. Walter Burleigh declared, "The wrath of Divine justice would be poured out upon us as a nation if we determined upon an act [extermination] so wicked. The civilization of the age would not tolerate it, while the sensibilities of the Christian world would revolt at such a thought."[27]

Americans were also highly sensitive to outside criticism. Perhaps the most common term used in relation to Indian policy after "farce" was "honor."[28] The string of broken treaties extending back through American history was a stain on the nation's honor. When Indian reformer Helen Hunt Jackson sought to shame the American people into action twenty years later in the drive for allotment, she entitled her book *A Century of Dishonor*. Given the wretched record of the 1860s made explicit in any number of official reports, there was a strong current of support in the summer of 1867 for yet another treaty-making venture, this one rooted in the exigencies of national honor. The practical effect of this obsession was to fix in the minds of Congress, as well as the commissioners appointed to the task, the necessity of devising a treaty that could be kept, an apparent flaw in most other U.S. Indian treaties.

This requirement coincided with the humanitarian impulse to establish a working settlement with the Indians, which was to be accomplished by expanding the scope of the treaty-making function. In 1867 the United States was still making treaties to extinguish land title, but on the plains the importance of this aspect had faded almost to irrelevance before the much more emphasized role of ending war. Now, in setting the agenda for 1867, Congress, under humanitarian influence, overlaid the basic war-and-peace function with that of civilization.

The several reports on Indian conditions had ascertained two facts: that the Indians were a dying people, and that whites were the cause of this precipitous decline. It was a common conviction that the former might be arrested, but only one senator ever hinted that white expansion might be restrained.[29] Neither "fact" had been taken into account in the negotiation of earlier treaties, thus the cause of all the trouble—white expansion—had never been satisfactorily handled. The peacemakers of 1867 were determined to address this failing of previous treaties by providing within their treaties a comprehensive solution to the Indian problem. This commitment, spurred by humanitarian sentiments to reverse the trend of Indian extinction—as well as to eliminate the press of the exterminationists in the West, the military, and occasionally in Congress—broadened the nature of treaty making and increased the stakes on the outcome of the already fragile process.

Two other more cynical compulsions bolstered the move for peace in 1867. Ever-present fiscal considerations, echoing the cries for peace in 1865, were the first of these. Always a cause guaranteed to win approval in a penurious Congress, particularly in the House of Representatives, which guarded the public purse, an appeal to frugality was a tool adroit humanitarians put to good use. In pressing for the creation of the peace commission he sponsored, Sen. John Henderson resorted shamelessly to the tactic: "This war, if it lasts during the summer and fall, will cost us $100,000,000. . . .We are expending from $125,000 to $250,000, perhaps, daily in this war, and these expenditures will be rapidly increased from day to day. . . . The war is but begun, and it will increase, and alarmingly increase, in its proportions of atrocity and also in its proportions of public debt. Now, it behooves the Congress of the United States in session to do something, if we possibly can, to put an end to it."[30] This statement is particularly revealing on two points. Undoubtedly, the army was an expensive operation, but Henderson's figures were not substantiated, although they were repeated elsewhere.[31] Like the scurrilous description of Indian treaty-making procedures employed by detractors, these numbers remained an effective propaganda tool regardless of their accuracy.[32] They complemented perfectly the "cheaper to feed them than fight them" mentality that pervaded even the ranks of those who had no sympathy for the Indians.

The other point of interest was the coupling of humanitarian sentiment with pecuniary concerns, the juxtaposition of "proportions of atrocity" with "proportions of public debt." The frequency with which these are matched in congressional discussions and administrative reports through to the end of treaty making in 1871 raises questions about the real basis of American concerns.[33] After his impassioned statement as to the immorality of extermination, delivered to the House in 1868, Congressman Burleigh added, "But, aside from the moral question, it would bankrupt the national Treasury."[34]

The second cynical approach to the wisdom of treaty making in 1867 was that embraced by those who believed that the peace therein made, bought, or bribed would be a useful measure for buying time. It was a position best exemplified in the person of Gen. William T. Sherman, the second-highest ranking officer in the U.S. Army and one of the commissioners appointed to the peace team in 1867. Despite his military position, Sherman willingly participated in the peace commission of 1867 because he saw that a window of opportunity would exist, even if only a few months of peace were won, to complete the transcontinental railroad, which he was confident would break Indian resistance as no army could. The railroad would usher in waves of emigrants that would make previous intrusions look like mere trickles. As important, this flood of settlers would bring about the quick extermination of the buffalo, and with that loss the Indian would be forced to conform or starve. Sherman was the railroad's most vociferous advocate for in it he saw a technological solution to what had become a military quagmire.[35]

Sherman's confidence in the railroad was in part confirmed by the anticlimactic dénouement to Red Cloud's War. It was the single but persistent demand of Red Cloud's Oglala Sioux that the Bozeman Trail be abandoned. As long as it was the primary link to the Montana mines the United States hesitated, and the talks with the Sioux in 1867 stalled on this point.

In 1868, however, the railroad moved beyond the contested area, opening up a new and more convenient access road to Montana, and American interest in the Bozeman Trail evaporated. The United States relented, the trail was abandoned, and Red Cloud retired in victory and signed the peace treaty on November 6, 1868. It was the single episode in United States history where an Indian treaty was signed on Indian terms, but in truth it was not much of a victory. It was simply that the railroad had made the battle obsolete. Making peace in order to buy time won advocates for the peace process in the most unlikely places.

War and peace, then, bolstered by a number of other factors determined the commitment of the United States to undertake yet another round of treaty making in 1867. The record of that decade meant that negotiation could only be viewed as the lesser of two evils, but it was certainly the less expensive of the two options. Treaty making was a tool chosen for pragmatic reasons, and American commitment to it wavered, dependent only on how effective it could be in achieving the ends sought. In 1867 both the cynical and the confident briefly put their faith in the treaty process, but expectations were greater than those imposed on previous treaties. The likelihood of disappointment, on any number of fronts, was high.

Canadians in 1867 had much less on their minds. On a superficial level, the situation in Canada was not so very different from that in which the United States found itself. In 1867 the two nations faced west and embarked on a course to bring under active jurisdiction vast territories to which they laid claim. The western lands in both countries were occupied by a significant population of various Indian nations whose rights, however limited whites perceived them, had to be acknowledged and extinguished. Treaties were the preferred method for this process because of a common heritage, but for somewhat different practical reasons. With the further exceptions of a painfully acute awareness of every cent spent to achieve their ends and a parallel interest in establishing transportation routes, the similarities between Canada and the United States, in terms of when and why they embarked on the ambitious treaty processes they did, ended here.

The developments that led to the negotiation of the Numbered Treaties in Canada between 1871 and 1877 were considerably less dramatic and less complicated than the intricate, bloody morass that prompted the United States to the same task in 1867 and 1868. While general war instigated American action, the Canadian process was precipitated in the first instance by a massive real-estate transaction. The ink of Confederation was hardly dry in 1867 before the empire-builders of central Canada, who had crafted that union in opposition to large segments of Maritime opinion, turned covetous eyes on the Prairie West. Rupert's Land, that vast tract of land encompassing the Hudson Bay watershed, held out the potential for empire, or at least the trappings of one. Under the leadership of John A. Macdonald and the Conservative Party, Canada set out to acquire this territory.

Many reasons impelled the negotiations, concluded in 1869, to bring this vast territory hitherto administered by the Hudson's Bay Company under Canadian jurisdiction, and much discussion resulted. In all of these debates, however, little thought was given to the existing inhabitants of this land. In Parliament, William Henry Chipman, elected from Nova Scotia on a Confederation-repeal platform, wondered if "all the inhabitants of this territory [were] willing to come into the Union, or were they to be dragged in against their will also." But his was a lone voice and may have had more to do with his own disgruntlement with Confederation than interest in the Indians.[36] Canada had made a commitment to do something about the Indians, at Britain's behest, under the terms of the purchase of Rupert's Land. Treaties were the traditional means, and imaginative alternatives were not the strong point of the men who forged Confederation. Treaties were not only a standard practice but, unlike in the United States, an unquestioned one. In a parliamentary debate in which the fate of Indians in the sought-after territory was discussed, one member remarked that "with a view of protecting those who may be attracted to this rich and fertile region, in search of either mineral or agricultural wealth, a large and comprehensive treaty will be found necessary. Of the accuracy of this statement, both Canada and the United States have precedents in previous treaties."[37] It is reasonable to believe that Canadian leaders in the early days of Confederation understood they would be obliged to make treaties with Indians sooner or later, although they would clearly have preferred to wait. There was no concrete point of departure for the Numbered Treaties comparable to the July 20 act of Congress in the United States. A general intent to treat with the Indians existed, but Canada's approach to treaty making was largely reactive rather than self-directed. As a result, in sharp contrast to the United States, there is little official documentation of the treaty process.

The low regard with which central Canadians viewed the peoples of the West became apparent in the procedures that joined Rupert's Land to the Dominion. The partners in the negotiations included Dominion representatives, Hudson's Bay Company officers, and British government officials. Neither the substantial "mixed-blood" population—known as the Métis—nor any of the several Indian peoples who resided in the territory were informed of, let alone consulted on, the transfer. Uncertain of the significance of this change for their future, they were quick to make their displeasure felt.

The Métis gained the lion's share of attention in short order by striking the Dominion government on several of its most vulnerable points—legitimacy, authority, and national security. The Red River Rebellion of 1869–70 did not arrest the acquisition of Rupert's Land by Canada, but it did forcefully alert Ottawa to the fact that there were other voices to be heard.

The Indians were somewhat less strident in articulating their concerns but no less persistent. The Dominion government was unknown to them, and its response to the protests from Red River was hardly reassuring. The Ojibwa people resident in that vast region from Lake Superior west to Rainy River and the Lake of the Woods were, perhaps, in the best position to negotiate. Their understanding of the strategic and resource value of their territory to Canadians, coupled with a keen appreciation of their own firm title to these lands and an awareness of American treaty terms just to the south, inhibited an easy Canadian advance west. In plotting an all-Canadian route to Red River in 1869, surveyor S. J. Dawson urged prompt treaty negotiations with the Ojibwas, observing, "They would be keenly alive to any imagined slight in opening a highway, without regard to them, through a territory of which they believe themselves to be sole lords and masters."[38] Three years later little had changed. Confronting Lt. Gov. Alexander Morris, Chief Mawedopenais reiterated the essential points of the Indian position: "*The sound of the rustling of the gold is under my feet where I stand*; we have a rich country; it is the Great Spirit who gave us this; where we stand upon is the Indians' property, and belongs to them."[39]

If Indians in the Canadian Prairie West had little direct knowledge of the implications of Dominion jurisdiction, they could at least extrapolate from events in the American West with which they were not unfamiliar. It was hardly a comforting picture. Developments on the prairies brought this point home to Canadian officials. In Manitoba, around the Red River area, the Ojibwas employed various tactics to gain Ottawa's attention. Hardly was Lt. Gov. Adams G. Archibald established at his post in 1871 when he received delegations seeking formal arrangements on the matters of land and the future of the Indians within the Dominion. When delays ensued despite his assurances otherwise, the Ojibwas persisted. Archibald reported: "They have sent repeated messages enquiring when the Treaty was to come off, and appeared very much disappointed at the delay. They have interfered with emigrants, warning them not to come on the ground outside the Hudson's Bay Company surveys, and lately they have posted up a written notice on the door of the church at Portage La Prairie, warning parties not to intrude on their lands until a Treaty is made."[40] As early as 1871 even the peoples of the North Saskatchewan region were petitioning for a settlement recognizing their rights and compensating them for losses that association with the Dominion would involve. Chief Sweetgrass of the Plains Crees informed the lieutenant governor that "We heard our lands were sold and we did not like it," and then proceeded to list a number of concerns, including agricultural assistance, which he suggested might form the basis for discussions.[41] This dissatisfaction with the supposed "sale" of their lands was most clearly expressed during the negotiations for Treaty 4, when the Crees demanded that the £300,000 paid for Rupert's Land be turned over to them rather than to the Hudson's Bay Company.[42] Until treaties were signed with them in 1874 and 1876, the Plains Crees continued to prompt the government through petition as well as the more effective means of intimidating settlers and disrupting the Canadian westward advance by obstruction of telegraph, survey, and geological crews.[43]

These Indian pressures to negotiate, precipitated by the presumptuous takeover of Rupert's Land without consulting those most directly affected by the move, were undeniably the most important factor in goading the Dominion government to treaty making in the 1870s. But Canada was receptive to the process, if not the timetable, for various other reasons as well. For the most part these motivations were but pale shadows of the forces that drove Americans to the treaty table. This divergence signaled the abrupt departure the Americans had taken very early in the process, and indicated too the remarkable consistency of treaty making in British North America. This difference between the two nations had a tremendous impact on the negotiations of the plains treaties and on the terms that resulted.

From the land transfers of the 1790s through the Robinson Treaties of 1850, there was little to be found in the Indian treaties of British North America aside from provisions for the surrender of territory. How much land and at what cost were variable factors in each agreement, but the central focus never wavered. Indeed, Canadian officials fully expected to concentrate on land cessions in 1871 with the negotiation of the first of the Numbered Treaties. There were some stirrings of a broader treaty initiative manifested in at least one instance in a report to the secretary of state that noted the possibilities: "Treaties may be made with them [western Indians] simply with a view to the extinction of their rights, by agreeing to pay them a sum and afterwards abandon them to themselves. On the other side, they may be instructed, civilized and led to a mode of life more in conformity with the new position of this country, and accordingly make them good, industrious, and useful citizens."[44] But the government did not embrace this second option and chose to continue the narrower format of treaties in keeping with past practice, although the goals suggested in this report were in fact in line with Indian policy elsewhere and with long-term intentions for the Indians of the Prairie West. Until required to do so by the very real negotiation pressures exerted by the Indians at the various treaty-making sessions, Canada's vision remained fixed on land alone.

In the United States in 1867, a consensus of opinion settled on treaty making as the most expedient means, in the circumstances of that year, to solve what were considered the critical problems of Indian relations on the plains—the necessity for peace and the means to keep it. Canada was not troubled by the conflict that haunted its neighbor. Events on the Canadian prairies might affect the timetable for negotiations and, in the end, also the outcome of those negotiations. Nevertheless, Canada's primary motive in embarking on treaty making was not the war-and-peace imperative of the United States but rather the much more narrow and traditional quest for land title. In American debates over the Indians in the late 1860s, land hardly ever emerged as an issue except when some compassionate advocate of Indian rights in Congress attempted to impart a historical lesson on how his countrymen had gotten themselves into this muddle in the first place.[45]

The Canadian emphasis on land is clear in documented discussions of each of the Numbered Treaties of the 1870s. This consistency is important because, unlike the American treaties, which were spawned by the enactment of the Great Peace Commission and concluded as a piece, Canada's treaties were individual affairs. There was a general intent to clear the entire Northwest of Indian title, but it was also recognized from the beginning that this had to be done in separate treaties according to distinct territories and the distribution of Indians over them. The treaties may be considered in a body but, with the exception of Treaties 1 and 2, which were negotiated simultaneously and on the basis of the same instructions, minor differences in circumstances led to somewhat different terms for the Indians. The single consistent fact from the government's perspective, from 1870 to 1877, was land.

The importance of land and the extinguishment of Indian title as the chief goal sought by Canadian authorities was indicated by the emphasis placed on this element in the treaties. After the initial preamble, each of the Numbered Treaties contained several extensive clauses on the subject of land. These included a statement of the queen's intentions with regard to the land, an extended statement of extinguishment and cession by the Indians to "all their rights, titles and privileges whatsoever to the lands included within the following limits" and an exacting description of the lands *to be ceded*. Treaties 4, 5, 6, and 7 also contained a provision of cession "to all other lands" to which these peoples might venture a claim.[46] These terms literally constitute the bulk of the text of the Numbered Treaties. This emphasis contrasts sharply with the format of the American treaties in which, in every instance, pride of place was given, in Article 1, to the termination of war and commitments to peace. The dual purpose of the American treaties was apparent in the remainder of each document, which was devoted almost exclusively to the measures of civilization. Only a single brief article, buried in the midst of these treaties, dealt with extinguishment of title, an indication of the weight Americans gave to this consideration. Therein the affected Indians agreed to "relinquish all rights to occupy permanently the territory *outside their reservation*."[47] The emphasis on the land in question was on what the Indians were to receive, not what they were surrendering, the opposite of comparable clauses in the Canadian treaties. In the American treaties, acknowledgment of Indian title was oblique at best, and the formal recognition and extinguishment of it were minor, if necessary, matters.

The Indians as well as the government recognized the centrality of land to the negotiations in Canada. It is clear from the pretreaty petitions of Indian leaders, the remarks of interested observers reporting on the scene, and the recorded speeches of Indians at the treaty talks that they, unlike the government, had a variety of preoccupations.[48] The Indians employed Canadian single-mindedness to advance their own concerns. After asserting his displeasure over the sale of Rupert's Land to Canada by the Hudson's Bay Company, Chief Sweetgrass noted in 1871, "it is our property, and no one has the right to sell them." He took the occasion to draw attention to the needs of his people: "We want cattle, tools, agricultural implements, and assistance in everything when we come to settle." To this he added aid in times of famine, a prohibition against alcohol, and some restriction of the American traders.[49] In areas with more immediate prospects for white settlement in the only region experiencing population growth remotely comparable to the American emigration pressures, the Manitoba Indians were also quick to take advantage of Canadian preoccupation with land to press their own concerns. The official memorandum documenting these demands, but not written into the treaty itself, included a list of domestic animals to be supplied as well as some agricultural equipment.[50] Similar terms, included for the first time in the treaty document, appeared in Treaty 3 after Indian negotiators, employing the power arising from their strategic geographic location, improved the deal. In addition to agricultural animals and implements, reserve lands were calculated on a higher scale. Instead of the 160 acres per family of five stipulated in Treaties 1 and 2, Treaty 3 Indians won an allotment of 640 acres.

Canada was not oblivious or immune to the other factors that moved the United States to treaty making, but the difference in degree is striking. The Dominion government too had dreams of a national railroad. Gaining clear land title in order to extend the railway was a recognized step in the process, not an unfortunate obstacle. Whereas the transcontinental railroad in the United States would be a link to existing and expanding population centers, the future Canadian Pacific Railway was viewed, in contrast, as the means to spawn such communities. Neither did railroads in Canada offer the means, envisaged by General Sherman, of a technological solution to the Indian problem. In the 1870s the Canadian government did not perceive the Indians in this way. While a minor complication and more a potential threat than a real one, Canada's aboriginal population was probably less imposing an obstacle than the sheer physical demands of a railway across the Canadian Shield or through the Rocky Mountains. There was no connection made between the Indians and the railroads in Canadian sources or literature except the request, in the negotiations for Treaty 3, for free railroad passage by the Indians. The treaty commissioner felt no compunction about denying it.[51]

If there was anything comparable to the American agonies over national honor, it emerged from Canada's commitment to continue the treaty-making process of British tradition, which brought with it the beginnings of that attitude of Canadian superiority toward Americans in the realm of Indian affairs. Canada had undertaken the obligation to negotiate with the Indians in the Northwest Territory as part of the deal by which it purchased Rupert's Land. The practice was thus traditional, required no revisions of policy, and was expedient. But it also stroked the vanity of the infant Dominion, which regarded the British record on Indian treaties as the main reason for the quiet state of Indian relations in Canada. In explaining to Parliament his resolutions on the acquisition of Rupert's Land, William McDougall added that he was "glad to say that in Canada we had no difficulty in dealing with the Indians, which was experienced in the United States, and the reason was that we had always acted justly towards them, and desired to continue to do so." [52] British North America had no "century of dishonor."

Canadian smugness in this regard was bolstered by the Indian pressures to treat. Canadians could well believe that for the Indians to sign a treaty with the Crown or its representatives was for them to be assured of a fair and honorable deal. The pomp and circumstance that accompanied the treaty process, the injection of the Crown at every opportunity, and the language of treaty making were manifestations of this type of national honor. The Dominion government had no more regard for Indian culture, Indian government, or even Indian responsibility than had its American counterpart.[53] Apart from treaty making, Canada effectively considered Indians as wards of the state, though this was not formally the case until the 1876 Indian Act. The Dominion simply was not troubled with the legal wrangles that gave the Americans so much grief, but Canada did have tremendous regard for the treaty process. It overcame the difficult issue of land title and also resolved so many other problems that plagued the Americans. In theory and practice, aided as always by the absence of settler pressure in Canada, which might have put their principles sorely to the test, Canada's treaties could mitigate the circumstances that led to friction in the United States. This was all understood by Canadian officials. Their commitment to treaty making had not wavered, as had that of the Americans, from the original purpose of the exercise. As such, treaties were a reflection of Canada's national honor, an as yet unstained commodity. If national honor did not serve as a major motivation to treaty making in the 1870s, it at least ensured that treaties would be the chief instruments in Indian relations.

The factors that fueled the American national missionary impulse were not entirely absent in Canada, but they were very faint by comparison. It is necessary to distinguish between the Christian religious orders, with their spiritual mission to evangelize and thereby save the Indians, and the secular "mission," which inspired government action. The former was widespread in the Canadian West well before the government embarked on its secular but no less zealous conversion of the Indians into whites. Canada may have absorbed the theory of the empire's "white man's burden," but insofar as it affected treaty making, this national missionary drive was dim indeed. There was truly no comparable vision to that of the American "city upon a hill." Ideas about the potential and necessity of civilizing the Indians, and at least a theoretical commitment to it, were in evidence in the policymaking circles of the Canadian government in the 1870s. In his annual report for the year ending in June 1875, Minister of the Interior David Laird declared that "I am firmly persuaded that the true interests of the aborigines and of the State alike require that every effort should be made to aid the red man in lifting himself out of his condition of tutelage and dependence, and that it is clearly our wisdom and our duty, through education and every other means, to prepare him for a higher civilization by encouraging him to assume the privileges and responsibilities of full citizenship." [54] But this issue was seen to be a problem of post-treaty times. The determination of the Canadian government and its commissioners to restrict treaties to limited traditional goals reflected this. The United States in the 1867–68 treaties had undertaken an extraordinarily ambitious program either to resolve every aspect of its Indian problem in one effort or to fail in the attempt. Canada stubbornly resisted pressure to take more than one step at a time, acceding with ill grace to any expansion of aims. As such, the missionary impulse did not form a major force in Canada's coming to the treaty table, although it did influence what happened when it got there.

One aspect unique to Canadian motivations was fear of complications occasioned by American conflict. This came to the fore in the move to engage the Blackfoot Confederacy in Treaty 7. Alone among the Canadian Indians treated with in the 1870s, the Blackfoot do not appear to have sought out the government in a desire for a treaty. Given the sluggishness of Canadian initiative in treaty making, this might have been expected to delay a Blackfoot treaty indefinitely. In 1876, however, events south of the border prompted the Dominion government to give the matter more attention. In 1876 the Americans had embarked on major campaigns in their Black Hills war with the Sioux. In the Fort Laramie Treaty of 1868, the Black Hills were designated part of the Great Sioux Reservation, but the discovery of gold there in 1874 relegated this treaty promise to the dustbin. The Sioux resisted this latest brazen invasion by the Americans and war resulted. Even as Canadian treaty commissioners were preparing to sit down with the Crees on the North Saskatchewan in the summer of 1876, the U.S. Army experienced its greatest disaster in the Indian wars with the annihilation of Lt. Col. George A. Custer's Seventh Cavalry at the Little Bighorn. The Canadian government was alarmed at these events, even more so when word came of a proposed alliance between the Sioux and their customary enemies, the Blackfoot.[55] Such an alliance threatened the security of Canadian lives in the sparsely settled West. The Northwest Mounted Police, a preventive force of law and order, not a true military organization, could not be expected to offer adequate defense in a real war. There was also the possibility of diplomatic complications as the Americans might decide, in order to quell the opposition, to cross into Canadian territory, a violation of sovereignty that Canada was not prepared to resist.[56] The necessity of emphasizing to the Blackfoot the difference between Canada and the United States and in binding the Blackfoot to good behavior suddenly took on greater significance. A treaty commission was subsequently dispatched to negotiate this agreement in 1877, employing the offices not only of the new lieutenant governor of the Northwest Territory, David Laird, but also the senior officer of the Northwest Mounted Police, Commissioner James F. Macleod, who was expected to wield his formidable personal influence in persuading the Blackfoot of the disadvantages of war.[57]

There were two points on which Canadian and American motivation did coincide. The United States was anxious to complete its transcontinental railway. Canada was less ambitious, but nonetheless was moved to treat in two cases, at least in part, because of transportation considerations. Treaty 3 covered a region that was recognized as an important transportation avenue during the 1869–70 Red River Rebellion. If an all-Canadian route to Red River and beyond were ever built, this territory was crucial. It was also an issue in Treaty 5, which dealt initially with the northern part of the abbreviated province of Manitoba. In this case, it was access to the great lakes of the province that attracted the government's eye. The Indians of this region, vulnerable to the vicissitudes of the fur-trade business that had long flourished there but was then beginning to fade, were particularly anxious to transform the means by which they made a living.[58] The government was unmoved by Indian interests, but it was very concerned about clear passage on the lakes in the days before the railroad eased transportation and quite interested in the mineral potential of the region.[59]

Whatever their differences on treaty making, both governments were equally preoccupied with financial matters. The Dominion government was no less concerned about the costs of Indian relations than was the American government. In fact, given the straitened state of the Canadian treasury and the fragile condition of the economy in the 1870s, there was probably more interest in economy in Canada, where "in the 1870s, when the United States was spending $20 million a year on Indian wars, Ottawa's entire budget was only $19 million."[60] Canadians feared an Indian war as much for the cost as for the turmoil. Prime Minister Alexander Mackenzie had hardly assumed office in 1873 before he was inundated with correspondence from the indefatigable Alexander Morris, lieutenant governor of the Northwest Territory, on relations with the Indians. Mackenzie, who represented a different political party, nonetheless assured Morris of his unfailing support in these matters and remarked, "I never doubted that our true policy was to make friends of them even at a considerable cost, as anything is cheaper and [sic] than an Indian war."[61] Mackenzie's choice of words echoed the often repeated American refrain on the same subject, that it was "cheaper to feed them than fight them."

Treaties may have been the accepted method by which relations with the Indians were conducted, but it was circumstances that brought the governments in Washington and Ottawa to employ these means when they confronted the problem of the Indians in the West in the late 1860s. In the United States, war was the precipitating factor, although a host of subordinate causes lent support to a renewed effort at negotiations in the West. Treaties were new in Canada, to the Dominion government if not in the history of British North America. Inexperience may have influenced the sluggish approach to Indian affairs taken by the new government in Ottawa, but more important was the overall lack of consideration given by the coterie of politicians to anyone or anything outside their immediate circle of concern. Nowhere was this more apparent than in the casual absorption of Rupert's Land, where national complacency was jarred by the vigorous reaction of those people most directly affected by the transfer—the Métis and Indians of the Prairie West. Scrambling for a response, Canada too turned to treaty making as the most effective means to address the Indian question.

4 The Making of the Medicine Lodge, Fort Laramie, and Numbered Treaties

The treaty sessions on the American Plains in 1867–68 and on the Canadian Prairies in the 1870s were among the largest ever held in the two nations. The governments of both took the meetings very seriously, reflecting both the physical magnitude of the conferences and the range of tasks to be accomplished. Their earnestness was indicated in the practical measures of treaty making, including the origin of and instructions to the commissions appointed, the caliber and competence of the men selected to serve on these commissions, and the locations chosen and security and social arrangements made to facilitate the negotiations.

The plains treaties of this era originated, in both countries, at the highest levels of government. The Great Peace Commission of 1867–68 came into being by a joint act of Congress signed into law on July 20, 1867. Although its credentials were seemingly unimpeachable, the commission did represent a new departure in treaty making. It was the president's responsibility under the Constitution to inaugurate such work, and yet the act opened with the statement, "That the President of the United States be, and he is hereby, authorized to appoint a commission."[1] In effect, Congress was directing the president and giving him a sanction he did not need. The point is not unimportant. In the contentious appropriations debates that followed the work of the commission, the legitimacy of the treaties was actually challenged in Congress on the basis of these "irregular origins."[2]

Canada was new to the practice of treaty making in its own right, but within the parliamentary system dissent was more controlled than in the divided authority of the American congressional system. All decisions regarding the Numbered Treaties rested exclusively with the prime minister and his cabinet. Parliament, like the House of Representatives, controlled the purse strings of these activities, but the party system, more rigidly constituted in Canada than in the United States, ensured that policies promoted by the prime minister in council would likely win advocacy in the House. Of course, such opposition would also have required interest, but Parliament engaged in none of the agonized self-examination that infused congressional consideration of Indian treaties.

The contrast in objectives sought from treaty making was nowhere more apparent than in the instructions that guided the commissioners sent to conclude arrangements with the Indians. These were made explicit in the U.S. Congress's authorization legislation of July 20 and in Canada in the several directives of the Privy Council, issued in a flurry before each of the Numbered Treaties. These documents not only defined the goals of each nation but also indicated the gulf by then existing between the two on the purposes of treaty making generally. The American legislation reflected a desperate need to solve the Indian problem. Canada's instructions were, by comparison, exceptionally narrow and continued to echo the traditional ends of Indian treaty making. The nature of these instructions would have some bearing on the direction negotiations and terms would take.

The Great Peace Commission went west with a comprehensive mandate of daunting proportions, delineated in the July 20 Act and worth citing at length. Congress authorized that the commission "shall have power and authority to call together the chiefs and headmen of such bands or tribes of Indians as are now waging war against the United States or committing depredations upon the people thereof, to ascertain the alleged reasons for their acts of hostility, and in their discretion, under the direction of the President, to make and conclude with said bands or tribes such treaty stipulations, subject to the action of the Senate, as may remove all just causes of complaint on their part, and at the same time establish security for person and property along the lines of railroad now being constructed to the Pacific and other thoroughfares of travel to the western Territories, and such as will most likely insure civilization for the Indians and peace and safety for the whites."[3] The act included an additional six sections dealing with reservations to be established (section 2); monies to be allotted to the purpose of treaty making (section 3); a requirement that the secretary of war provide adequate logistical assistance (section 4); an "or else" clause threatening military action in the event of failure and specifying the forces to be used in that contingency (sections 5 and 6); and a demand that the commission submit a comprehensive report on its activities (section 7).

The goals of the commission could not have been clearer, nor could they have been any broader. They encompassed most of the concerns that plagued American Indian policy on the plains—war and peace, settler and railroad security, and the compulsion to "civilize" the Indians. The humanitarian influence was starkly apparent in the expressed desire to determine the causes of Indian hostility and to ameliorate those conditions. This commitment was a direct response to the several commission reports flooding Congress in 1867 fingering unrestrained settlers, miners, and army personnel as the chief instigators of Indian hostility. The intent "to make . . . such treaty stipulations . . . as will most likely insure civilization for the Indians" was an understated expression of the other significant humanitarian impulse and hardly indicated the critical impact of this element as the resolution of the vexing Indian problem. In addition, it failed to anticipate the importance that the commissioners would place on civilization. The secondary articles promising military action in the event of failure served as a sop to those in Congress and in the West who would have preferred an all-out war of extermination instead.[4]

For all its thoroughness, the act was severely flawed by several critical omissions, perhaps more clear in retrospect than at the time. The most basic of these was the absence, outside the assignment of monies to pay for the actual negotiations, of any fiscal limitations or requirements. The 1865 treaties had sparked furious debate in the Senate over the outrageously extravagant nature of the annuities awarded therein, and yet less than two years later, Congress itself was constituting a peace commission for which it failed to establish fiscal guidelines on acceptable expenditures. As the treaty system in the United States would fall in a conflict over the Indian appropriations bill meant to pick up the tab for the 1867–68 treaties, this was a significant oversight indeed.

This omission nicely complemented the ambiguous and anomalous position of the commissioners themselves. They were given, as the instructions imply, sweeping authority and responsibility, and yet they really had very little power and even less direction. Congress had essentially unloaded a very contentious problem into the hands of a few men, only one of whom—Sen. John Henderson—had a direct connection to the body that would approve or disallow the work. Congress had created the commission but had no obligation to support or approve the action taken in its name, and few members would feel any compulsion to do so later.[5] The commissioners were also told very clearly what to do but, aside from the section authorizing the establishment of reservations—and even these instructions included a wide degree of latitude—there were no practical guidelines as to how their objectives should be met. The Great Peace Commission not only labored under the burden of over-whelming, diverse, and conflicting expectations imposed on the treaty-making process, but also set out to achieve unprecedented, ambitious ends with neither explicit guidelines nor unequivocal support.

The Numbered Treaties had more nebulous, but no less prestigious, origins in the considerably less structured surroundings of the prime minister's cabinet. These treaties were not negotiated in a body and therefore were undertaken in each instance as the result of individual orders of the Privy Council. In contrast to the American treaty instructions, which were typed and printed in an appendix to the *Congressional Globe* of the appropriate session (among other places), the Privy Council's orders were handwritten and copies of the orders exist in the records of the Privy Council Office as well as in the public papers of some of those involved in the treaty process. Frequently, more than one order was issued on each occasion, dealing with different aspects of the particular treaty proposed. The three matters that regularly warranted attention in these transmissions, and in supplementary communications from the appropriate minister, were the appointment of the commissioners, a statement of the point of the treaty (which was always and exclusively to extinguish Indian land title, sometimes detailing the territory under question), and some very detailed dickering over the price to be paid, in the form of annuities, for this prize.[6] The simplicity and directness of the Canadian instructions are startling in comparison to those given to the American commissioners, and they reflected the different priorities established by the two governments. There was no mention in the orders of any object other than that of extinguishing land title. What concerns the Dominion government may have had about the disaffection of the Plains Indians were expected to find amelioration in the process settling the trouble-some land question. The conflict that did exist, and there was some, only accelerated the timetable for treaty making. Thus the veiled threats at Portage la Prairie and the very real interference with telegraph and survey crews on the prairies did draw Ottawa's attention and encourage action.

Canadians were both more confident of the appeal of British policy as a pacifying force and less able to recognize a threat that did not come in the direct form Americans experienced. There was no war to end, no peace to be made, and no outstanding grievance that could not be re-solved within the narrow confines of the government's conception of the treaties, whatever other ideas the Indians may have had. There was no need to ensure the security of railroads specifically as, again, extinguishment of land title would decide this. The lack of evidence implying cabinet discussion of a civilization policy for the Plains Indians and the absence of any reference to such a program as a treaty goal in the Orders of the Privy Council reflect the constancy of Canadian treaty policy. From the government's perspective, treaties would precede civilization, not organize it.

The reiteration of the extinguishment of land title as the chief objective was only a minor point in comparison to the constant refrain over how much this objective would cost. In this the Canadian government was influenced both by the terms of earlier treaties in British North America and the American example. There was some insistence that no more than four dollars per head had been paid previously in central Canada.[7] Treaty 3 annuities were initially restricted to this sum, but the failure to conclude a treaty for two years at these rates, and information that the Americans paid much higher annuities to Indians just across the border, forced a grudging concession.[8] A change in commissioners, from the less energetic and certainly less powerful Wemyss Simpson to Lt. Gov. Alexander Morris, resulted in a compromise solution that won the government's approval.[9] Ottawa's desire to maintain a constant rate in annuities filled subsequent instructions to treaty commissioners. The ability of these officials to adhere to the stingy government guidelines was the basis on which treaties and negotiators were adjudged successful or not.[10] Thus Canada, unlike the United States, dispatched its representatives with some general idea of what the process was going to cost the government on an annual basis.

Canadian treaty instructions, as manifested in the Orders of the Privy Council, were really no clearer than the American directions on the power and authority of the appointed commissioners to make binding agreements. The cabinet formally embraced no more responsibility to act on the work of its commissioners than did Congress the efforts of the Great Peace Commission. In the seven Numbered Treaties, the lieutenant governor of the Northwest Territory played an active role, but in terms of the power structure of the federal government, he was a negligible influence. The Canadian government in the 1870s was, however, a much smaller, more informal organization than the congressional system. This ensured an intimacy of acquaintance among the power brokers not as apparent in the American context. Treaties 4, 5, and 6 were negotiated by a lieutenant governor who did not belong to the same political party as the government he was representing, yet he was nonetheless well-acquainted with the members of the cabinet who directed him, and he corresponded extensively with some of them. Alexander Morris, lieutenant governor of Manitoba and the Northwest Territory from 1872 through 1876 (and Manitoba alone through 1877), had the support of his immediate superior in Indian matters, the Conservative minister of the interior, Alexander Campbell, and of Prime Minister Sir John A. Macdonald. But Morris also enjoyed the confidence of their Liberal successors, Minister of the Interior David Laird and Prime Minister Alexander Mackenzie. The Liberals warmly enjoined Morris to keep them informed of matters in the Northwest Territory both privately and officially.[11] Laird, in dispatching instructions extra to the Privy Council orders on the making of Treaty 6, remarked that, "Your large experience and past success in conducting Indian negotiations relieves me from the necessity of giving you any detailed instructions in reference to your present mission."[12]

The Canadian treaties did garner some criticism from the government, however. Minister of the Interior Laird adjusted the terms of Treaties 1 and 2 to dispel charges made by the Indians with regard to the unfulfilled terms of the "Outside Promises." Complaints of this nature were registered almost from the signing of Treaty 1, bouncing from the desk of the lieutenant governor to the office of Indian affairs and to the minister of the interior. After investigating the matter himself in 1874 while attending the negotiations for Treaty 4, Laird supported a modification of Treaties 1 and 2, adding to them as an official supplement the memorandum of the "Outside Promises" produced by the original negotiators.[13] There was also some consternation—although hardly comparable to American disputes—over the extraordinary provisions in Treaty 6.[14]

In general, though, the government accepted almost without question the work of its commissioners. This may have been a reflection of the parliamentary system, in which delegated authority was not subject to such critical second-guessing. The personal element evident in the close association of all parties involved could also have had some bearing on this confidence. Another factor, pointed out heatedly by Alexander Morris when his work on Treaty 6 was criticized, was that the Privy Council was very far from the scene of negotiations, and thus a certain flexibility with terms of the treaties on the part of the commissioners was to be understood.[15]

The practical results of the level of responsibility, power, and latitude given the commissioners in both countries were not immediately apparent, as the commissioners' authority was somewhat vague and definitely not binding. But, in fact, Canada's commissioners made treaties that won easy ratification with little hint of dissension, while the work of the American commissioners generated stormy debate and precipitated the end of the U.S. treaty-making system. Under their instructions, the American treaty makers had tremendous freedom to introduce radical changes in American Indian policy, and they certainly tried to exercise that mandate. The rejection of their work was a considerable surprise to many, even in Congress, where the irony of rejecting what they themselves had wrought was palpable.[16] The Canadian commissioners had a much narrower mandate, but some latitude nonetheless. While their work also was not considered binding until approval, they enjoyed a measure of confidence not accorded their American counterparts.

This difference in confidence is interesting given the caliber of men involved in the negotiations for both governments. Under the Act of July 20, seven men were appointed to the Great Peace Commission. Congress named the four civilians, leaving it to the president to appoint the three army officers "not below the rank of brigadier general."[17] The civilians included the sponsor of the bill to create the commission, Sen. John Henderson, as well as the commissioner of Indian affairs, Nathaniel G. Taylor. Henderson was a westerner from Missouri yet stood in the Senate, where he chaired the Committee on Indian Affairs, as a committed humanitarian. Taylor, a former Methodist minister, personified the American missionary impulse, secular and religious, to save the Indians. Samuel Tappan, a third appointee, also exemplified the missionary spirit. He had been an ardent abolitionist in "Bleeding Kansas" in pre–Civil War years, and in the wake of the war he had focused his attention on the Indian reform movement, exhibiting all the zeal he had hitherto devoted to the abolitionist cause.[18] Tappan had chaired one of the commissions investigating the Sand Creek Massacre and was the sort who would vilify U.S. Indian policy as a "national sin." The fourth civilian, John Sanborn, a volunteer officer in the Union army during the Civil War, had fought Indians in the West. But he had also been a negotiator of the 1865 treaties on the southern plains and cochair of the influential commission that had investigated the Fetterman Massacre and pointed an accusing finger at the military. The willingness of Congress to appoint men so clearly disposed to the humanitarian impulses in Indian policy was indicative of the strength of that position, for the moment, in Congress and northeastern public opinion. During the treaty negotiations themselves, Sanborn, who was addressed as "General" in recognition of his Civil War service, in fact sided with his military colleagues on crucial decisions.[19]

The commission was balanced by three military officers appointed by the president. The most important of these, indeed the most powerful figure on the commission, was Gen. William Tecumseh Sherman, whose stature in post–Civil War America was second only to future president Gen. Ulysses S. Grant. Sherman carried the authority vested in his own reputation as well as that of his official position as commander of the Division of the Missouri (virtually the entire Plains West). He had intimate ties with the War Department through his association with General Grant as well as in Congress, where his brother was an influential senator and a strong voice in criticism of the Indian treaty-making system.[20] Sherman had some military experience in prewar California but little on the plains before 1866.

He was supported by two lesser known generals, Alfred Terry and William S. Harney, and later Gen. Christopher Augur. Of the three, only Harney was well acquainted with the Plains Indians, especially the Sioux and Cheyennes, against whom he had led armies. After the Civil War, both Terry and Augur would forge their reputations as Indian-fighting generals on the plains, but neither had had much exposure to the Indians there before the treaty-making ventures of 1867–68.[21] Nonetheless, all had impressive military records and none were considered exterminationists.

It was an impressive array of talent, and "with the combined skills of the statesman, the soldier, the lawyer, the frontiersman, and the veteran Indian negotiator, the commission expected to produce a final solution to the Indian problem for those who lived east of the Rocky Mountains."[22] Certainly the professional standing and experience of these men suggested that such a resolution was at least actively and sincerely sought. But they represented exactly the uneasy mélange of disparate motivations that had driven the United States to the bargaining table. Their prestige, like the exalted expectations imposed on the treaty-making process, set the system up for a crushing defeat should they fail to achieve their objectives, for if these intelligent, informed, and committed men could find no solution, then perhaps there was no solution to find.

The comparative stature of the Canadian and American negotiators is difficult to assess. There simply was no Canadian equivalent to General Sherman. The most prestigious negotiator of the Numbered Treaties representing the government was David Laird, in his capacity as minister of the interior, who served as cocommissioner of Treaty 4. A lieutenant governor was present at all seven treaties and took the leading part in the negotiation of five of them. Lt. Gov. Adams Archibald's role in Treaties 1 and 2 was limited to observation and perhaps some unwarranted interference with the work of the chief commissioner, Indian Superintendent Wemyss Simpson.[23] More significant was Alexander Morris, the lieutenant governor who conducted the negotiations of four of the Numbered Treaties and the revision of the first two. Laird, who succeeded Morris as lieutenant governor of the Northwest Territory in 1876, concluded Treaty 7, wherein he took a more active role than he had at Treaty 4 but operated in the less-powerful office of lieutenant governor than as a cabinet minister. Indian Superintendent Simpson, the least significant of the chief negotiators, gained his appointment by virtue of his having been present at the negotiation of the Robinson Huron Treaty in 1850, and thus he was expected to have a more informed appreciation of what treaty terms were supposed to be than did the Privy Council members who had dispatched him.[24]

Subordinate treaty commissioners included S. J. Dawson, William J. Christie, James McKay, and Northwest Mounted Police commissioner James F. Macleod.[25] As Dominion surveyor, Dawson had laid out the vital road across the Canadian Shield in 1869–70 and urged the government to initiate treaty talks afterward.[26] His knowledge of the area and acquaintance with the Indians there resulted in his participation in the drawn-out negotiations that ended with Treaty 3 in 1873. Christie was a retired Hudson's Bay Company factor with extensive experience in the West, where he had spent twelve years in command of the Saskatchewan District. He was employed as a commissioner for Treaties 4 and 6 because "'his intimate acquaintance with the Indians of the Saskatchewan, their wants, habits and dialects'" was recognized as a valuable asset in the business of treaty making.[27]

A greater role was played by James McKay, an English-speaking Métis trader and former Hudson's Bay Company employee who moved into provincial politics in 1870. His knowledge of all facets of western life made him an asset to the government at each of the six treaty councils he attended, and his presence lent some continuity to the proceedings. As a commissioner for Treaty 6, he took an active role in the formal negotiations. McKay and Christie had the distinction of being the only treaty commissioners in either Canada or the United States to speak the language of the peoples with whom they were negotiating.

The only Canadian figure comparable to the American military officers was James F. Macleod, commissioner of the Northwest Mounted Police and himself a significant force in the Prairie West. Though not a man of national stature on Sherman's level, Macleod nevertheless held greater influence among the Indians than did the American general, and it is not an understatement to attribute the successful conclusion of Treaty 7 to his presence.[28]

A significant difference between treaty commissioners in the two countries, however, was their connection to the territory and the people with whom the treaties were being made. General Sherman's offices were in St. Louis, but he had only just arrived there and would shortly be reappointed to Washington. Senator Henderson represented Missouri but did his work in Washington. Of the three subordinate generals, only Harney could boast of an extended association with the Plains Indians. In Canada the lieutenant governors, in contrast to the senior American negotiators, lived and worked in the Prairie West. These officials were at least superficially acquainted with many of the Indian chiefs and headmen and had received some of them or their supplicants in their gubernatorial offices.[29] Superintendent Simpson was criticized by Lieutenant Governors Archibald and Morris because he exhibited a distinct reluctance to take up residence in the territory where his charges, the Indians of the Prairie West, lived.[30] Commissioners McKay and Christie were much better acquainted with various Indian bands and their leaders because of their careers in trade, and James Macleod had the closest relationship of a treaty negotiator with the Indians through his friendship with Blackfoot chief Crowfoot.

In both countries the treaties were negotiated in Indian country itself. This was the standard practice in British North America but not always the case in the United States. Americans had long recognized the psychological impact of transporting Indians from their home territories via modern means of transportation through increasingly populous centers of the burgeoning American West, to the metropolises of the East Coast, and finally to the home of the "Great Father" in Washington.[31] Neither Britain nor Canada indulged in this practice. It was not practical to take large bodies of Indians to London to meet the queen for treaty-making purposes. Ottawa would not have served these purposes, being neither an impressive metropolis in the 1870s nor the home of the "Great Queen Mother," although member of Parliament John Christian Schultz did suggest it as the proper venue in which to resolve the quagmire of the Outside Promises.[32] British and Canadian leaders were less pressed by the need to awe the Indians into submission, which was really the purpose of American ventures of this kind. Cost would also likely have been a consideration for the Canadians, where it was not for the Americans.

The commissioners not only went to Indian territory but also to locations favored by the Indians. Medicine Lodge Creek was a regular gathering place for the Indians of the southern plains and had been suggested by Ten Bears, a Comanche chief.[33] The Fort Laramie treaties were actually negotiated over several months at a series of military forts and trading posts, including Forts Sully, Rice, and David Russell, and concluded at Fort Laramie. The latter was an established military and trading post and easily accessible to the Americans. Medicine Lodge, in contrast, was particularly inconvenient for the commissioners. It lay in the heart of untrammeled Indian country, seventy miles from the nearest outpost at Fort Larned, and thus vulnerable should the conference turn sour. It was also difficult to transport the tons of treaty presents, trade goods, and food supplies to such an isolated location.

The Canadians chose similar places for similar reasons. The Stone Fort and Manitoba Post served for Treaties 1 and 2, Fort Frances for Treaty 3, Fort Qu'Appelle for Treaty 4, and Forts Pitt and Carlton for Treaty 6. All were outposts of the Hudson's Bay Company and thus as conveniently located for Indian and government access as was possible in these often remote regions. The commissioners went to the Indians themselves in the Treaty 5 negotiations, landing at various communities on Lake Winnipeg to secure this agreement. Treaty 7 was negotiated at Blackfoot Crossing, a site chosen by Blackfoot chief Crowfoot.[34] Fort Carlton had been added to the locations where the assemblies of Treaty 6 were to take place at the specific request of one of the Cree chiefs, Mistawasis, since it was more convenient to the Crees of central Saskatchewan.[35] These places were not always convenient for the government commissioners, though. The Stone Fort required a trip of only twenty miles from Fort Garry, but the negotiations at Fort Frances compelled the lieutenant governor to travel more than one hundred miles. By his own reckoning, Lieutenant Governor Morris traveled a thousand miles to complete Treaty 5. An even more extensive undertaking was required for Treaty 6, with the lieutenant governor traveling from Fort Garry to the North Saskatchewan and in the course of that summer covering sixteen hundred miles.[36]

A final matter of some interest to a comparison of treaty-making procedures was the distribution of presents. The different approaches of each nation toward this important aspect of Indian diplomacy reveals yet again the divergence in the meaning of treaties to the two governments. The United States was famous among the Indians for its lavish gift-giving, and the promise of presents was an alluring inducement in getting Indian crowds to gather. Gifts were distributed to all in attendance, not just to important figures, and at Medicine Lodge the bounty consisted of "bales of beads, buttons, bells, iron pans, tin cups, butcher knives, blankets, bolts of gaudy calico, pants, coats, hats, and, most enticingly, pistols and ammunition."[37] In fact, it was believed to be the promise of guns to be distributed that brought the Sioux to the peace table in the ill-fated negotiations of 1866 and encouraged them to try again in 1867.[38] Although this practice was condemned as a waste of money and tantamount to bribery, its defenders in Congress tried to invoke its historical precedents as a common feature of treaty making, pointing to the potentially unpleasant ramifications if it suddenly came to an end.[39] It remained an aspect of the treaties of 1867 and 1868, but the details of presents distributed do not figure in either the treaty text or recorded deliberations.

Canadians took a more formal position on presents. All communications to the Indians, especially those either promising or postponing treaty negotiations, were accompanied by presents for the chiefs or other leaders.[40] It was an accepted part of Indian relations. Presents, which in Canada were as likely to include money as well as gifts in kind, were specified in each of the treaties. The role of presents as an element in the formal proceedings, as opposed to a general pacifier or bribe, is suggested by the fact that not everyone was accorded a gift in Canadian practice. Regarding presents to be sent to calm the Indians of the North Saskatchewan in 1872, it was proposed that the gifts include everyone, indicating that this was not the usual practice.[41] Gifts were more commonly made to the chiefs and headmen. Each of the Numbered Treaties did include a one-time monetary gift to all who accepted the treaties, but even then the chiefs and headmen were accorded more money as well as specific gifts of clothing, medals, and flags.

All of the practical factors—origins of instructions, stature of the commissioners, and goals of the process—as well as the extensive accoutrements of negotiation suggest a formal and serious diplomatic exchange between peoples in the several treaty meetings of 1867–68 and the 1870s. At the same time, however, it was clear that American disillusionment with the practice was reaching a crisis point for the future of the policy. In Canada the chief attitude of those responsible for Indian affairs in Ottawa was disinterest. The peoples of the Prairie West had been ignored as irrelevant in the transfer of their lands to Canadian jurisdiction. Ottawa remained inattentive to their concerns until such matters were coupled with persistent and threatening protests. Only then was indifference overcome. The implications of these attitudes become more apparent in an examination of the treaties themselves, wherein it can be seen that the diplomatic balance affected by the formal proceedings gave way to a relationship heavily weighted in favor of the white governments involved.

5   The Role of "Others" in Treaty Making

Officially there were only two parties to the treaties, the governments and the Indians. But treaty councils were grand affairs and attracted a host of others to the proceedings. Some, like the interpreters, were integral to the process itself. The U.S. Army and its Canadian equivalents, the militia and the Northwest Mounted Police, served a variety of support functions, from logistics and organization to security, but occasionally played a formal or ceremonial role as well. Missionaries too were drawn to the councils, which proved a natural magnet to those dedicated to a civilizing mission in all its aspects. The "mixed-blood" population, the Métis as they were known in Canada, also attended the treaty sessions, which had significant implications for their future. Each of these groups participated in the treaty-making ventures of 1867–68 and the 1870s.

As critical to successful treaty making as the commissioners and their Indian counterparts were, they would have been unable to proceed without effective interpreters. Government and Indians alike recognized this need, and in several cases both parties sought out competent translators. Interpreters were an eclectic group that included frontiersmen with long-standing Indian connections through their Indian wives, the mixed-blood adult children of such unions, and occasionally missionaries. One of the most contentious points in subsequent assessments of the validity of both the American and Canadian treaties has been the question of interpretation. As Robert Utley has noted, "Exact meaning is extremely difficult to convey from one language to another and the average [frontier] interpreter . . . was scarcely proficient in the science. . . . Even the honest seeker of truth encountered enormous obstacles stemming from the differences in cultural background."[1] This is true to a point, and yet to emphasize the shortcomings of the interpreters would be a disservice to their very real contributions and obscure the nature of the misunderstanding that has plagued historical interpretation of the treaties.

The Americans faced a momentous challenge of communication at the Medicine Lodge gathering, where several languages were spoken. However, the United States also had experience with treaty councils with the Plains Indians, and both the army and the Department of the Interior had employed interpreters for these peoples previously. The interpreters hired by the American government divide easily into two categories—men married to Indian women and the mixed-blood children of these marriages. Especially on the southern plains, these interracial relationships produced a surprising number of people who moved easily between cultures and exhibited a sound grasp of at least one Indian language as well as English.

The Southern Cheyennes were particularly well served in this capacity. Competent interpreters of their language included three mixed-blood children of long-time plains trader William Bent and his Cheyenne wife (or wives). George, Charlie, and Julia Bent were all on hand at Medicine Lodge, although only George was listed as an official interpreter. John S. Smith, another interpreter, was married to a Cheyenne woman and lived among her people. Edmund Guerrier, like the Bents, was the son of a similarly mixed union. Smith and Guerrier had served as translators at the 1865 Treaty of the Little Arkansas. The Bents and Guerrier had attended school, and Guerrier had even gone on to St. Louis University.[2] George and Charlie Bent and Guerrier had been in the Cheyenne camp when the militia attacked at Sand Creek in November 1864, and afterward the Bent brothers remained among the Cheyenne hostiles until the council at Medicine Lodge. The interpreters in this instance, then, were well equipped to deal with both languages and cultures, and if sympathies were closely examined they would likely have fallen in Indian favor.

More instructive than the Cheyenne situation at Medicine Lodge was the experience of the Kiowas, with whom interpretation was expected to be a major problem. The distinctive nature of the Kiowa language, which was unrelated to other Plains Indian languages, made it difficult to find anyone other than the Kiowas themselves who spoke it—there is some confusion in treaty reports as to whether anyone else did.[3] At worst these participants had to function through a Comanche intermediary, as Comanche was the common trading language of the southern plains and known to the Kiowas. The Comanche interpreter at Medicine Lodge was Philip McCusker, a scout and interpreter who had the distinction of an exceptionally close association with that tribe through his Comanche wife. He had worked for the Department of the Interior before and at Medicine Lodge was acknowledged as principal interpreter.[4]

McCusker's skill in conveying the treaty terms, in either Comanche or Kiowa, is best assessed by the Indians' understanding of those terms, insofar as this can be determined from council records. During the discussions a Kiowa leader, Satanta, took a major role in rebutting the government position. After listening to Senator Henderson's promises of "civilization, religion, and wealth" based on relocation, agriculture, education, and farming assistance, Satanta responded, "All the land south of the Arkansas belongs to the Kiowas and Comanches, and I don't want to give away any of it. I love the land and the buffalo, and I will not part with any."[5] At a later meeting, he rejected other elements of the commission's program, declaring, "This building homes for us is all nonsense; we don't want you to build any for us. We would all die. . . . This trusting to the agents for my food, I do not believe in it."[6] Such statements indicate an appreciation of the demand for a land surrender and for what the civilization terms implied for the Kiowa way of life. This understanding also suggests an effective bridging of the language barrier, even with the Kiowas.

Such a conclusion cannot be drawn with certainty from the treaty discussions at Fort Laramie, where the Indian participants did not give an informed rejection of the civilization measures entrenched in the treaties, at least as recorded in the council transcripts. Seven men were identified in the Fort Laramie treaties as interpreters, about whom little is known. Most had Sioux wives and French names and were traders and frontiersmen.[7] Their backgrounds were likely narrower than, for instance, those available to translate for the Southern Cheyennes. This was not necessarily the most serious problem that hampered understanding, however.

The treaty council minutes with various Sioux peoples also suggest that the two parties involved were able to communicate their interests effectively. The commissioners explained the benefits of "civilization" and the measures of that nature written into the treaty. The leaders of the different Sioux peoples offered unenthusiastic responses to those provisions but lent their voices eagerly to an insistence on a series of other terms of more interest to them. These demands included a desire for peace, objections to the Bozeman Trail and other transportation routes cutting up their territories and chasing off the game, the delivery of annuities promised in earlier treaties, and a persistent appeal for ammunition and guns.[8]

The Sioux rejection of the civilization terms was muted in comparison to that made by the southern plains peoples, but may perhaps be attrib-

uted as much to the commissioners as to a failure on the part of the interpreters. At Medicine Lodge, Senator Henderson did most of the talking,
and his speeches focused almost exclusively on the civilization aspects of
the treaty.[9] In the early councils with the Sioux in 1867, General Sherman
was the central figure, and in 1868 the commission lost Taylor and Henderson to responsibilities in Washington, leaving a preponderance of
generals to conclude the negotiations. Thus, in the final stage of treaty
councils, the Sioux dealt almost exclusively with Generals Harney and
Terry, and with John Sanborn, who proved a supporter of the army's position. The generals, as evidenced in the treaty minutes, were intent on
making peace. As a result they dealt largely with the issues raised by the
Indians as the causes for discontent rather than flogging the civilization
program in which they had less confidence.[10] When Red Cloud came to
Fort Laramie in November 1868, the officer accepting his adhesion reported that "the provisions of the treaty in answer to questions of Red
Cloud, were explained to them, but in answer to whether he wished to
hear all the points in regard to the reservation and farming. He [sic] stated
that he had learned from others all he cared to know about that." [11] In
this instance, Red Cloud did not even test the interpreters. He was not
interested.

Canada did not have the treaty-making experience of the United States
but could claim other advantages when it came to communicating with
different cultures in different languages. The centuries-old presence of the
Hudson's Bay Company in the West, the half-century of Christian missionary experience there, and the existence of a large mixed-blood population—the Métis—ensured a significant resource base from which potential interpreters might be drawn. The government turned to these
sources for assistance when it opened negotiations for the first of the
Numbered Treaties in 1871. So did the Indians. One of the notable characteristics of the making of those agreements was the care taken by the
Indians themselves to ensure effective translation.

At the Stone Fort in 1871, the government and Indians alike employed
as interpreters Indian men who were also ministers in the Anglican
church, although the report of the treaty session in the local newspaper
remarked that it was the government interpreter, the Reverend Henry
Cochrane, who "did nearly all the translating during the Treaty." [12] Little
information was recorded about the negotiations of Treaty 2, although it
was negotiated under the same instructions and by the same commission
as Treaty 1, and possibly the same interpreters were used. The official in-

terpreter at Treaty 4 was also an Indian, Charles Pratt, and like Cochrane, he was a missionary under the auspices of the Anglican church.[13] Cochrane divided interpretation duties with James McKay in the several stops made by treaty commissioners for Treaty 5.[14]

An immediate controversy arose in the wake of Treaties 1 and 2 with Indian charges of government failure to fulfill treaty terms. This problem, the Outside Promises issue, was likely a result of the commissioners' narrow interpretation of their mandate rather than any inadequate translation, because many of the terms that caused the furor were recorded in a separate memorandum.[15] But when the matter was addressed in official councils in 1875, the Indians were not prepared to risk further misunderstanding. In addition to the three government interpreters on hand, there were also "three Indians, who understood English, and who had at an early period been selected by the Indians to check the interpretation of what was said."[16]

The government went to the final Treaty 3 negotiations with Nicholas Chatelain, a Métis employee of the Hudson's Bay Company, identified by Lieutenant Governor Morris as the government interpreter, although James McKay was credited in the treaty text with explaining the terms. Looking out for their own interests, the Indians "had also an Indian reporter, whose duty was to commit to memory all that was said. They had also secured the services of M. Joseph Nolin, of Point du Chene, to take notes in French of the negotiations."[17] The Treaty 3 Indians may have acted cautiously in light of the experience of those who had signed Treaties 1 and 2, or perhaps they were exhibiting a facet of the negotiating skill they had employed in their own protracted negotiations with Canada. At Treaty 3 there was also an array of Métis observers from Manitoba as well as from the Rainy Lake–Rainy River region, and thus there was no shortage of potential translators on hand to ensure understanding.

The government went to the Treaty 6 negotiations at Fort Carlton and Fort Pitt with two official interpreters, Peter Ballendine and the Reverend John McKay. According to Peter Erasmus, who would be appointed chief interpreter, Ballendine was not competent to translate, and John McKay was proficient only in Swampy Cree and thus could not adequately convey Plains Cree.[18] James McKay and William Christie were also present, and although neither were officially designated interpreters, Morris noted that they played a role nonetheless, "watching how the answers were rendered, and correcting when necessary."[19] Having come with two possible interpreters, Morris was unenthusiastic when confronted by the translator hired by Chief Mistawasis, the Métis trader Peter Erasmus. Erasmus assumed that Morris objected to an additional interpreter because of the expense, but Mistawasis insisted, assuring the lieutenant governor that "We will pay our own man and I already see that it will be well for us to do so." The chief added, "I can speak Blackfoot and know what it takes to interpret. If you do not want the arrangement, there will be no talks." [20] Morris failed to record this exchange, perhaps because he quickly recognized Erasmus's merit, later describing him as "a most efficient interpreter." [21] Mistawasis's insistence on and Morris's endorsement of Erasmus suggest an earnest desire by both parties to ensure the clearest communication and best understanding of terms possible.

Three names were associated with interpretation at the 1877 treaty council at Blackfoot Crossing. The mixed-blood son of a Blood woman and white man, Jerry Potts was a scout and interpreter who had worked for the Northwest Mounted Police since 1874. His name has been the one most often mentioned in connection with this treaty, although he was not the chief interpreter. On the treaty itself James Bird was recorded as having read and explained the terms. Lieutenant Governor Laird, acknowledging interpretation problems, noted in his official report that "the Commissioners at first had not a good interpreter of the Blackfoot language" but then hired Bird, who "has been many years among the Piegans and Blackfeet, and is a very intelligent interpreter." [22] Laird also noted with approval the assistance of Jean L'Heureux, a Quebec native with some formal education and an extensive if bizarre career among the Blackfoot. [23] L'Heureux served as interpreter for Blackfoot chief Crowfoot. In addition to these men, two missionaries, Father Constantine Scollen and the Reverend John McDougall, were on hand. Scollen had worked among the Blackfoot, although he may have been more adept with the Cree language. McDougall operated a mission among the Stony Indians and interpreted for them. [24]

Interpretation at the Blackfoot treaty, then, was likely of a reasonable caliber. The official minutes of the gathering suggest a problem similar to that which characterized the American councils with the Sioux. Lieutenant Governor Laird was the chief commissioner and main spokesman. He imparted the treaty terms, and yet in his major speeches Laird did not emphasize the land surrender element that constituted most of the treaty. Because the Blackfoot, unlike the Plains Crees at Treaty 6, did not press the issues of agriculture or education, neither did Laird. The lieutenant governor may have shaped the discussion to accord with Blackfoot demands, as Morris had done at Treaty 6, but Laird might also have been concerned to avoid the additional expenditures Morris had undertaken and which had incurred displeasure in Ottawa.[25]

Instead, Laird told those gathered at Blackfoot Crossing what they wanted to hear, explaining the buffalo preservation measure passed under his direction by the Council of the Northwest Territory, extolling the virtues of the Northwest Mounted Police, and detailing the annuities to be provided under the treaty.[26] These included a general issue of ammunition and a Winchester rifle for every chief and subchief, a term not included in any of the other Numbered Treaties. Like the Sioux who listened to treaty commissioners read off the civilization terms and then moved on to their own concerns, the Blackfoot had other things on their minds. Along with buffalo preservation, they wanted their lands secured from intruders. In this they trusted to the good will of the Northwest Mounted Police, who had already rid them of the American whisky traders. Indeed, Blackfoot spokesmen talked more of the police than they did about the terms for stock raising and farming.[27]

The interpreters employed at Blackfoot Crossing may well have been up to the task of communicating the terms even in their crosscultural complexity, but they were not asked to do so in great detail. In the Blackfoot treaty, as in the Treaty of Fort Laramie with the Sioux, little emphasis was given to the essence of the documents and neither side pressed the issue. The interpreters could do only what was asked of them, and in some cases this was not very much.

Christian missionaries were a fact of life in North American Indian relations and had been from the beginning. The first missionary order, the Recollets, had arrived in New France in 1615 with the Jesuits not far behind. After that, missionaries spread west across the continent on the heels of the fur trade, a pattern still discernible in the location of mission settlements in the 1860s and 1870s. Because of this, some Indian nations, among them the Canadian Blackfoot and the American Plains Indians, who were less involved in the fur trade, had little if any contact with them even by the 1860s.[28]

Missionaries in what would be by 1870 the United States and Canada had similar goals and served comparable functions in the treaty-making ventures of the 1860s and 1870s. In both places missionaries were employed to spread the word of upcoming treaty councils and were expected to encourage attendance. The religious orders were considered by the national governments as the spearhead of civilization among the Indians, and thus it was assumed they would have a part to play in the implementation of such a policy in the West.

Missionaries, though, were not just unofficial representatives of the government. Evangelization had always been the goal of the missionary religious orders, and they came to treaty councils as much with this in mind as anything else. As well, many individuals saw themselves as intermediaries, representing Indian interests to governments that might not otherwise be sensitive to Indian concerns. In this capacity missionaries in Canada played a role in prompting the government to treat with the Indians. Despite the similarity of means and goals, the role and impact of missionaries in the treaty-making enterprises on the plains of the two countries were quite different. This was the result of their previous missionary experience in the West.

The settlement at Red River drew a formal religious presence as early as 1818, when the Roman Catholic Church in Quebec dispatched priests to minister to the French-speaking Catholic Métis population who had begun to settle there. The Church of England responded by sending its first missionary and minister in 1820. More venturesome were the Methodists, who inaugurated their mission to the Indians of the West in 1840. In the course of the ensuing decade, Methodists established themselves on the fur-trade routes across the Northwest as far as Norway House at the head of Lake Winnipeg and Edmonton House on the North Saskatchewan River. Unlike the two more established churches, which existed at Red River on the sufferance of the Hudson's Bay Company, the Methodist effort operated under company auspices. Like their missionary counterparts in other faiths, the Methodists saw education and agriculture as fundamental to their ambitions for evangelization. Gardens were introduced at the missions, and the Reverend James Evans tried to raise livestock at Norway House. He was more successful in his educational endeavors, though, and his development of the Cree syllabic system was effective in disseminating the Bible and other religious literature among the Plains Crees.[29] The Roman Catholics established their own mission on the North Saskatchewan in 1844. Although operating with less enthusiastic support from the Hudson's Bay Company, the Catholic Church had a legitimate calling in the Northwest, again because of the Métis there.[30]

This foundation of missionary efforts in the Canadian West was important, but it was the next generation of religious practitioners who were to play a part in treaty making there. At Red River the Anglican Church had undertaken not only to minister to the Indians of the region but also to find among them suitable candidates to be trained to minister to their own people. In this they had some success. At Treaty 1 negotiations the Anglican presence was significant. The Reverend Henry Cochrane and Henry McCorrister, identified respectively as Indian missionary and Indian clergyman, had both been raised in the Indian settlement of St. Peter's.[31] The influence of the religious presence is difficult to determine, but Cochrane was in a particularly advantageous position as the chief interpreter. Also in attendance was the Venerable Archdeacon Abraham Cowley, who had managed the Anglican mission at St. Peter's from 1857 to 1866. One of the more vocal Indian spokesmen at Treaty 1 was Henry Prince, identified as chief of the Christian Ojibwa and a resident of St. Peter's. Prince, among others, made the case for agricultural assistance and advanced a series of demands that included clothing, a house, agricultural supplies, stock, a horse and buggy for chiefs, hunting supplies, and freedom from taxation.[32] In the face of these demands, the treaty commissioners yielded to other speakers to argue the merits of the treaty terms as offered.[33] Cochrane spoke up to express his dismay at the extravagant demands.[34] Archdeacon Cowley also addressed the Indians, and one official participant attributed to him the confusion of terms that later led to Indian discontent.[35] On the basis of such superficial evidence, the Anglican influence in winning Indian assent to the treaty the next day cannot be determined, but that the Anglicans were present in force and in a position to exert what influence they could cannot be ignored. Cochrane, McCorrister, and Cowley all signed Treaty 1 as witnesses.

The impact of missionaries at the subsequent three treaties—2, 3, and 4—is more difficult to ascertain. Nobody identified as an Anglican missionary or clergyman showed up as official treaty witnesses and no mention is made of any in official accounts, although it is unlikely these events passed them by altogether. The Methodists had a firmer grasp on the northern edge of Manitoba and beyond, thanks to missionary efforts on the fur trade routes in the 1840s. Egerton Ryerson Young witnessed Treaty 5 at Berens River and two additional missionaries, John H. Ruttan and O. German, both identified in the treaty as Methodist ministers, signed as witnesses at Norway House. Henry Cochrane again served as interpreter at adhesions to this treaty in 1876, where his services were acknowledged as valuable.[36] But there is little evidence to suggest that the missionaries at any of these councils exercised influence over either the Indians involved or the terms that resulted.

By 1870 the religious pioneers at Red River had expanded their networks along the fur-trade routes on the northern fringes of the prairies and had been joined by the Presbyterians. Each faith had their established centers and all yielded a number of men who came to play important roles in the treaty-making process on the plains in 1876 and 1877. These included George and John McDougall, father and son Wesleyan Methodist missionaries to the Crees at the their Victoria mission and to the Stonies in the Rocky Mountain foothills; Roman Catholic Fathers Albert Lacombe and Constantine Scollen, who worked among the Crees on the North Saskatchewan and also, with less success, among the Blackfoot; and John McKay and James Nisbet, Presbyterians operating out of Prince Albert. Of these, George McDougall and Albert Lacombe were noted for their itinerant missionary efforts. Like their counterparts in Manitoba, these missionaries made agriculture and education integral aspects of their missionary work, and these practices flourished at the various mission posts of all denominations.

Most missionaries submitted reports to government officials, with or without government prompting, on the state of affairs among the Indians on the plains. In 1872 George McDougall issued stern warnings about the disruptive effects of alcohol among the Plains Indians, a report that Wemyss Simpson used to discourage the pursuit of treaties on the Saskatchewan at that early date.[37] Observations on the necessity of making treaties as soon as possible came from a variety of missionaries, including James Nisbet in 1873, George McDougall in 1875, and John McDougall and Father Scollen in 1876.[38] The range of roles missionaries played is suggested by the 1875 communication from George McDougall. Though he doubtless believed for his own reasons that a treaty with the Plains Crees was a necessity, he also served in this instance as a tool of the Crees themselves, reporting that "Though they deplored the necessity of resorting to extreme measures, yet they were unanimous in their determination to oppose the running of lines or the making of roads through their country until a settlement between the Government and them had been effected."[39] Such warnings were probably not sufficient in themselves to stir the Canadian government to action, but these voices, in conjunction with similar clamoring from other sources, lent support to demands the Indians were communicating more directly.

In making a case for negotiations with the Blackfoot to the minister of the interior in 1876, Alexander Morris cited reports from Scollen and John McDougall to support the necessity. The lieutenant governor noted that the missionaries were "both strongly of the opinion, that a Treaty should be made with the Blackfoot next year" in the interests of peace on the southern plains. He then drew attention to the insidious influence of American traders in alcohol and also to the potential of a Blackfoot alliance with the American Sioux before adding, "The reasons assigned by Messrs. Scollen and McDougall, for making a Treaty, are very strong, and they both assured me, that this warlike race, are now very well disposed and anxious to be treated with, as the Crees have been." [40] Blackfoot concerns about American traders and the ill effects of liquor had been noted by George McDougall in an article in the *Wesleyan Missionary Notices* of 1874 as well as in a letter to Hudson's Bay Company director D. A. Smith earlier that year. [41] These missionary reports, however, confuse an understanding of Blackfoot motives for treaty making. The Blackfoot stand apart from other treaty Indians on the plains in what they hoped to achieve from the treaty offered them in 1877. They were concerned about buffalo preservation measures and the security of their territory in the face of outside incursion, and they were emphatically not interested in being treated with "as the Crees have been." The pressure on Blackfoot territory was not as yet sufficient to convince them of the necessity for formal arrangements to "share" their lands with intruders. They did not recognize the precarious state of the buffalo as inevitable and sought only ways to restore that resource. The Blackfoot remedy, an objective they shared with the "hostile" peoples of the American Plains, was the expulsion of all intruders from their lands. [42] These Indians might have had some basis for believing that the Canadian government would cooperate with their wishes given their experience with the Northwest Mounted Police. If one form of Canadian authority had ended the liquor plague, it might be reasonable to expect a treaty agreement to end another problem. It is not clear in reports by the lieutenant governor to the minister of the interior or in other official correspondence, however, that the government left room in its negotiations with the Blackfoot for anything other than the aims of the government itself. Missionary reports of Blackfoot enthusiasm may have obscured official understanding of these issues.

George McDougall played an important role in the critical effort to communicate government treaty plans to the plains people of the North

Saskatchewan. While passing through Winnipeg on his way west in 1875, McDougall was enlisted by the lieutenant governor to spread the word among the Crees of the planned treaty councils on that river in the summer of 1876.[43] McDougall was zealous in carrying out his mission on behalf of the government and by his own reckoning visited almost four thousand Indians.[44]

From the beginning of Christian missionary efforts in America, missionaries had counted success in the number of conversions won, but they were never able to measure the depth of commitment thus made. The influence missionaries exercised in treaty-making councils has been perhaps even more nebulous. They clearly helped bolster government inclination to come to terms with the plains peoples and also assisted in bringing the two parties together. Of more long-term significance, however, was the preparatory work of "civilization" they had done in the West. Their schools, churches, and model farms, operating without official support until the government turned its attention to the implementation of the treaties at the end of the 1870s, made missionary institutions the logical foundation on which to structure the transformation of the Plains Indians.

The missionary efforts among the Indian signatories of the U.S. treaties of 1867–68 were far less substantial by comparison. Official support came earlier in the United States than in British North America through the "civilization fund," but it was still meager. As in British North America, missionaries to the south had long sought to evangelize the Indians, and they moved west with the advancing frontier in pursuit of this goal. When the Santee Sioux of Minnesota erupted in the massacre of 1862, it was Minnesota's Episcopal bishop who interceded with President Lincoln to diminish the backlash. Bishop Henry Whipple, who was determined that "it should never be said that the first bishop of Minnesota turned his back upon the heathen at his door," was perhaps more dedicated than many, but his interest in the Indians was not uncommon in his calling.[45] The westward drift of the Santee population after 1862 drew the first Protestant missionaries into the orbit of the hostile Sioux to whom the 1868 treaty efforts were directed, although it was only after 1869 that any measurable progress among them was registered.[46] Spanish missions had made inroads within Comanche territory much earlier, but their major contribution to southern Plains Indian culture was the horse, not Catholicism. By 1867, then, an effective American missionary presence among the Plains Indians was almost negligible.

Yet Catholic missionary efforts were marginally more successful than those of other denominations through the single-handed efforts of the legendary Jesuit missionary, Father Pierre-Jean De Smet. Comparable to the Canadian missionary Albert Lacombe in his penchant for an itinerant mission, personal dynamism, and faith, De Smet nonetheless outshone his contemporary with the magnitude of his achievements. Devoted to the resolution of intertribal warfare, he attended the historic 1851 treaty council at Fort Laramie, where he employed his skills as a mediator to promote understanding among the major parties.[47] Remembering this service, the government again sought his assistance in 1867 when the Great Peace Commission embarked on its work. One of the commission's first official acts was to interview De Smet in order to determine "the feelings, disposition, and wants of the Indians he had recently visited in the Upper Missouri Country together with his views of the policy that should be adopted towards said Indians, looking for their improvement and civilization."[48] After making this report, De Smet ventured into hostile Sioux territory once more, deliberately seeking out the Hunkpapa band of Sitting Bull as one of those that refused to consider treating with the United States. Though De Smet met a friendly reception from the distinguished chief, Sitting Bull sent only a representative to the council in April 1868. The Jesuit's efforts in this regard hardly equal those of George McDougall in advertising the Treaty 6 councils. Generally in the United States, though, the Indian agents of the Department of the Interior and army officers, working in conjunction with "stay-around-the-fort" Indians and long-time frontier traders, announced the coming of the peace council.[49] Missionaries in the American West were in no position to do so. De Smet was on hand in November 1868 as was Samuel Hinman, an Episcopal missionary to the Santee Sioux, when the leading hostiles, among them Red Cloud, signed the treaty. But there is little to suggest that missionaries exercised any influence in acceptance of treaty terms.

When Americans turned to the implementation of their detailed civilization policy after the 1867–68 treaties had been signed, there was little in the way of educational and agricultural infrastructures in existence among the nomadic plains people on which to build, a contrast to the situation in Canada. Missionary power was, however, a growing force in Indian policy, and when President Grant devised his Indian Peace Policy, inaugurated in 1869, missionaries were assigned a prominent role in its implementation.[50]

As in Canada, it is difficult to pinpoint the influence of missionaries at the treaty councils themselves or to define their impact. The lack of a substantial missionary presence at the American treaties obscures, however, the religious contribution to the atmosphere of treaty making, imbued as it was in 1867–68 by the need to make a permanent peace based on the "civilization" and evangelization of the Indians. Only well afterward did the significance of the missionary movement to Indian policy become apparent.

Both nations felt obliged to add military forces to their treaty commissions as support staff. Under the July 20 Act, the U.S. Army had been directed to handle treaty-making logistics, a task it shared in part with the Indian department. The army contributed 150,000 rations to the Great Peace Commission's efforts and transported these supplies, which were then distributed, at least at Medicine Lodge, by the Indian department.[51]

At Medicine Lodge the commissioners were accompanied by two companies of the Seventh Cavalry and a battery from the Fourth Artillery, the latter equipped with Gatling guns, in total over two hundred men.[52] This military presence reflected the very real security concerns involved in venturing into territory acknowledged to be hostile in an attempt to sign a treaty of peace. The Cheyennes in particular gave the commissioners an uneasy time, camping well away from the main treaty grounds and persistently delaying negotiations. Twice betrayed by the American military in recent memory, first at Sand Creek and then in early 1867 by Gen. Winfield Hancock, Cheyenne suspicions were well founded. General Harney, who was well known among the Cheyennes, exercised great care in dealing with them. He advised the more impatient Senator Henderson not to hurry them and imposed strict control on military behavior so as not to give offence.[53] The army was equally important in treaty councils with the Sioux, although negotiations for the Fort Laramie treaties took place in the more secure facilities of established forts rather than on the open plains. The treaty commission, unable to wait out the strategic delaying tactics of some bands of Sioux, signed up as many as they could before handing the task over to the commander of Fort Laramie. On November 6, 1868, it was the honor of the Fourth Infantry's Maj. William Dye to accept the signature of Red Cloud.

Canada also employed military forces and for a number of reasons. Here too the militia and later the Northwest Mounted Police played a logistical role in organizing and distributing supplies, although the Hudson's Bay Company, like the U.S. Army, had the greater part in procurement and transportation.[54] But there were also other practical responsibilities. The distribution of annuities always attracted traders anxious for profit, and treaty commissioners found the militia a deterrent to those who dealt in illicit goods such as alcohol.[55] Alexander Morris was very concerned about the number of militia men assigned to accompany him on his quest to conclude Treaty 3, noting that "Governor Archibald took a hundred men to 'The Stone Fort,' twenty miles from here." In contrast, Morris was "going upwards of a hundred miles into a wild country where there will be a large gathering of Indians and no authority. I did not choose to expose myself to be insulted, as I am informed Simpson was, on a previous occasion, moreover. I wish a sufficient force to preserve order and prevent illicit trading with the Indians, by the hangers on who will be sure to be there."[56] He also had some warning from the archbishop at Red River "that the Riel party had sent couriers to the North West . . . also to prevent a treaty at the angle."[57] Militia commander Col. Patrick Robertson-Ross apparently sympathized with Morris's concerns for ceremony, security, and law enforcement, recommending that the accompanying force "consist of not less than 150 Infantry and 50 Artillery soldiers with four 7-pounder field-guns."[58] This was equivalent to the force sent by the U.S. Army to Medicine Lodge, minus the Gatling guns.

More interesting was the deployment of troops at the Treaty 4 gathering. There, dissension between the Crees and Ojibwas (also known as Saulteaux) broadened the scope of the militia's role to keeping the peace. Morris, ever anxious to justify the large retinue of militia he demanded, emphasized one incident in his report: "The Saulteaux, one day went the length of placing six 'soldiers,' armed with rifles and revolvers, in the conference tent to intimidate the other Indians, a step which was promptly counteracted by Lieut.-Col. Smith, calling in six of the militiamen who were stationed in the tent. . . . [T]heir presence exerted great moral influence, and I am persuaded, prevented the jealousies and ancient feud between the Crees and Saulteaux culminating in acts of violence."[59]

By 1875 the Northwest Mounted Police were established on the plains and already a force with a reputation among the Crees as well as the Blackfoot. The influential role of this force at Treaties 6 and 7 can hardly be overstated. Interpreter Peter Erasmus, who had come to Fort Carlton at the behest of Chief Mistawasis, noted, "The Police, dressed in their smart scarlet uniforms and riding well trained horses, made a big impression with the Indians."[60] An observer at the Indian councils, in which terms were debated among the Indians themselves, Erasmus recorded Mistawa-

sis's perceptions of the force and its impact on the success of treaty making. The chief remarked that the police were men as the Crees were, and
few in number too, yet had driven the American liquor traders from
Blackfoot country as well as mounting an exhausting search for the perpetrators of the Cypress Hills massacre. "Let me tell you why these things
are so. It was the power that stands behind those few Red Coats that
those men feared and wasted no time in getting out when they could; the
power that is represented in all the Queen's people, and we the children
are counted as important even as the Governor who is her personal
speaker. The Police are the Queen Mother's agents and have the same
laws for whites as they have for the Indians." [61]

The reputation of the Northwest Mounted Police for fairness and justice was even more deeply rooted in Blackfoot country, where the direct
experience of the exodus of the liquor traders resulted in a good relationship between the police and the Indian inhabitants. Although the Blackfoot had had less contact with white society and were often described as
"war-like," the commissioners were not daunted by the prospect of going among them for treaty purposes. So confident were they of their circumstances that Colonel Macleod and other officers brought their wives
to the council at Blackfoot Crossing. Lieutenant Governor Laird had such
a positive impression of the pleasant relationship between the police and
the Indians that he recommended that the force be charged with the task
of distributing annuities in compliance with a Blackfoot request to that
effect. [62] The Northwest Mounted Police were singled out because of their
relationship with the Blackfoot, unlike the U.S. Army, which was recommended for the same role as a way to check the corruption of the Indian
department. [63]

As interpreters, mixed-blood men and at least one mixed-blood woman
made a mark at American treaty councils, especially on the southern
plains. [64] Apart from this, mixed-bloods were probably marginal at best
to the considerations of either the American government or the Indians
involved. At the Fort Laramie treaty council in May 1868, there was some
discussion, initiated by the Oglala Man-Afraid-of-His-Horse, on whether
or not the "half-breeds" were to join the Indians on the reservation to be
established by that treaty or to remain where they were. The mixed-
blood community itself, represented by traders Joseph Bissonette and
John Richard Jr., was divided on the question. [65] For their part, the American negotiators were not prepared to address the matter definitively but

offered the opinion, voiced by commissioner John Sanborn, that "We require no half-breeds to go to the reservation, but simply promise to those that do go there with the Indians that they will there be assisted and protected. There will be no more assistance given here."[66] This approach reflected American practice, which ignored the possibility that the mixed-blood population might form a distinct entity and dealt with them as white or Indian. There was no recorded discussion in the southern-plains talks on this subject, despite the numbers of people in attendance who would have fallen into this category. The lack of interest suggests that perhaps the Indian and the mixed-bloods themselves did not object to the government's position.

The situation in Canada was somewhat different, perhaps because the Métis population there lived in established communities, notably at Red River and on the Saskatchewan River, distinct from Indian settlements and considered themselves a separate entity. Because of this it was easier for the Canadian government to distinguish them from the Indians. The Métis had also asserted their own political will in the Red River Rebellion, an act of independence the Canadian government could not overlook. Under the act establishing the province of Manitoba, the Métis were accorded land rights on the basis of their unique claim. Their position at treaty negotiations was somewhat ambiguous, but their interests were addressed in two ways: in appeals, advanced by the Indians, to include them or make arrangements for them, and as facilitators of the treaty process, usually in the interests of the government.

Indian spokesmen at Treaties 1, 3, 4, and 6 expressed concern over the future of the Métis, whom they considered a part of their own communities. For the most part, the government tried to resist these appeals, a position consistent with the financially straitened outlook of the government and the unwelcome expense of adding untold numbers of Métis to the bill. At Treaty 1, Commissioner Simpson, who always seemed ill at ease operating outside his specific mandate, drew attention to the land provision of the Manitoba Act for the Métis. He allowed, however, "that any person now electing to be classed with the Indians, and receiving the Indian pay and gratuity, would [he] believed, thereby forfeit his or her right to another grant as a half-breed," and that the choice was up to the individual.[67] Alexander Morris had the opportunity to entrench the government's stance at subsequent treaty councils, where he reassured the supplicants that the government would look after the Métis.[68] When Chief Mistawasis raised the subject during the Treaty 6 negotiations at

Fort Carlton, Morris's response was somewhat more equivocal. "The Half-breeds of the North-West cannot come into the Treaty," he said, although those who lived with the Indians as Indians might be considered on an individual basis.[69] In his official report, however, Morris urged the Privy Council to more concrete action: "There are a few who are identified with the Indians, but there is a large class of Métis who live by the hunt of the buffalo, and have no settled homes. . . . [W]hile I would not be disposed to recommend their being brought under the treaties, I would suggest that land should be assigned to them, and that on their settling down . . . some assistance should be given them to enable them to enter upon agricultural operations."[70] The government proved less receptive to the problems of the Métis than either the Plains Indians or Lieutenant Governor Morris, and little came of such appeals.

More significant was the active role of Métis individuals at the treaty councils. Among these, James McKay stood out as a special favorite of government treaty commissioners. In outlining the characteristics of the ideal treaty commissioner in 1870, Lieutenant Governor Archibald suggested that such an official "should have mixed with our Indian Tribes, should understand their language and habits, and have personal influence among them." He recommended McKay.[71] McKay attended Treaties 1 and 2 as an observer but became an official participant at Treaty 3, where he was embraced with enthusiasm by Alexander Morris. Morris's accounts of the four treaties he negotiated and the two he revised bear ample evidence of McKay's instrumental role on behalf of the government. As interpreter at Treaties 3 and 5, commissioner at Treaty 6, and general adviser to the government all along, McKay was indispensable.[72]

But there was more to the Métis contribution than the efforts of James McKay. Large numbers of Métis were present at each of the councils for the first six treaties, but much of what they did there went unrecorded in government sources. Of course, they served as interpreters on occasion, but it was during the Treaty 3 negotiations that they had a major impact. Morris came to the Treaty 3 talks with a retinue of Manitoba Métis, including McKay, Pierre Levailler, Charles Nolin, and a M. Genton. Faced with an impasse in the talks, Morris dispatched these men to the Indian council in an effort to encourage a reconsideration of the terms offered. When they returned the next day, an intense discussion of specific terms was held, but agreement in the end was won. Chief Mawedopenais confirmed Morris's confidence in the Métis influence when he declared, "I wish you to understand you owe the treaty much to the Half-breeds," to which Morris responded, "I know it . . . and I am proud that all the Half-breeds from Manitoba, who are here, gave their Governor their cordial support."[73]

With these remarks Morris overlooked the possible contribution of the Métis population of the Northwest Angle. The official government interpreter, Nicholas Chatelain, was among these. It was the welfare of the Angle Métis that the Ojibwas sought to assure in their inquiries about the treaty and that Morris turned aside with a promise to refer the matter to Ottawa.[74] In fact, a "Half-Breed Adhesion" was later negotiated in 1875, wherein the Métis were acknowledged in their claim to treaty rights as Métis, though the agreement was neither ratified by Ottawa nor implemented.[75] Morris made a more sweeping acknowledgment of their role during Treaty 3 negotiations in his final report, noting: "the hearty co-operation and efficient aid the Commissioners received from the Métis who were present at the Angle, and who, with one accord, whether of French or English origin, used the influence which their relationships to the Indians gave them, to impress them with the necessity of their entering into the treaty."[76]

How the Métis may have assisted the Indians or obstructed the government is not as easily determined as the aid they gave treaty commissioners, who did not dwell on such instances in their official reports. At Treaty 4 Métis participants imparted to the Indians the more favorable terms won at the Northwest Angle over those written into Treaties 1 and 2.[77] Later recorders, though, did not mention their contributions at other councils. Ignoring the legitimate claims and difficult plight of the Métis population of the northwest, Canadian officials preferred to idealize them in a role their acknowledged part in the treaties only encouraged. In this connection, Lord Dufferin in 1877 described the Métis as "the ambassadors between the east and the west," and declared, "they have done for the colony what otherwise would have been left unaccomplished, and have introduced between the white population and the red man a traditional feeling of amity and friendship which but for them it might have been impossible to establish."[78]

Treaty making attracted a myriad of interested parties to the proceedings. Interpreters and the mixed-blood or Métis populations, from which many of them sprang, often had personal concerns in the outcome of the councils, which bore implications for their futures as much as for that of the Indians. But Christian missionaries, the U.S. Army, and even the Northwest Mounted Police, all of whom could expect to play a role in the implementation of these treaties, could not remain aloof. Still, these groups had little immediate impact on the overall course that both governments had set for the future of the Indians of the Great Plains and Prairie West. These fundamental plans were already firmly cast in a policy of assimilation that manifested itself—in detail in the United States, while still only in outline in western Canada—in the form of reserves and guidelines for civilization.

6 Reserves

Settlement was the primary reason for expansion into the West. In 1867 Americans were already there, and Canadians were beginning to dream of similar growth. The problem in both countries was that Indians already occupied these lands. Both the United States and Canada recognized, in keeping with age-old practice and tradition, the necessity of extinguishing Indian land title, which was acknowledged in some form in each nation. Treaties were the effective instrument for that purpose and were employed in 1867–68 by the United States to the broader ends of ending war and establishing peace. But they also embodied other, far-reaching implications for Indian policy, instigated specifically by the problem of what to do with the occupants once the land was under the legal jurisdiction of the national governments. The two central components of Indian policy expanded in the treaties of 1867–68 and the Numbered Treaties were those of setting aside lands exclusively for Indian habitation (called "reserves" in Canada and "reservations" in the United States) and civilization.

The idea of reserves was not new when the North American nations faced west at the end of the 1860s. The French had established Indian reserves, after a fashion, in New France, and New England and Virginia also had their own versions of such enclaves.[1] Both Britain and the new United States continued sporadic efforts in this direction in the latter half of the eighteenth century. A significant divergence in policy between the two regions took place in the wake of the War of 1812. Confronted by populations no longer of military utility, Britain embraced the practice in earnest. The desire to secure British North America's southern boundary was a consideration after the war, given the indifferent and occasionally treasonous behavior of border residents in that conflict. The solution to this problem required more Indian land cessions in Upper Canada to accommodate new and, it was hoped, more loyal settlers. This in turn fueled the necessity to find lands for the dislocated Indians in the territory of yet other Indian nations.

At the same time, the United States embarked on what might be described, given the overall direction of reserve policy in the nineteenth century, as a detour. Even before the War of 1812, the United States had begun to expand rapidly, pushing into the territories of the Old Northwest and the Old Southwest, and in both regions encountering sizable indigenous populations. Unrestrained American growth sparked the usual problems of friction and the blatant disregard by white settlers of aboriginal rights. These Indians, unlike those in the older states, were too numerous to absorb into irrelevance, but another solution was at hand. In the first quarter of the new century, the United States formulated the policy of removal. Applied erratically in the Old Northwest in the 1810s, it was implemented on a national scale during the 1830s. The Louisiana Purchase of 1803 had provided the nation with a substantial holding ground for the peoples thus expelled, and government officials deemed the vast territory west of the Mississippi River well beyond the grasp or interest of the white population for generations to come.[2]

American optimism was short-lived. By the 1840s the United States found itself on the brink of yet another major expansion and confronting yet another Indian barrier, a situation that approached crisis proportions a generation later following the Civil War. Canada, perched on the edge of its own vast western territory in Rupert's Land, was by then in a comparable position. The numbers of Indians in both places were considerable, but this time removal was no longer a possibility.

The only British effort at removal had taken place in Upper Canada in 1836, under Lt. Gov. Francis Bond Head. Bond Head raised havoc in a number of ways in Upper Canada, and Indian policy was no exception. Convinced that Indians were doomed to extinction and beyond any effort to revive the population, the lieutenant governor devised a plan to ship the Indians of Upper Canada to Manitoulin Island in Lake Huron.[3] This destination would serve as one large reserve where the Indians might live out their existence in peaceful and unfettered isolation. As with American removal plans, Bond Head's scheme would also free up thousands of acres of prime real estate for white settlement. Like the American experience too it was widely criticized, and in British North America the practice was swiftly abandoned as an aberration, as was Bond Head himself.[4]

The more conventional approach, at least in Upper Canada, was the establishment of large reserves, but by the 1850s Indian policymakers had come to the conclusion that these were ineffective in promoting "civilization" among the Indians and were considering smaller reserves adjacent to white population centers as an alternative.[5] The United States came to a similar decision point in the 1850s, leading to reservation experiments during that decade on the tribal remnants of peoples who had been removed from the Northeast and were now on the fringes of the American frontier once more. Smaller reservations awash in a sea of white settlement were established, and an allotment system was even implemented in some cases. The disastrous results of this approach in the American Midwest, which dispossessed and impoverished several Indian peoples, encouraged the search for a different solution to the problem of Indians and land reserves.[6] By the 1860s the United States, faced with large numbers of Indians in newly acquired territories, required a more comprehensive and systematic policy.

Canada also had to adapt to a new situation. Prior to the Robinson Treaties of 1850, territory had been acquired piecemeal on the basis of the advance of settlement, and Indians resident in these regions were removed to lands bought from other Indian nations. Once British North America, and then Canada, began acquiring land in huge cessions, it was necessary to revise the policy. Now it became a requirement of treaty making to set aside a quantity of land for the Indians from that surrendered, and the commitment to establish reserves became an essential component of the treaty process.

The sophistication of the reserve policy in each nation was paralleled by the development of the function reserves were to serve. Protection and civilization were central elements to the idea, more acutely so after the War of 1812 when it was understood that Indians, no longer an equal partner in national affairs, would require not only protection because of their weaker, vulnerable status, but also a transformation if they were to survive. These two functions remained at the core of the reserve system during the nineteenth century, although the balance between them shifted over time.

Crass greed propelled the American removal policy of the 1830s. Even Indian sympathizers in the United States during that decade seeing the villainy, particularly in the Old Southwest, could appreciate the argument for the protective aspects of removal. It was disillusionment with the apparent lack of advancement toward civilization exhibited in the Indian Territory that led to a shift in the size of reservations to smaller and sometimes allotted parcels in the American Midwest.[7] Britain too had ini-

Fig. 1. Chief Red Cloud. As the undisputed victor in the war of 1866–68, Red Cloud saw little of value in the treaty-making process. Nebraska State Historical Society, RG2845, 3:4, J. E. Meddaugh (photographer)

Fig. 2. The Great Peace Commission. *From left to right*: General Terry, General Harney, General Sherman, an unknown Sioux woman, Indian Commissioner N. G. Taylor, Samuel Tappan, and General Augur. U.S. National Archives and Records Administration, U.S. Signal Corps, III-SC-87714

Fig. 3. Treaty 6 with the Saskatchewan Crees at Fort Carlton, August 1876. *Canadian Illustrated News*, December 16, 1876. National Archives of Canada, C64741

Fig. 4. Satanta, Kiowa chief. Satanta had nothing but contempt for the Americans and their treaty promises, which he ridiculed at the Council of Medicine Lodge. U.S. National Archives and Records Administration, Indian List #130

Fig. 5. David Laird, minister of the interior, October 1876. Laird stressed buffalo-preservation measures over provisions for agricultural assistance in order to smooth the negotiations of Treaty 7 with the Blackfoot. National Archives of Canada, PA33430

Fig. 6. Indian Visit to Ottawa, 1886. Ahtahkakoop (seated at left) and Mistawasis (seated at right) saw Treaty 6 and its agricultural provisions as the best option for the future of the Plains Crees. National Archives of Canada, C19258

Fig. 7. Adams G. Archibald. As lieutenant governor of Manitoba, Archibald presided over the negotiation of Treaties 1 and 2 in 1871. National Archives of Canada, PA26322

Fig. 8. The Manitoba Indian Treaty. Treaty I was negotiated at the Stone Fort in August 1871. *Canadian Illustrated News,*

Fig. 9. Alexander Morris, 1871. Morris negotiated four of the Numbered Treaties and renegotiated two others. Though a representative of Canada, he proved receptive to Indian concerns for the future. National Archives of Canada, C7104

tially favored reserves for their protective rather than civilizing function, although increased interest in the latter role as the final purpose grew after 1830 with the transfer of Indian affairs to civilian authority. The protective function did not disappear but became instead, along with the idea of reserves themselves, a necessary step on the road to "civilization" rather than an end in itself.[8]

There was a basic contradiction in the framing of reserve policy as it was expressed in the Treaties of Medicine Lodge and Fort Laramie and the Numbered Treaties. Both sets of treaties promised "permanent" Indian land holdings, and yet equally clearly, the architects of these documents were committed to the view of reserves as what some have called "laboratories of civilization."[9] Inherent in the idea of civilization was the transformation of Indians into whites. But whites did not have reserves. Thus, with their common land holdings and extensive territory (even the Canadian government thought the reserves it established were too large), these set-aside lands were by definition temporary.[10] Even though the contradiction was obvious, this arrangement made complete sense to the governments, reformers, and humanitarians who supported the reserve policy at the time.

The process of "progress" was conceived of as a linear development, with peoples advancing from an existence as nomads on unrestricted land holdings, to nomads on restricted land holdings, to semi-agriculturalists on limited territory, and finally to yeoman farmers on allotted parcels of land.[11] Whites viewed this as inevitable, although the timetable imagined for the process might vary from place to place, people to people, and country to country. The inviolability of Indian lands promised in treaties, and the stress on the permanence of these holdings, "as long as the water flows and the sun rises," were not so much hypocritical (although they may seem so in retrospect) as understood differently. It would be impossible to "save" the Indians from extinction unless reserves were established, a fact that was widely accepted in both countries. It would also be impossible for these peoples to achieve "civilization" if their new lands were overrun by white settlers. Thus reserves had to be made impervious to control by whites. If Indians required this assurance, perhaps to induce them to take up these restricted land holdings in the first place, then it was there for them as well. They could hardly be expected to understand that progress and civilization were inevitable, although a few whites did try to explain it to them.[12]

Many Indians likely found this contradiction confusing. Given treaty promises of the permanence and inviolability of their reserves, it may have appeared to some that they were getting what they wanted or needed: permanent lands where whites would not be permitted to go and the right to continue to pursue their usual practices of hunting, fishing, and trapping unhindered. The treaties in both countries did recognize these things. Without the conviction, which whites held to firmly, that reserves were a temporary holding place until civilization dawned on them, it is understandable that Indians believed that "permanent" actually meant "forever."

These views of reserves—permanent, but not permanent, stepping-stones to civilization—governed the approaches that the United States and Canada adopted in their treaty-making ventures in the 1860s and 1870s. The necessity to set aside lands was included in the instructions imparted to the Great Peace Commission by statute in 1867 and formed the second article in each of the treaties signed at Medicine Lodge Creek and Fort Laramie. Somewhat further down the list in the Numbered Treaties was the commitment wherein the queen "hereby agrees and undertakes to lay aside reserves [for farming lands]" for the use of her Indian subjects.[13] The reserves (or in the United States, reservations) that resulted from these efforts were notably different, at least in size, with the American areas constituting huge blocs of territory, while the Canadian lands were considerably smaller. Reserve acreage as established in the 1860s and 1870s, as well as the much-altered physical dimensions of present-day reserves, have disguised the shared motive upon which the two countries acted.[14] The similarity of approach and coincidence of purpose inherent in both Canadian and American policies emerge in an examination of the original premises underlying reserve policy. An understanding of national motivations, in conjunction with an analysis of treaty terms, helps clarify the discrepancies between Canada and the United States.

In both countries, reserve policy bore some relation to the official disposition of public lands through legislation designed to encourage settlement. By the time the United States and Canada came to treaty making on the plains, both had homestead policies in place to organize the settlement, in progress and proposed, envisioned for the Prairie West. The American Homestead Act, passed in 1862, allotted 160 acres for a nominal fee after five years' occupation. Canadian law, through the Dominion Lands Act of 1872, also permitted a 160-acre claim after three years' residence.

Table 1: Summary of terms for farmlands and
citizenship in the Sioux Treaty of Fort Laramie

ARTICLE 6

Lands for farming

Heads of families can select a piece of reservation land to start farming, not exceeding 320 acres.

On doing so, this piece of land will cease to be held in common.

Land to be held by this person as long as it is cultivated.

Any person (including women) over 18 can choose land not exceeding 80 acres.

These transactions to be recorded in a Land Book.

The status of the land is not fee simple but may be made so at the president's discretion.

The United States can make laws on the alienation of this type of property and other matters relating to it.

Any *male* Indian over 18 who shall occupy a piece of land *outside* the reservation that shall not be mineral lands or any other reserved for use by the United States, and who has made improvements of more than $200 value and occupied this land for 3 years continuously, shall be entitled to receive a U.S. patent for 160 acres, including his improved land.

After providing written application and proof of 2 disinterested witnesses, the Indian can register this land at the General Land Office and hold it as long as he continues to live there.

Citizenship

Any Indian receiving a patent under the above rules may become a citizen of the United States entitled to all rights of citizenship and shall "at the same time, retain all his rights to benefits accruing to Indians under this treaty."

Note: For a complete summary of American treaty terms see appendix 3. Note that all terms are summaries of original terms, not the terms themselves.

The United States established reservations in the actual treaties and laid them out in exacting detail. They were huge territories, with the exception of that awarded the Northern Cheyennes and Northern Arapahos, who were expected to share the lands assigned to others.[15] The designation of such extensive territories accorded with both the recommendations of the Senate Committee on Indian Affairs and the instructions given the Great Peace Commission, and consisted of the two remaining "empty" regions within the Great Plains north of Nebraska and south of Kansas. Americans very deliberately conceived of this concentration of the Indians as the first step in a gradualist policy toward the specific ends of acculturation and assimilation.[16] Agriculture was an instrumental part

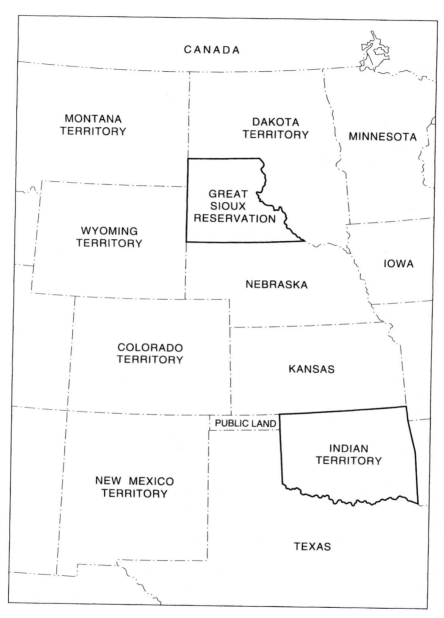

Map 1. The Great Plains after the implementation of the 1867–68 treaties, illustrating the Great Sioux Reservation and Indian Territory. Adapted from Prucha, *Atlas*, map 102.

of this policy, and the emphasis on this way of life in subsequent articles within the treaties made clear the fact that there was nothing inconsistent in an American assimilationist policy that began with the allotment of territories larger than some states.

In comparison to homestead allotments of 160 acres, treaty terms granting 320 acres were generous indeed. But Indians endured restrictions imposed by treaty on the lands they thus acquired that no other settler faced. Only heads of families could acquire the maximum allotment of 320 acres. Individuals were restricted to 80 acres, although unlike the Homestead Act provisions both men and women were eligible. Land could be held only as long as it was cultivated, a reinforcement of one of the central purposes of the reservations in fostering an agricultural existence. Only if the individual concerned embraced citizenship, a possibility explicitly allowed for under the Sioux treaty but probably understood to apply to the others as well, could he as a matter of course enter into full and unhindered possession of this land. These restrictions were intended to serve the protective function of Indian policy, but they also impeded the advance of "civilization" by differentiating between Indians and non-Indians. (See table 1.)

In Canada the connection between land and agriculture was more direct. In determining the size of reserves, Canada applied an exacting mathematical formula of either 160 or 640 acres per family of five, prorated for families of different sizes.[17] These terms were at least the equivalent of the Dominion Lands Act's provisions, and in the cases where 640 acres were allotted the terms were more generous than not only the homestead allotments but also those given by the Americans. But the object remained the same and was, in fact, more deliberately stated. In explaining to the Indians of Treaty 1 the amount of land to be set aside for them, Lieutenant Governor Archibald explicitly invoked farming as a justification. "These reserves will be large enough," he said, "but you must not expect them to be larger than will be enough to give a farm to each family when farms shall be required."[18]

The Canadian government continued to emphasize the agricultural purpose of the reserve lands, insisting that the Indians surrender their rights to the vast bulk of the western plains. However, under pressure from Indians in the negotiations for Treaty 3, the government was obliged to relent on reserve size. Indeed, the Canadian government seemed more concerned with consistency than the amount of land. Once the Treaty 3 Indians had forced an accommodation of 640 acres to be allotted per family of five, the commissioners applied this amount across the board without further thought, except in the case of Treaty 5. In the latter treaty it was acknowledged, and used as a justification for the amount of land assigned per family, that the land in question in northern Manitoba was of limited use for agricultural purposes.[19] It might have been expected, then, that lands of lesser quality might have induced a more generous settlement from the government, but this was not the case. The Canadians' emphasis was on farming. If the lands available were not to be used for farming, then there was no purpose in burdening the Indians with territory that might be fit for other uses such as mining or lumber. These enterprises did not accord with the intent to "civilize" the Indians, and Indian involvement in them might interfere with the government's own exploitation of these lands. It was easier on the prairies to hand over 640 acres to the Indians there, as no purpose other than agriculture was thought possible at the time the treaties were made. The only occasion when the questionable nature of the land for farming purposes and the government's desire to retain it for other uses came into conflict was in Treaty 3, and there the Indians were quite aware of the potential additional values of their land and therefore drove a harder bargain.[20] The fact that they were in a position, in the early 1870s, to exert strategic pressure on the Canadian government may account for the success the Indians achieved in winning the larger acreage allotted per family.

There were no provisions in the Canadian treaties for allotment in severalty or the assumption of title in fee simple. Like the various American restrictions on individual land holding, the absence of such terms was meant to assure the protection of the Indians' land base until such time as they were deemed capable of undertaking the responsibilities of private property.[21] The guidelines for that stage of Indian development in Canada were governed by statute, not treaty. That allotment and private property were things to come to the Indians in the West was clear from the direction already plotted in central Canada. The 1857 Gradual Civilization Act, introduced into the colonial legislature by John A. Macdonald, inaugurated these measures in pre-Confederation Canada. The policy was extended across the new nation by Macdonald's government in the 1869 Gradual Enfranchisement Act, which promised fee simple title to heirs of those who had become enfranchised and received an allotment.[22] The comprehensive Indian Act of 1876 confirmed these government goals once more, but in Article 94 the law explicitly excluded the Indians of the West from the enfranchisement and allotment provisions.[23] This deliberate prohibition reflected a lack of confidence in the ability of as yet "uncivilized" Indians to cope with European institutions. But it also complemented the leisurely approach of the Canadian authorities to the settlement of western Indians, a process that was not, from an official standpoint, an immediate concern. Civilization measures were understood to come later, although when exactly they would be applied to the West, no one could say in the 1870s. The United States, having no legislative equivalent, had to incorporate whatever measures it envisaged into the treaties.

Canada and the United States shared the vision of Indians settled on individual lots, reflected in the similarity of treaty terms to homestead provisions. The difference in the size of the territory allotted in the two countries, however, does not immediately indicate this impulse on the part of the United States. The Americans initially carved huge chunks from the public domain to be set aside for the Indians. Their first concern was to get the Indians off the remaining lands and only afterward to break down the extensive regions into more conventional land holdings. The Canadian government was more determined on the single-minded goal of acquiring title to the whole territory at once but felt no immediate compulsion to relocate the Indians. The Dominion government could reasonably say at the treaty negotiations that reserves were for farming only and were to be established permanently for Indian use when they wanted to turn to agriculture, whenever that might be.[24] But because reserves were to be used for farming purposes, this was how they were calculated. The results may have been substantial in the eyes of Canadian land speculators or aspiring farmers or the Canadian government, but the acreage hardly amounted to half of South Dakota as did the Great Sioux Reservation, even had the reserves under each of the Numbered Treaties been consolidated.

Both Canada and the United States designated lands in excess, considerably in excess in the American case, of what they believed would be necessary for Indian use with the objective intended — agriculture on individual farms.[25] But they also believed the excess lands would serve the purpose of providing a source of income to Indians who could not possibly farm such extensive territory.[26] Indeed, such was American optimism on this score that all treaty annuities and assistance were finite, restricted to a period of ten or twenty years, because it was expected that by that time the Indians would begin to sell off their excess lands and so could fund their own purchases of seed and implements and hire their own instructors.[27]

Thus in both nations the agricultural purpose of reserve lands was unquestioned and was in fact simply understood. The United States had no more inclination than did Canada, and in reality probably had considerably less, to encourage a continuance of Indian ways. Circumstances in each nation dictated the policies. By promising huge territories the United States made it easier to convince Indians to retire to reservations, although this was not entirely successful in practice. Canada had more success in convincing the Indians to accept much smaller reserves by not insisting on immediate occupancy. There the establishment of limited reserves and an agricultural existence for the western Indians were concerns for the future, not the present.

Decisions on location of reserves also reflected the narrow purposes and beliefs of governments at the time rather than a considered policy, which in retrospect may appear more insidious. The American Plains reservations, though no longer the united territories they initially were, have remained relatively adjacent, while Canadian reserves have always been scattered. How these lands were chosen and by whom determined the patterns of allotment and modern demarcation.

In the United States, the Senate Committee on Indian Affairs established the general outlines of the western reservations, which were to be located "so as not to interfere with travel on highways located by authority of the United States, nor with the route of the Northern Pacific railroad, the Union Pacific railroad, the Union Pacific railroad eastern division, or the proposed route of the Atlantic and Pacific railroad by way of Albuquerque."[28] The idea of consulting with the Indians on this matter was not considered. Poring over maps of the West, the commissioners determined that this left only two substantial empty territories, and they decided to concentrate the Indians in those regions even before a single Indian had been encountered. This meant the removal of all the peoples concerned. The southern plains nations of the Kiowas, Comanches, and Kiowa-Apaches, as well as the Southern Cheyennes and Arapahos, would be relocated to areas within the Indian Territory on lands surrendered by treaty by the Five Civilized Nations as a result of the active participation

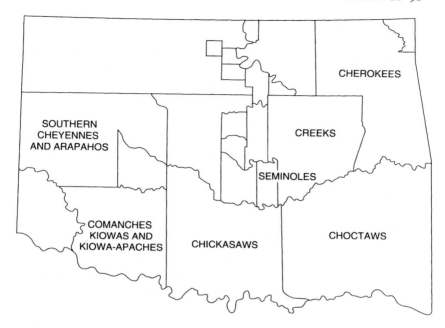

Map 2. Indian Territory after the implementation of the 1867 Medicine Lodge Creek Treaty. Reservations were assigned therein to the Southern Cheyennes and Arapahos and to the Kiowas, Comanches, and Kiowa-Apaches. Adapted from Prucha, *Atlas*, map 60.

of some individuals among them on the losing side in the American Civil War.[29] The Sioux would be shifted east to a reservation in present-day South Dakota, although they retained, under a unique provision, rights to the Powder River country in Montana.[30] Others, specifically the Northern Cheyennes and Northern Arapahos of the central plains, would be required to abandon not just their lands but the entire region. They did not gain their own reservation but were offered the alternative of joining either of those established for northern and southern plains peoples. (See map 1 and map 2.)

Congress and the peace commissioners did engage in some discussion on the number of reservations to be created, pondering the advantages of one, two, or more. A single area would have meant removing the Sioux to the south, and although this remained a point of discussion until the late 1870s, it was generally accepted that this would probably cause a war.[31] When Little Raven of the Southern Arapaho requested a separate reservation from that promised the Cheyennes and Arapahos together, he was denied.[32] Given the extensive nature of the civilization provisions, which required various instructors, implements, buildings, and agents for each reservation, it was in the economic interest of the United States to keep the number of reservations to a minimum. Eventually, three were formed.

Territory was assigned to peoples, not to bands, although the size of the set-aside lands did not preclude settlement on the basis of bands, and in practice this is what happened. Theoretically, the Indians were free (that is, not directed) to choose where they could live within the reservation, but this was constricted indirectly as the United States arbitrarily established posts to dispense rations and annuities and assigned particular bands to each, thus obliging some accommodation.[33]

Canada treated with various peoples—among them the Ojibwas in northwestern Ontario, the Crees on the plains, and the Blackfoot in the foothills of the Rocky Mountains—but reserves were assigned on the basis of bands within each nation. Instructions as to specific locations did not come from the highest authority, as was the case in the United States. Instead, treaties included either terms specifying the regions wherein the Indians concerned expressed a desire to settle or provisions promising the selection of reserves at a later date "in consultation" with the people concerned.[34] In theory this left the Indians with considerable latitude as to where they wished to live, a more relaxed arrangement than that accorded the American Plains Indians. It also implied that Indian consent was important. In practice, however, it was not always honored, particularly over time and as the Dominion government began to see the disadvantages of permitting the Indians to make these selections. Those who managed to have their reserves surveyed shortly after the treaties were made were more successful in obtaining their choices.[35] Government reluctance to survey reserves was one factor in impeding the exercise of this right. In Manitoba, the ongoing dispute over the contentious Outside Promises delayed reserve surveys in some cases more than five years, and when the Indians finally came to settle on the lands they had chosen, they discovered in at least one instance that they had already been surveyed for Hudson's Bay Company and homestead purposes.[36] A

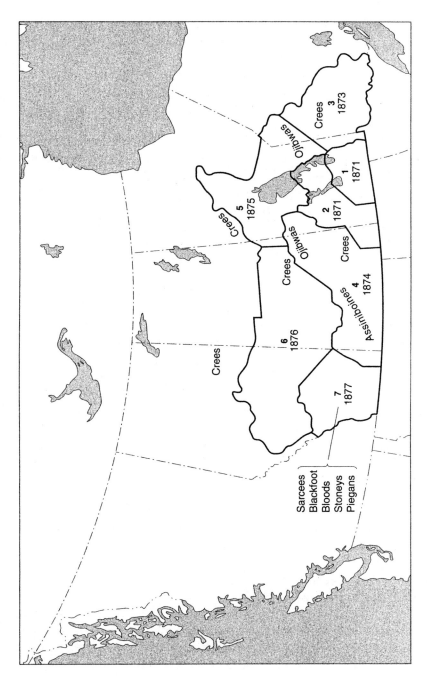

Map 3. Territories ceded in the Numbered Treaties, 1871–77. Adapted from Miller, *Skyscrapers*, p. 166.

more direct and heavy-handed interference by the government was apparent in the selection of reserves in Saskatchewan under Treaty 4, where Indian choices were vetoed for railroad considerations.[37]

In both nations at least some concerns were raised about the quality of lands involved. A few American senators wondered about the possibilities of transforming the already recalcitrant Sioux into farmers when their reservation consisted of a territory long known as the Badlands.[38] Such critics could be soothed by assurances that there was enough arable land even in this region to accommodate the existing, and declining, Indian population.[39] The commitment in Article 3 of the Sioux and Kiowa-Comanche treaties to acquire additional arable land outside the reservation also assuaged doubts. In Canada careful instructions were made in the creation of Treaty 7 reserves to ensure that some arable land was available in the arid tract the Blackfoot had chosen because of its proximity to the buffalo ranges.[40]

American policy in these treaties was explicitly one of concentration. This concept was rather loose since the reservations comprised vast tracts of land. But the theory was that it would be easier to cultivate civilization when the Indians lived closer together, as the "civilized" would influence the "uncivilized." Furthermore, it would be cheaper to provide the necessary elements of civilization—that is, education and agricultural instruction—to many at once. The impulse to concentrate as the first step was the reason for the large reservations. The Indians were to be moved along gradually, but there was also some concern that potentially hostile peoples not be crowded on top of one another.[41] The negative strategic implications for white security apparently did not occur to American policymakers until later. Despite the emphasis on reservations as incubators of civilization, little attention was given to the fact that isolation from railways and travel routes would impede market access when the ideal of individual farms came to fruition. Agriculture was seen in the first instance as a means to self-support, not as an avenue to mainstream American society.

Canada was more ambivalent about both agricultural marketing potential and security. Treaties stipulated that reserves were to be selected by individual bands, making possible a "scattering" of reserves across a wide area, but it did not preclude concentration either, leaving at least the initial inclination up to the Indians themselves. In Manitoba, under Treaty 5, in which bands seemed the preferred choice as the unit for reserve organization, the only instruction given was to avoid the surveying of reserves that were too small.[42] Farther west there were at least three requests for consolidated reserves. Pakan, a noted leader among the Treaty 4 Crees, received a noncommittal and confusing response to his request, which was never realized.[43] Big Bear, a major Plains Cree leader who initially declined to enter Treaty 6, tried to forge a consolidated reserve, first in the Cypress Hills in 1878 and then on the North Saskatchewan in the early 1880s, but he was thwarted in both attempts ostensibly for security reasons.[44] Blackfoot chief Crowfoot won the right to a consolidated reserve for the Blackfeet, Bloods, and Sarcees, only to have one of his own compatriots, Blood chief Red Crow, foil his plan.[45]

Apparently, Canada was willing initially to permit the Indians a degree of latitude, especially as there was a great deal of land and very few settlers. Lieutenant Governor Morris underscored the value of settling them on familiar lands, acknowledging the connection that they felt to particular regions: "The Indians, have a strong attachment to the localities, in which they and their fathers have been accustomed to dwell, and it is desirable to to [sic] cultivate this home feeling of attachment to the soil." [46] Only as conflict with railway and settler demands and increasing security concerns grew did Canada begin to interfere and reject choices the Indians had made. One result of these later considerations was a disinclination to support concentration.

Alexander Morris also suggested the utility of small reserves for agricultural marketing, but this was not a Canadian priority, indicating a divergence between the man-on-the-ground official in the West and the long-term interests of Ottawa.[47] Again, self-sufficiency at best seems to have been the highest goal of the government. Even this was later transformed into agriculture as a character-building exercise.[48] Morris's views in this and other things indicated some belief on his part that Indians would be a part of the settlement of the West, whereas government policy viewed Indians as irrelevant to that settlement once they had been pacified.

There was nothing either particularly thoughtful or venomous in American or Canadian reserve policy. The differences emerged out of the circumstances facing the two nations. In the long run, concentration might have had advantages. Canada, which chose to avoid it, should have insisted on concentration as the cheaper alternative, while the United States would have found scattering a more suitable strategy in the face of potential Indian aggression. But in neither place were policymakers thinking this way. In the United States a scattering policy would have countered desires to move Indians out of the line of settlement and defeated the compulsion American officials felt to protect the Indians from the extermination or extinction they would face outside of consolidated reservations. For the Dominion government any hurry to establish reserves would place undesirable strain on the fragile national economy. Concentrated settlements might have proven more economical for Canada, but in the 1870s, with the conviction that reserves were to be a temporary phenomenon, there was no need to make arrangements for unforeseen long-term consequences.

How reserve policy was framed in the treaties of both nations was an indication of motive and commitment. The American treaties specified the lands the Indians could *retain*. Although confinement to reservations was not compulsory at first, Americans wanted the Indians to move there promptly. The absence of a compelling element may have resided in the recognition that to require adherence would have induced conflict. In addition, some Americans, perhaps even the treaty commissioners, possibly believed that the extravagant offers of food and assistance on reservations could not be turned down by a sensible people.[49] Getting the Indians onto their assigned lands would have solved the American problems of racial friction as well as setting the scene for the civilization policy that was an important humanitarian concern.

The Canadian treaties specified the land to be *ceded*, reflecting the primary Canadian goal of extinguishing Indian land title. Canada also believed in civilization, and so saw reserves as an alternative to extinction, but did not face the pressures that made this an imperative in the United States. There was time enough to save the Indians and to "civilize" them. Canada's priority was the economy, and reserves would be expensive since they would require the accoutrements of "civilization," especially once the Indians called for the fulfillment of the terms they had required be added to the treaties. (See map 3.)

The American decision to create extensive reservation territories was an explicitly temporary arrangement designed to facilitate the overtly gradualist approach the U.S. government embraced. Over the century and a quarter since these reservations were established, their lands have been significantly diminished. The Great Sioux Reservation of 1868, which once comprised fully one-half of South Dakota, has been pared down to five much reduced areas, although they still retain vastly more "excess" lands than any of the western Canadian reserves. This was not the intention of the framers of the treaties, the reform organizers who supported them, or the Congress that ratified them. As historian Francis Prucha has observed, "The modern concern of Indians to protect a community land base has led to an emphasis on land arrangements of these treaties (especially the 1868 treaty with the Sioux at Fort Laramie) that distorts their meaning in the context of the circumstances under which they were signed. These treaties were reformist documents aimed at attaining the humanitarian civilizing goals of the Peace Commission, even though the reforming tendencies were probably not well understood by the Indians and have been overlooked by historians *because they were not effective.*" [50]

The Canadian approach was, by this definition of the reformist mission, more direct and perhaps more successful. Reserves were allotted on the basis of the current population, leaving no room for future growth and certainly not for subsequent generations to enjoy the same extensive land holdings in common as had their ancestors. The result, a century later, is a series of many tiny and inadequate reserves.[51]

From a late-twentieth-century perspective, and without looking at the historical context, it is hard to escape the conclusion that the Canadian government, which imposed such puny and inadequate land holdings, was villainous at best. This observation is particularly acute in comparison to the current American Indian land holdings on the plains, although it does not take into account the many American Indian peoples whose collective land holdings disappeared altogether in the allotment-in-severalty drive that persisted from 1887 through the 1930s under the terms of the General Allotment Act. But to condemn Canada is to ignore the guiding principles of 1870s reserve policy as it existed in both countries. The two nations were convinced that reserves were a temporary holding action that would disappear under what both believed was the unchallenged and unalterable destiny of a linearly defined Progress. Reserves were explicitly recognized as the cradles of Indian civilization, something to be cast off once a social maturity had been attained. The decisions to create reserves on the different dimensions of the Canadian and American models were made in direct response to existing conditions in each nation. The United States had pressing problems to resolve: settler pressures, Indian wars, and the imminent (so it was believed) extinction or extermination of the Indians. It was important to get these people out of the way first and easier to get them to swallow this accommodation if a gradualist program were adopted. The commitment of the United States to a formal civilization program leaps out from the treaty texts where such provisions predominate. Canada had no comparable pressures. But to open the West legitimately to settlement, the nation needed title to the land, and thus the sweeping extinguishment clauses embodied in each treaty.

Canada's commitment to "civilizing" the Indians was less certain in the treaties, more implied than apparent in the size of reserves that were established on the basis of adequate farming lands, and manifested in the willingness of the government and its commissioners to accede to demands for farming implements. The difference is a subtle one. Canada could afford to avoid a policy commitment in the West. In fact, as far as the government was concerned, this was all it could afford. This method was not an option for the United States. A century later this difference in pace has resulted in physical differences that overshadow the similarities of approach. A twentieth-century perspective and understanding of Indian issues has cast the American and Canadian reserve experiences in a different light that should not be allowed to obscure their original purposes, which were quite clearly not that far apart.

7 Civilization

The second major component of Indian policy manifested in the treaties of 1867–68 and the Numbered Treaties was that of civilization, a wide-ranging program aimed at the social transformation of Indians into replicas of their white neighbors. By 1867 civilization, as it was applied to the North American Indians, was a familiar idea. The French had attempted it among the Indians in their colonies along the St. Lawrence River and in Acadia.[1] In the United States its ideological origins could be traced almost to the birth of the Republic and its earliest philosophical underpinnings to Pres. Thomas Jefferson. In British North America policy lagged somewhat behind the Americans in this regard. There civilization first appeared as an official commitment only after 1830, following the transfer of Indian administration from military to civilian hands after the realization that these people were no longer of strategic value.[2] This change came harder to the British, for it jarred with their long-time approach to Indian affairs. All of the European nations that had struggled for control of the North American continent solicited the military aid of the various Indian peoples, but "the great distinguishing feature of English relations with the Indian groups was replacement of the Indians on the land by white settlers, not conversion and assimilation of the Indians into European colonial society."[3]

There was no doubt that the United States from the beginning shared this original English purpose. Indeed, the Royal Proclamation had emerged out of an appreciation of American eagerness to expand. But almost from the earliest days of that nation's existence, a competing philosophical approach to the Indians had developed. The citizens of the Republic envisaged it very much in the old Puritan image of a "city upon a hill," leading the rest of the world to redemption through its own shining example. This conception of national exceptionalism, grounded in the tenets of the Enlightenment and then subsumed in an evangelical fervor that swept the United States in successive waves in the nineteenth century, spilled over into Indian relations too. Americans were bent on seizing Indian lands, and some rationale had to be devised not only to justify that seizure but also to celebrate it. Such an attitude led to many contradictions in American society, slavery in the land of the free being only the most glaring. In the case of the Indians, American absorption of the land would be balanced by the quid pro quo of civilization, which would render extensive Indian use of the land obsolete. From this perspective, removal could be interpreted as a positive good for the Indians as it was considered an encouragement of civilization among them.

Canada, in its approach to a civilization policy in the 1870s, was truer to English antecedents in its single-minded zeal to acquire land title. Britain too was swept in the early part of the nineteenth century with an evangelical religious fervor, which animated such organizations as the Aborigines' Protection Society, an influential body in the reorientation of British Indian policy.[4] Some have suggested that Britain came to this change in policy for rather more mundane reasons, perhaps as an imaginative bureaucratic solution to the threatened elimination of jobs in the Indian affairs office in England.[5] Whatever the motive behind the change, civilization measures did take shape in British North America over the next forty years, the most notable characteristics of the process being the constant lack of proper funds and the sluggish nature of the exercise.[6] The government established reserves, missionaries expanded their operations, and education and agriculture were encouraged, if not well financed. Britain took advantage of Indian interest in these aspects of civilization and encouraged and accepted Indian contributions to the funding of such initiatives.[7] Britain may have been receptive to the idea of civilization and to gradual assimilation of aboriginal peoples, but the imperial government of the mid–nineteenth century was preoccupied with disentangling itself from administrative responsibilities at home and abroad, including North American Indian affairs. It was left to the colonies to fill this gap and, especially in Upper Canada where legislation that shaped later Canadian practice was implemented, the task was eagerly embraced. British and colonial policy set precedents for the Dominion's foray into the West in the 1870s, but did not itself directly apply to the Northwest. Until Canada purchased Rupert's Land in 1869, the Hudson's Bay Company held sway there, and an official civilization policy remained a matter for the future.

American commitment to a civilization policy was more solidly rooted. Congress had established the "civilization fund" in 1819, its explicit purpose to promote actively the education and "civilization" of the Indians. Although the American Republic had been founded on a strict adherence to the principle of separation of church and state, this money was none-theless frequently channeled through missionary societies.[8] Legislation devoted to a civilization policy was otherwise negligible, and the ten-thousand-dollar-a-year fund was not augmented over the next several decades despite pleas from the Office of Indian Affairs and the increase in the number of Indians under American jurisdiction who were expected to benefit from it.[9] The treaty terms offered to those peoples pushed West by the ever-encroaching American frontier provide more conclusive ev-idence of American interest in "civilizing" the Indians. After the War of 1812, as the United States embarked on westward expansion in earnest, Indian treaties began to incorporate terms providing for education and agricultural assistance.[10]

In approaching the treaty-making sessions on the plains and prairies in 1867 and the 1870s, then, both nations had precedents for civilization as a core element of their Indian policy, although the structural forms they chose for implementing this policy were different. In the United States, civilization was almost exclusively a matter of treaty arrangements, while in Canada it was entrusted to legislation. Two basic assumptions sup-ported the entrenchment of civilization as a major feature in the Indian policy of Canada and the United States. The nations shared these ideas, although they were more acutely felt in the United States, where all mat-ters dealing with Indians were of more immediate consequence, the re-sult of the advanced stage of white expansion in that country.

The first of these assumptions was the conviction that the Indians were a dying race, although the term most often employed was that they faced "extinction." In the United States this was attributed to a number of causes, including disease, alcohol, and internecine wars, all indirectly the result of contact with whites, as well as the possibility of deliberate extermination by whites.[11] Canada recognized the same indirect causes as diminishing the numbers of its own Indian populations in the West.[12] That the Indians were dying out was thus an established fact by the mid-nineteenth century. Popular opinion in both countries was convinced of it, and the formulation of Indian policy was affected by it, although at least in Canada there was some reason to doubt the validity of the claim.[13]

The impact of white migration on Indians was cast in both countries, although with somewhat less insistence or repetition in Canada, as the inevitable result of the clash between "civilization" and "savagery." [14] This pat answer to the dilemma of one race's recognized responsibility for another's endangerment, cloaked in the overtones of "divine Providence," largely relieved the culprits of doing anything to address the real issue — the intrusion of whites on Indian lands. When the Great Peace Commission embarked on its mission in 1867, this conviction was made explicit: "We do not contest the ever-ready argument that civilization must not be arrested in its progress by a handful of savages. . . . We earnestly desire the speedy settlement of all our territories. None are more anxious than we to see their agricultural and mineral wealth developed by an industrious, thrifty, and enlightened population. And we fully recognize the fact that the Indian must not stand in the way of this result. We would only be understood as doubting the purity and genuineness of that civilization which reaches its ends by falsehood and violence, and dispenses blessings that spring from violated rights." [15] One senator did raise his voice in favor of restraining American citizens, citing as proof of the ability of the United States to enforce regard for Indian rights, the fact that "we have in subjection, absolute subjection . . . ten States with a white population of eight or nine millions." [16] It was an allusion to the military control of the post–Civil War South, but this formula found no application in the West, where it was a lone cry among the many forces — pioneer, capitalist, humanitarian, and military — that accepted the inevitability of white expansion. Neither did Canadian policymakers, plotting the colonization of the Canadian West, doubt the inevitability of this conflict, although they were consistently more concerned about avoiding the violent aspects of such a collision. [17]

The second assumption underlying the emergence of a concerted policy of civilization was the belief that race was at the bottom of the difficulties. As they existed, whites and Indians were incompatible, a logical conclusion from the effects of contact on aboriginal societies. The solution was not, however, a nineteenth-century form of cultural plurality. It was instead to make Indians like whites, to assimilate them into the settler societies. As one senator informed his colleagues, "the only ultimate solution of this whole question is, that the Indian shall take his place among other men and accept the march of civilization, as he must ultimately, or there is nothing except his destiny that awaits him, which is extinction." [18] Policymakers posed the dilemma exclusively in terms that put the onus for change on the Indians. The perplexing quandary in each nation was how to achieve this.

The first step was admitted to be the establishment of reserves, which served the purpose of protection, a necessary preliminary on the road to "civilization." The critical element of reserve policy was the assumption that these landholdings were, by the definition of the governments that established them, temporary, and in the long term the container in which the crucial civilization elixir would be concocted and administered. Americans and Canadians differed on how they chose to implement civilization, but almost everyone agreed that there were three essential components to such a policy: Christianity, education, and agriculture.[19]

The Christian faith, particularly in its evangelical Protestant form, was recognized by policymakers, governments, and humanitarians as one of the pillars of white civilization and as one of the benefits to be imparted to the Indians as a matter of course.[20] General Pope understood that the goal of American policy was to make the Indian "a good citizen and a good Christian."[21] In a discussion of the future status of Indians in the United States, Senator Henderson remarked, "I understand that the object is to have these Indians Christianized; to have them become citizens of the United States; to have them become in all respects civilized like white men."[22]

Despite this linking of Christianity with civilization, there was nothing in either the treaties of 1867–68 or the Numbered Treaties to give tangible support to such implied intentions. Neither set of treaties even mentioned Christianity. This suggests the possibility that both nations embraced the rhetoric of the faith because it so neatly served narrow official ends. Christianity, as employed by governments, offered a vital rationalization for what otherwise might be suspected as an unwarranted eviction of the Indians from their own lands. James Harlan informed his Senate colleagues, "it has been maintained from the beginning that Christian nations had a right to the soil occupied by other nations."[23] He neglected to mention that this argument was one originating entirely within and recognized only by Christian nations themselves. Lt. Gov. Adams Archibald also invoked this conviction of the superior claim of Christian countries, founded in their more appropriate use of the land as an agricultural resource, during 1871 treaty talks. Confronted by the reluctance of Treaty 1 Indians to surrender the bulk of their land, a local newspaper reported, "His Excellency, put the matter in its true light. God, he says, intends this land to raise great crops for all his children, and the time has come when it is to be used for that purpose."[24]

The churches understood the advantages religion offered to the self-serving purposes of the government and sometimes used this attitude to further their own efforts. Commenting on President Grant's Indian Peace Policy, which assigned to the churches a significant official role, the Anglican archbishop of Rupert's Land told Lieutenant Governor Morris, "I do not at all suggest that it is desirable to adopt such a course but still I believe the Government may materially further its own ends and what is necessary with the Indians by working harmoniously & sympathetically with the Missions." [25] With this suggestion, Archbishop Robert Machray provided what may be a more persuasive explanation for the seeming indifference of treaty commissioners to entrenching Christianity in the text of the treaties. By 1871 organized religion was well rooted in Manitoba, and missionary outposts across the Canadian prairies were two generations old. Missionaries, Indian and white alike, were present at treaty councils and often played important roles, occasionally as interpreters. Their assigned mission stations, representing Roman Catholic, Methodist, Anglican, and Presbyterian faiths, had established schools and model farms. Thus missionary activity in the Canadian West had already found secure footholds for the promotion of the three-pronged policy of civilization—Christianity, education, and agriculture. All four denominations had representatives at Treaty 6, and when ministers were requested by the Fort Carlton Crees, Alexander Morris responded, "You see missionaries here on the ground, both Roman Catholic and Protestant; they have been in the country many years. As it has been in the past, so it will be again, you will not be forgotten." He also noted, in a telling commentary on official attitudes toward spiritual matters, "With regard to ministers I cannot interfere." [26]

The government could accept, however grudgingly, that it must supply concrete aid to further the practical goals of education and agriculture, but there was little the Dominion could or should do to promote faith. The widespread missionary presence in western Canada precluded the necessity of official organization and financing of the effort, but this did not necessarily mean a lack of appreciation for the effort itself.

The American situation was different. Here too Christianity failed to surface as a stated objective in the treaties. In contrast to Canada, the role of missionaries at the treaty-making councils on the plains was minimal. Two missionaries, the Jesuit Pierre-Jean De Smet and Episcopalian minister Samuel Hinman, witnessed some of the signing sessions of the Fort Laramie Treaty, but there is scant evidence to suggest that there was a missionary presence of any sort at Medicine Lodge. Yet the evangelical impulse in Congress and the Northeast, which had supported a peace initiative in 1867 and an emphasis on civilization as the central component of that overture, pervaded the civilian members of the commission itself in a way that was not as obvious among Canadian treaty makers. This connection was clearest in the president of the peace commission and former Methodist minister Nathaniel Taylor and likely a strong influence in reformers Samuel Tappan and Sen. John Henderson, "all of whom strongly believed that applying Christian principles would do much more to solve the Indian problem than would using military force."[27] Aware of the embryonic state of missionary affairs among the Indians of the plains, Taylor castigated American religious bodies for ignoring these peoples: "While our missionary societies and benevolent associations have annually collected thousands of dollars from the charitable, to be sent to Asia and Africa for the purposes of civilization, scarcely a dollar is expended or a thought bestowed on the civilization of Indians at our very doors."[28] Taylor perhaps failed to take into account the kind of infrastructure necessary for a successful missionary venture. In Canada missionaries had followed the fur trade, and if the Hudson's Bay Company was ambivalent about the advantages of missions for fur-trade operations, it nonetheless lent its organizational and transportation networks to these efforts. American missionaries had gone west with settlers and were very early established in the Oregon Country, but the plains remained untouched by such activity. Like the Blackfoot territory in Canada, which lay outside the fur-trade range, the country of the American Plains Indians was slow to attract American settlers and was thus relatively ignored by missionary overtures. Even the indefatigable Father De Smet failed in his attempts to establish a mission on the Upper Missouri River before 1870.[29]

At the treaty discussions themselves, missionaries were insignificant. It has been suggested that the American negotiators understood the antipathy of the Plains Indians in particular to the Christian religion and therefore left it out of their talks.[30] This explanation seems unlikely since nothing the Americans offered in the treaty negotiations appealed to the Indians, and yet as the treaty terms illustrate, there was no compunction about filling the document with equally obnoxious provisions for reservations, agricultural assistance, and other elements of "civilization." More likely, as in the Canadian case, treaty commissioners had confidence that missionary work was a natural concomitant of the civilization structure they had written into the treaties, and this proved to be the case in practice. In 1869 President Grant broke with conventional Indian office practice to employ as Indian agents and superintendents men nominated by specific Christian denominations, initially Quakers only but soon also Episcopalians, Methodists, and even Roman Catholics. Bolstered by this formal endorsement as well as by the development of some official infrastructure, missionary efforts on the American Plains blossomed after 1870.[31]

Education was the second fundamental aspect of a policy of civilization. In the United States education was considered vital for the resolution of the Indian problem. In its first report, the Great Peace Commission confronted this question: "What prevented their [whites and Indians] living together? First. The antipathy of race. Second. The difference of customs and manners arising from their tribal or clannish organizations. Third. The difference in language." This was a reasonable assessment, but the solution was, of course, entirely one way: "Now, by educating the children of these tribes in the English language these differences would have disappeared, and civilization would have followed at once." The announced object was "to fuse them into one homogeneous mass. Uniformity of language will do this—nothing else will."[32]

In a way, Indians were the preferred minority in the United States. They were distinctly different from the white population, but their differences could be eliminated. It was possible to assimilate them. This could not be said for the more-numerous black population, for whom only the most radical of humanitarian sympathizers would have suggested a similar solution.

Education was the route to the eradication of these troubling differences, and assimilation was the goal. Agriculture might physically save Indians by providing them a means of subsistence, but only education could solve the fundamental conflict of "civilized" and "savage" because the "inferior" population could thereby be elevated. It would make Indians more like whites and, as well, persuade them of the superiority of the white culture they were to embrace.

Education had many elements, but the single most important of these was the teaching of the English language. This would dissipate, in the first instance, the differences among the tribes, creating that sought-after "homogenous mass." But it would also obliterate what were described as "barbarous dialects" that impeded instruction in further arts of "civilization," like agriculture.[33] Whites held no respect for Indian languages or culture as things of value in themselves, at least for the Indians. In his annual report of 1864, the American commissioner of Indian affairs remarked, "The Indian race, by what seems to be the law of its existence, is fast passing away, and in contact with the white race the tribes are rapidly losing their distinctive features, in language, habits, customs, &c." This was the ostensible object of American policy, yet the commissioner was somewhat troubled by an anthropological problem and suggested that "a modest appropriation, judiciously expended, would enable the office, through its agents, teachers, missionaries, and others interested in the various tribes of red men, to collect annually a large and increasingly valuable collection of the memorials referred to," including "portraits, implements of industry or of warfare, specimens of apparel, &c."[34] Indian culture would be preserved only for white educational purposes, not because of any use Indians might have for it. Inherent in this approach, naturally, was an almost universal rejection of Indian modes of education, which encompassed a multiplicity of means and ends as complex as non-Indian educational practices. But the absence of institutional forms, such as schools, permitted missionaries and secular authorities to ignore them.[35]

Another aspect of education was the value of this program for imparting to Indians the superiority, and therefore attractions, of white culture, thereby winning them to an acceptance of their transformation. Although American treaty commissioners had been accused of treachery in the past, and with some justification, the Great Peace Commission was at pains to make clear to the Indians what they were being offered, since Americans believed it was an offer that could not be refused. The terms were laid out as bluntly in the negotiations as they were in the treaty documents themselves:

In lieu of the buffalo, you must have herds of cattle, sheep and hogs like the white man. In order to have these, you must have a reservation of rich land, and now set aside for you, before the white man settles upon it. We will help you select it. . . . On that reservation we will build a house to receive the clothing and goods to be sent you every year. Your agent shall live among you and hear your complaints. At the same place you will have your trading houses, also a physician to cure you of sickness, and a farmer to help you cultivate the soil. We will send you a mill to grind your corn and teachers to educate your children. In addition to these things, your Great Father will send you every year such goods as you may need.[36]

Reviewing these terms, the *New York Times* understood the role that education would play in the process of persuasion. "If we can show the savages . . . that the white man's mode of living is easier, better and more satisfactory to the physical man than theirs, the young savages will speedily adopt it. The Indians, as a rule, have good sense."[37] This left the Americans a comfortable rationalization for the distinct lack of enthusiasm for these terms among the Indians they faced at the treaty talks. If they did not immediately appreciate what they were being offered, English would eventually make them see the light.

American seriousness in the realm of education, perhaps an indication of the more straightforward nature of this element of civilization policy, was clear through the identical articles included in each of the treaties signed at Medicine Lodge and Fort Laramie in 1867–68, indicating both the consistency of the commission and the fact that the terms originated with the government. These were ideas the commissioners took to the treaty talks, not ones that were inspired by Indian input. Article 4 suggests a possible loophole in implementation, permitting the United States to delay fulfilling obligations in a "so soon as" clause, but in practice the government's zeal, or at least that of the Indian office, led them to begin constructing buildings before even ascertaining whether children would go. This elicited some criticism in Congress from economy-minded representatives.[38] (See table 2.)

In many aspects of Indian relations—violence, conflict, secular missionary impulse, reserves—Canada seemed a pale shadow of the American experience, and the Canadian approach to education in the West was no different. Both countries viewed education as a vital element of civilization. Understanding was recognized as an important factor in persuading the Indians to change. Minister of the Interior David Laird put this into words in 1874: "Even under the most favorable circumstances time must be given him [the Indian] to understand the motives and acquire the habits of the white man. . . . But when these motives come to be understood and acted upon by the Indian, the evidence of which is the possession of considerable property acquired by his own industry and thrift, it shows that he may safely be entrusted with the rights of full citizenship."[39] In 1875 Indian Commissioner J. A. N. Provencher was emphatic

Table 2: Summary of terms for education in the Kiowa
and Comanche Medicine Lodge Creek Treaty

ARTICLE 4. BUILDINGS ON RESERVATION

A schoolhouse or mission building is to be built "so soon as a sufficient number of children can be induced by the agent to attend school."

ARTICLE 7. CIVILIZATION AND EDUCATION

"In order to insure the civilization of the tribes . . . the necessity of education is admitted." Children (ages 6–16) will be compelled to attend school.

For every 30 children, the United States will supply a house for the teacher and a teacher "competent to teach elementary branches of an English education."

This article will continue "for not less than 20 years."

ARTICLE 14. PERSONNEL TO BE PROVIDED

The United States will hire the teachers (among other professionals) and provide money to pay for them.

Note: Terms have been summarized. Quotation marks indicate exact wording.

on the role of education in this process for reasons similar to those advanced by American advocates: "All those who have taken an interest in the future welfare of the Indians have directed their minds to their education and have insisted on the necessity to raise the level of their knowledge, to enlighten their minds and above all to act early on the minds of the children so as to give them . . . intellectual habits, which are the most striking feature of civilization."[40] Yet this conviction was not nearly as evident in the Numbered Treaties as in the American treaties. Six of the seven Canadian agreements contained a commitment to establish a school "on each reserve." The timetable for founding such institutions was predicated on when the Indians concerned "desire it" or when the Indians were "settled and prepared." In Treaty 7, the Blackfoot treaty, the promise made was to pay teachers' salaries when deemed advisable after the Indians settled.[41]

The absence of detail may cast the Canadian commitment to this aspect of civilization into some doubt, but other explanations suggest themselves. The vague references to schools would have been consistent with Canada's constricted view of treaties as title-extinguishment documents alone and a manifestation of Canadian reluctance to expand the function of such documents. As well, civilization was acknowledged to be a costly enterprise, and the parsimoniousness of the Canadian government in all things in the 1870s was a factor of which commissioners, through treaty-making instructions, were ever mindful. Joseph Howe, in directing the commissioners originally appointed to conclude Treaty 3, reminded them, "The Powers intrusted to you are large, and they should be used with constant reference to the responsibility which the Government owes to Parliament and to the country for the judicious and economic expenditure of the funds and supplies intrusted to your charge."[42]

Another difference with the American approach to education was the dissenting voice, perhaps the only one, of the Indian commissioner on the value of Indian languages. In a thoughtful critique of many aspects of Canadian Indian policy in the West, Commissioner Provencher questioned the value of making English the centerpiece of an Indian education program. Remarking on the likelihood of Indians continuing to use and maintain their own languages anyway, and on whether it was indeed "the duty of a civilizing Government to throw its influence to extinguish a language spoken by thousands," he offered a pragmatic rationalization for the use of Indian languages. "The first principle in education is to attract the attention of the pupil to what he is taught," a goal not likely to be successful in a widespread program of language repression.[43] Provencher's suggestions bore no fruit but were an indication that no matter what the policy in Ottawa, whether planned or haphazard, some people, including even persons in the bureaucracy of Indian affairs, were giving thought to Indian matters. Provencher's concerns fit perfectly with a logical, rational, planned civilization program. The question lurking in the shadows of any discussion of the Canadian program, however, is whether a plan existed at all.

Canada's treaty terms in the matter of education raise some doubts. The commitment to education hardly seems more concrete than the official promotion of Christianity, although at least there is some acknowledgment of this responsibility. From correspondence after the treaties were signed, it is evident that many Indian communities were interested in schools and instruction, an impulse that the lieutenant governors supported and encouraged.[44] In the published newspaper account of the Treaty 1 proceedings, the subject of schools and education did not arise until the sixth day of the council, four days after Lieutenant Governor Archibald's opening statement, which by the same report did not mention the subject. The intervening time had been spent in ongoing discussion of the terms offered, among them those that would come to constitute the Outside Promises. Only after repeated insistence from Henry

Prince on the question of security for the future was it reported that the lieutenant governor, not treaty commissioner Simpson, responded, "showing that the Queen was willing to help the Indians in every way, and that besides giving them land and annuities, she would give them a school and a schoolmaster for each reserve."[45] But this meager report does not make clear the source of the initiative. Unlike the terms for agricultural assistance, however, the commitment to provide schools was included in the treaty, which suggests that the commissioners believed this to be part of the package they were authorized to offer. Perhaps Indian and government interests coincided on this point.

In Alexander Morris's published accounts of the treaty negotiations, an explicit reference to education appears only in the Treaty 6 talks, and this incident sheds no light on whose idea it was. "You ask for school teachers and ministers," Morris is recorded as having said. "I had already promised you that when you settled down, and there were enough children, schools would be maintained."[46] The ambiguous evidence makes it difficult to ascertain whether education, like agricultural implements, was a demand originating with the Indians and accepted as standard by Treaty 6, or whether it had always been included as a fundamental part of the treaties. No matter who initiated the terms, one thing is certain — the Indians who expressed interest in education did not view it, as Canadian officials did, as a tool of civilization. Nor did the Indians likely intend to surrender control of the process even as they embraced it.

Christianity and education had both their strengths and their advocates as pillars of civilization, but agriculture was arguably the most important component of the three. Aside from the "God-given" mandate of an agrarian existence that justified the seizure of Indian lands, agriculture had any number of practical functions that made it a centerpiece of the civilizing effort. It was an education in itself, for by it one learned the value of work, acquired the rewards of private property, and gained a sense of individualism. All of these were believed central to the success of the white world and essential to the transformation of the Indian. For troubled consciences, the gift of agriculture, imparted to peoples dependent on such an insecure means of subsistence as the buffalo, would prove payment enough for the land surrendered in the process. On top of everything else, agriculture would solve the perplexing and very basic problem of how the Indians were to survive once the buffalo was gone.

Americans and Canadians alike were disgusted with what they perceived as an unwillingness of Indian men to "work," as they defined it. Congressman Benjamin Butler objected to an appropriation for the subsistence of one group of Indians by denouncing the practice: "I do not understand why it is that the Indian alone, of all the people on the globe, should be exempted from the penalty of the primeval curse of man to earn his bread by the sweat of his brow. We have to tax our constituents to feed lazy Indians."[47] In Canada, Department of the Interior employee M. G. Dickieson substantially agreed with Butler in a report to the Minister of the Interior in 1873: "One of the greatest impediments . . . is the belief inherent in the minds of every Indian that it is derogatory to the dignity of a man to work."[48] Agricultural labor was perceived as an answer to this problem, as it would naturally involve the absorption of the values of discipline and reliability essential to white civilization.[49] In the period before reserve life became a compulsory aspect of Indian relations, sooner in the United States than in Canada, policy critics could only grumble about the inequity of benefits extended to the Indians that were not available to citizens. Once Indians had been successfully confined to reserves, both governments were in a position to use heavy-handed measures to overcome this alleged resistance of Indians to work by employing the distribution of rations in a coercive fashion.

The ideas of private property and individualism were connected and of similar importance in both nations. The intent of the two nations to absorb rather than coexist with the Indian populations was clear in their views on these matters. Communal property inhibited an appreciation for private property, the fundamental element of the burgeoning capitalist societies in North America. Holding lands in common also encouraged tribal relations in a society fixated on the individual. Private property was also seen as a remedy to Indian internecine conflict, the tendency to which whites objected and identified as a character trait to be eliminated.[50] American conviction of the role of private property in diminishing such conflicts was first apparent on the plains in the 1851 Treaty of Fort Laramie, wherein each of the Indian peoples was assigned a specific district in the hopes that they would remain on their own territory and thereby avoid conflict with each other.[51] Tribal relations were interpreted as a serious impediment to both of these things—individualism and private property—and thus were an object of particular scorn by policymakers both north and south of the forty-ninth parallel.[52]

Although reserves were granted in blocs, extensive in the United States and more limited in Canada, neither nation ever envisioned communal agriculture. The American treaty terms, which focused on the individual and private property, did not encourage the communal or tribal basis of Indian life. Canadians were not as clear about this, as reserve lands in Canada were to be held in common. This was not, however, meant to impede individual farmsteads. By granting the lands en bloc, explained Commissioner Provencher, "we preserve the property intact, which thus belongs to the whole Band. A portion will afterwards be divided into lots, according to circumstances, and such families as may desire it shall be put in possession of one of these lots. The rest of the Reserve shall remain undivided to satisfy new demands, or be converted into a common for pasturage, firewood, building wood, and hay." [53] In commenting on the extensive size of the reserves allowed to the Treaty 6 Indians, Lieutenant Governor Morris told them they could not possibly farm such an extent — 640 acres per family of five — but suggested that they might sell the excess to establish for themselves an annual income such as Indians in Ontario had done. [54] The devotion of government policymakers and treaty commissioners toward these elements was apparent in the treaty terms accorded, which again reflected the different emphases and priorities, perhaps even levels of commitment, of the two nations.

Four articles in the American treaties dealt extensively with matters relating to agriculture. Article 6 designated "Lands for farming," and the strictness of the term "farming" was made more explicit in the extended conditions of the Sioux treaty, wherein Indians were permitted to select off-reserve lands so long as they did not include mineral lands or any other reserved for use by the United States. Indians were to undertake property only in an agricultural framework as this was the only road to advancement Americans would accept. [55] Under these terms, Indians who did not choose the agricultural option could not acquire individual property rights, limited as they were. (See table 3.)

The stipulations detailed in Articles 6 and 8 made it clear that the basis for distribution of lands was the individual or, perhaps, the family. Agriculture was to be an inducement to white civilization, the basis of which was the individual and the family farm. These terms stand out in greater relief when compared to the Canadian provisions for implements, animals, and financial assistance wherein aid was more likely to be distributed to a number of families or to bands than to a single family and never to an individual.

The seriousness of the Americans in their commitment to introducing agriculture was apparent too in the voluntary provision of a farming in-

TREATY WITH THE KIOWAS AND COMANCHES	TREATY WITH THE SIOUX

Article 6
Lands for farming

Heads of family can select a piece of reservation land not exceeding 320 acres to start farming.	Heads of family can select a piece of reservation land not exceeding 320 acres to start farming.
On doing so, this piece of land will cease to be held in common.	On doing so, this piece of land will cease to be held in common.
The land will be held by the person as long as it is cultivated.	The land will be held by the person as long as it is cultivated.
Any person (including women) over 18 can choose up to 80 acres of land.	Any person (including women) over 18 can choose up to 80 acres of land.
These transactions will be recorded in a Land Book.	These transactions will be recorded in a Land Book.
The status of the land is not fee simple but may be made so at the president's discretion.	The status of the land is not fee simple but may be made so at the president's discretion.
The United States can make laws on the alienation of this type of property and other matters relating to it.	The United States can make laws on the alienation of this type of property and other matters relating to it.
	Any male Indian over 18 who shall occupy a piece of land *outside* the reservation that shall not be mineral lands or any other reserved for use by the United States, and who has made improvements of more than $200 value and occupied this land for 3 years continuously, shall be entitled to receive a U.S. patent for 160 acres, including his improved land.
	After providing written application and proof of 2 disinterested witnesses, the Indian can register this land at the General Land Office and hold it as long as he continues to live there.

Citizenship

Any Indian receiving a patent under the
above rules may become a citizen of

Table 3: *continued*

the United States entitled to all rights of citizenship and shall "at the same time, retain all his rights to benefits accruing to Indians under this treaty."

Article 8
Agriculture

Once an Indian selects land for farming, he/she is entitled to:
    up to $100 worth of seeds and implements [unspecified], for the first year and up to $25.00 worth for the next 3 years;
    farming instruction by a farmer provided by the United States.
For every 100 persons cultivating, a blacksmith will be provided, as well as iron, steel, and other materials.

Once an Indian selects land for farming, he/she is entitled to:
    up to $100 worth of seeds and implements [unspecified], for the first year and up to $25.00 worth for the next 3 years;
    farming instruction by a farmer provided by the United States.
For every 100 persons cultivating, a blacksmith will be provided, as well as iron, steel, and other materials.

Article 10
Other necessities

$25,000 will be provided each year for 30 years to be spent by the secretary of the interior, at the commissioner of Indian Affairs's recommendation, on necessities (unspecified) for Indians.
If during the 30 years it is found money can be better spent on the Indians in some other way, Congress may change the purpose of the appropriation but may not change the amount of or withdraw the appropriation for 30 years.
An army officer will be appointed to inspect goods and supervise their delivery.

Persons who continue to roam and hunt will receive $10.00 per year for 30 years.
Persons engaged in farming will receive $20.00 per year for 30 years.
The money will be used by the secretary of the interior to purchase articles deemed to be of necessity for the Indians.
If during the 30 years it is found money can be better spent on the Indians in some other way, Congress may change the purpose of the appropriation but may not change the amount of or withdraw the appropriation for 30 years.
Food Provisions
Every Indian over 4 years of age who has settled permanently on a reservation and adhered to the treaty will be provided with 1 pound of meat and 1 pound of flour per day for 4 years if they cannot furnish their own subsistence at an earlier date.

continued

Table 3: *continued*

	Cows and Oxen The United States will give each family (lodge) who has settled to farm "1 good American cow and 1 good well-broken pair of American oxen" within 60 days of their settlement.

Article 15
Reward for crops

$500 will be awarded annually to the 10 best agricultural producers.	$500 will be awarded annually to the 10 best agricultural producers.

Note: Terms have been summarized.

structor, something the Canadian government would offer reluctantly when disaster struck the West after the complete disappearance of the buffalo from the Canadian prairies in 1879.[56] The general nature of the agricultural assistance offered in Article 8, unspecified implements or amount of seed as well as short-term monetary assistance, left room for adaptability to circumstance and did not circumscribe the forms this assistance might take in the future. (Again, this is something that is made clearer in comparison to Canadian treaty terms.)

Each of the Numbered Treaties contained some provisions for agricultural assistance, and these terms came as the result of pressure from the Indians.[57] The government—the treaty commissioners in the first instance and Ottawa itself in that no objections were raised to the introduction of agricultural terms—was receptive to expanding treaties to incorporate such demands. After this had been established as a standard aspect in the Treaty 3 negotiations, subsequent treaties involved haggling over the specifics of such terms rather than over whether or not to include them at all.

The most notable thing about the agricultural aid offered in the Numbered Treaties is that these sections read like a hardware store inventory list. This is a contrast to the American treaties, in which aid was delineated in dollars' worth rather than specific implements. These articles appeared in the Numbered Treaties undoubtedly because of the insistence of the Indians on agricultural aid, but it was the government that determined the form that aid should take. Here the commissioners, in operating without clear instructions from Ottawa, may have done more harm than good in the long run by their concessions. This practice of listing specific items narrowed the commitment to agricultural assistance and permitted a future literal-minded and mean-spirited bureaucracy to continue to convey to the Indians items, under treaty promises, that were no longer recognized as particularly helpful in the circumstances of agriculture on the prairies. The more general American terms theoretically allowed for some flexibility, although whether this was the case in practice is another matter. But the Canadian terms permitted an ungenerous interpretation that accorded with the attitudes of the men who oversaw Indian affairs in the early reserve period.

Another striking point about these enumerated items was the distribution of materials. Unlike the United States, where the individual was the basis for goods allotted, the Canadian treaties stated that all implements and stock would be shared. How many or how few families were to share these things depended on the pressure the Indians brought to bear on the commissioners or on how much regard or fear the commissioners had for those with whom they bargained. As a result, Treaty 6, which involved protracted negotiations on these points from the aware and insistent Plains Crees, and Treaty 7, with the Blackfoot who were held in fearful awe by Canadians, contained the most generous distribution of implements and stock. The Swampy Crees of Treaty 5, on the other hand, posing no threat to the government and making few demands, were awarded less generous terms. (See table 4.)

The agricultural policy of the government, as imparted in the Numbered Treaties, inaugurated what historian Sarah Carter has called a "period of indifference and neglect."[58] But the receptiveness of the commissioners, and the lack of objection by the government especially to terms that in one instance would be described later as "onerous" (financially) and yet ratified nonetheless, also suggests an uneasy compromise between accepted practice and "necessary innovations." Again, the Canadian government viewed the treaties only in the narrow terms of land title extinguishment but learned through the negotiations that Indians demanded more. Because the government wanted the treaties signed, it acceded to demands that fit the pattern, if not of previous treaty terms, then at least of past general intentions and practice in Indian policy. Thus terms that accorded with the civilization measures implemented in cen-

Table 4: Summary of terms for agricultural aid in Treaties 4–7

TREATY 4	TREATY 5	TREATY 6	TREATY 7
		Farming Equipment	
To every family "actually cultivating":	To every family "actually cultivating":	To every family now or later cultivating:	For those who want to cultivate (per family):
2 hoes	2 hoes	4 hoes	1 less cow than below, BUT ALSO
1 spade	1 spade	2 spades	2 hoes
1 scythe		2 scythes	1 spade
1 axe	1 plough per 10 families	1 whetstone	1 scythe
		2 hayforks	2 hayforks
1 plough per 10 families		2 reaping hooks	
2 harrows per 10 families		1 plough per 3 families	1 plough per 3 families
		1 harrow per 3 families	1 harrow per 3 families
		1 handmill, when amount of grain warrants it	
Per chief for use of the band:		Per Band:	For each chief, minor chief, and Stony chief for their bands:
1 crosscut saw		2 axes	10 axes
5 handsaws		1 crosscut saw	5 handsaws
1 pitsaw		1 handsaw	5 augers
the necessary files		1 pitsaw	1 grindstone
5 augers		the necessary files	the necessary files
1 chest of ordinary carpenter's tools		1 grindstone	1 whetstone
		1 auger	
		1 chest of ordinary carpenter's tools (per chief for use of the band)	

tral Canada through legislation, the commissioners, and by ratification the government, shifted from legislation to the treaties themselves. Perhaps because this was a break with past practice or because Alexander Morris wanted to acknowledge the Indians' demands without overstepping Ottawa's limits, the agricultural terms offered proved an unsatisfactory compromise during the subsequent implementation phase. The Indians discovered that their paltry terms, which they had to fight to get to

Table 4: *continued*

TREATY 4	TREATY 5	TREATY 6	TREATY 7
		Seed	
"enough" seed, oats, wheat, barley, and potatoes to plant the land "actually broken up"		"enough" wheat, barley, potatoes, and oats to plant the land "actually broken up"	"enough" potatoes, oats, barley, and wheat (if suitable) to plant the land "actually broken up"
		Livestock	
Per chief for use of the band: 1 yoke of oxen 1 bull 4 cows		Per band: 4 oxen 1 bull 6 cows 1 boar 2 sows	1 bull per chief 2 cows per family of 5 or less 3 cows per family of 6 to 9 4 cows per family of 10 or more

begin farming since the treaties promised the materials only when the Indians were *actually* farming, were insufficient in either quantity or appropriateness to the tasks at hand. Had the government interpreted its own treaties in the spirit in which such terms were negotiated by both the Indians and the commissioners, this would not have posed such a problem. But there were different men, a different spirit, and different circumstances abroad in the land in the matter of Indian relations, especially in the wake of the 1885 rebellion, and literal interpretation of the treaties upheld both these attitudes and Canadian smugness about honoring treaty terms.

The single greatest contradiction in the American treaty provisions, given the emphasis on private property and the individual as the centerpiece of the transformation to civilization, was the restriction on fee simple title set out in Article 6 of the 1867–68 treaties. (See table 3.) Surely if the object was a property-holding individual, a proper "Jeffersonian yeoman farmer" of the American ideal, then the final piece of the puzzle was missing here. The creation of freehold farmers was the ultimate goal of this article, and the Sioux treaty went the furthest in actually establishing grounds for citizenship for those who fulfilled the stringent requirements of property holding. But there was a distinct air of reluctance to impart to the Indians full ownership and fee simple title, apparent in the emphasis that such lands were to be held only as long as they were cultivated or as long as the person involved remained in occupation of them. The Americans, so optimistic in other aspects of their civilization policy, could not overcome this disinclination. Indeed, a hesitance to convey full title on the Indians appeared again in the General Allotment Act of 1887, the purpose of which was explicitly to break up tribal relations and induce private ownership among the Indians.[59] In part this reluctance stemmed from the American conception of Indians as immature and unready for such responsibilities, which proved a self-serving and useful characterization.

But Americans had other fears that might have justified this hesitation. One was that Indians likely would be swindled out of their property in short order, a prospect that alarmed those humanitarians and reformers who sought a gradual evolution of the race. American Indian relations held enough precedents to make this a viable fear. The Royal Proclamation of 1763 had specifically reserved the surrender of Indian title to Crown oversight because of this very tendency by Americans. Implementation of severalty under the General Allotment Act would prove the validity of this fear yet again. In this instance, the waning protective function of the American treaties edged out the more strident civilization impulse.

The Americans had other reasons to fear fee simple title by the Indians. As suggested by the citizenship provisions of Article 6, those Indians who received a patent under the established rules might become citizens of the United States, and this, by definition and under the Fourteenth Amendment to the Constitution adopted in 1868, would have won such Indians the right to vote. Some American congressmen would have applauded this advance as it would also have included the right of the government to tax these Indians. The tax-free status of American Indians remained a sore point with economy-minded members of the House.[60] But the voting rights of domestic minorities—blacks and Indians—as well as of racially dissimilar immigrants—Chinese, Japanese, and even southern and eastern Europeans—was an increasingly troublesome issue in the United States in the post–Civil War era. In 1867 and 1868 the most pressing of these questions was the matter of black voting rights and, in the midst of the Reconstruction and Fifteenth Amendment debates, this was a particularly sensitive issue. American treaty commissioners may well have shied away from any direct commitments to fee simple title and the citizenship it implied for fear of compromising larger questions. The restrictions on Indian landownership under treaty provisions, therefore, echoed the ambiguous strains of conflicting American reform movements.

As in the terms for education, the American program for the promotion of agriculture among the Indian signatories to these treaties reflected a comprehensive bid to advance civilization. All the means necessary to establish a family farm—a lot of an appropriate size, seed, implements, instruction, and sometimes even stock—were provided. American generosity reflected in part the conviction that even Indians would recognize a good deal when they saw one. General Sanborn told the Sioux he met with at Fort Rice in the summer of 1868: "The terms we propose are more liberal than you have ever had. Perhaps more liberal than any Indian Nation. You should not think of rejecting them, for so liberal terms are not likely again to be offered." [61] Congressional critics heartily agreed and decried the generosity shown the Indians when blacks, whom some believed to be a much more deserving minority, were given nothing at all. [62] The extent of these terms clearly demonstrated the commitment of the peace commissioners (at least the humanitarian reformers among them) to a system of agriculture that Americans believed would be as effective as education in destroying the cultural barriers that led to conflict. Agriculture offered a practical route to the acquisition of several of the fundamental values whites held dear—a work ethic, an attachment to private property, and the development of individualism—all traits supported by specific treaty terms.

Unlike the Americans, who clearly devised and imposed agricultural terms without the interest, input, or enthusiasm of the Indians, Canada did not initiate the agricultural aspects of its Numbered Treaties. With the exception of the Blackfoot treaty, the impetus for agricultural assistance as it appeared in the treaties belonged in every instance to the Indian participants. In light of Canada's subsequent pathetic record in agricultural assistance and encouragement of Indian farmers, characterized as obstructive at best if not downright sabotage, one could interpret Canadian treaty commitments to agriculture as having been less than sincere—perhaps they were just lip-service concessions to people who would not otherwise have signed the treaties, promises to be abandoned once Canada was in a position to ignore Indian demands. Evidence for Canada's performance in the implementation phase under reserve conditions is certainly suggestive of the government's willful undermining of Indian agricultural efforts.[63]

It is difficult, however, to accept this conclusion extrapolated back into the negotiation of the Numbered Treaties. Opposition to this point of view emerges from an examination of several pieces of evidence that suggest, at least in the treaty-making phase of Canadian Indian relations, some significant voices among government officials and treaty commissioners believed there was an intent to introduce a practical agricultural policy to address the future situation of the Indians in the West.

In a report to the governor general in August 1873, then Minister of the Interior Alexander Campbell offered a brief assessment of the situation on the plains west of Manitoba, urging that treaties with all of the peoples in these territories be made the following year. He noted the diminishing numbers of buffalo, the increased population pressures as a result of the westward migration of the Manitoba Métis, and how both of these factors were likely to exacerbate an already difficult situation when the buffalo, the single means of Indian subsistence, failed. In view of these things, Campbell stated his belief "that it is expedient with reference to the maintenance of the peace of the country to expedite the negotiations of treaties with these tribes so as to afford them the means of subsistence in exchange for their surrender of the Indian title of the lands over which they roam."[64] With this statement Campbell made explicit the nature of the treaties as understood by the cabinet minister responsible for Indians and may be assumed to be making a policy statement reflecting the will of the government he represented. The extinguishment of Indian land title remained, as it always had, the point of Canadian treaty making, but Campbell coupled this with a specific commitment to pay for it with a program that would ensure the subsistence of the Indians involved. This was not as clear a statement of intent as that given in the American act of July 20, 1867, but it was significant in advertising the intentions of the Canadian government. Campbell did not identify agriculture as the means to be supplied, nor did he link it with the concept of civilization, but he did not have to do so: these elements went together in contemporary thought.

Treaty commissioners in the field, through their actions and statements, provided the most apparent evidence for this interpretation. It seems clear from the government's reports and records that the Crown's representatives did not inaugurate any of the agricultural terms, but neither were they resistant to them. Commissioner Simpson objected to the extra demands of the Indians of Treaty 1, reluctant to go beyond that which he knew the government would accept.[65] However, Lieutenant Governor Archibald's opening remarks at the Stone Fort (Treaty 1) surely illustrated the government's receptiveness to such demands. He assured the Indians present that "She [the queen] wishes them [the Indians] to live in comfort. She would like them to adopt the habits of the whites—to till land and raise food, and store it up against a time of want." He also indicated the lethargic pace that the Canadian government was willing, indeed perhaps hoping to follow, by insisting, "the Queen, though she may think it good for you to adopt civilized habits, has no idea of compelling you to do so."[66]

Archibald was the lieutenant governor of Manitoba and the Northwest Territory, but he had only recently been appointed to this position from Ottawa and continued to correspond cordially with Prime Minister John A. Macdonald. Given this, he likely would not have advocated a course out of keeping with the government's position. Archibald supported Simpson's reluctance to include terms reflecting these intentions in the actual treaty, but nevertheless put his name, along with that of the Indian commissioner, to the memorandum of additional items, including the sought-after agricultural provisions that became the root of the Outside Promises fiasco.

The government's response to Indian complaints over the nonfulfillment of these additions, which the Indians understood to be part of the treaty but which the government did not, lends some credence to the interpretation that Ottawa was unsympathetic to the demands contained therein. However, this more likely reflects the existence of an inefficient and skeptical bureaucracy and a parsimonious government inclined to suspect Indians of wanting more than they had been promised, especially in light of the more "extraordinary" demands put forth by the Indian signatories of Treaty 3. Simpson, in his capacity as Indian Commissioner, did in fact distribute some of the assistance called for in the memorandum, although he did so unevenly and unsatisfactorily.[67] When Minister of the Interior Alexander Campbell discovered the memorandum in the annual report on Indian affairs for 1872, he expressed dismay at never having seen it before and issued instructions that it be implemented immediately, although complaints continued.[68] Archibald's successor as lieutenant governor, Alexander Morris, took the Indians' part from the beginning and repeatedly urged a resolution to what he considered a vexing problem.[69] During a visit to the West in 1874, Minister of the In-

terior David Laird made his own inquiries on the still outstanding grievances, and upon his return to Ottawa acted on the promises he had made
to the Indians concerned. Belatedly, the Privy Council accepted the Outside Promises as an official part of Treaties 1 and 2 and further instructed
Morris to notify the Indians that the promised action had been taken
and to gain their acceptance of the terms.[70]

Alexander Morris served as chief negotiator of the four subsequent
treaties and thus offered a degree of consistency to these arrangements.
He accepted the demands of the Treaty 3 Indians for agricultural assistance, although they were outside the purview of the limited instructions
he had been given as well. It was these terms that won Indian acceptance
of the treaty they had rejected twice before.[71] In the next four treaties, the
question of whether to include agricultural provisions was not disputed
by the commissioners, who included them in treaties as a matter of
course, or by the government, at least as such things are recorded in the
Privy Council minutes, parliamentary debates, and the governor general's records.

That the government and even the commissioners had their limits
was apparent in other instances. During the Treaty 6 negotiations, Lieutenant Governor Morris confronted perhaps the most prepared Indians
he had encountered in his offices as treaty commissioner. The Plains Crees
of the North Saskatchewan were keenly aware of the passing of their current way of life and anxious to find a means to subsist when the buffalo
disappeared altogether. The negotiations at Fort Carlton were the most
contentious Morris would face. As was the case in each of the Numbered
Treaties, the Indians won more concessions than the government had
been prepared to offer by presenting a list of demands and arguing their
case. On the fifth day of the proceedings Morris, having heard an extended list of Indian proposals presented by their own interpreter, responded with the government's counteroffer. Impressed by their concerns for the future and their expressed desire to embark on an agricultural
life, Morris expanded the list of agricultural implements to be supplied,
increased the amount of stock offered, agreed to provide a handmill to
each band settled and raising sufficient grain, and offered, of his own vo-
lition, a thousand-dollar payment for each of three years to the Fort Carlton bands after they had settled. It is possible to explain this as simply a
response to the pressures at hand. Morris himself concluded that the success in persuading the Indians to sign rested exclusively on his response
to the "food question," which so plagued these people.[72] But he was re-

ceptive to the terms because they were not out of keeping with his understanding of the spirit of Canadian intent with regard to the Western Indians. That Morris had an agricultural future in view rather than just capitulation to any demands made in the heat of the moment, is clear in his refusal of other things for which the Fort Carlton Indians asked, including, "responsibility of promising provision for the poor, blind and lame," which he evaded by emphasizing that "in all parts of the Queen's dominions we have them." Morris also denied the requested free passage on bridges and scows.[73] These things were not as crucial, perhaps, as direct agricultural assistance, but they also did not accord with conventional white views of a civilization policy, while the agricultural provisions did.

Morris was sympathetic to the Indian point of view, an attitude that grew on him during the course of his lieutenant governorship and five years' service in the Northwest, and is suggested by the evolution of his receptiveness to the Indians as he negotiated four treaties and renegotiated two others. But if his concessions were out of keeping with the general purposes of the government, he likely would have been censured for it. As it was, he enjoyed the full confidence of Liberal Minister of the Interior Laird and Prime Minister Mackenzie. Treaty 6 did elicit some criticism on the basis of the expanded terms he offered. In response, Morris reiterated the basic approach enunciated four years earlier by Campbell: "We were seeking to acquire their country, to make way for settlement, and thus deprive them of their hunting grounds and means of livelihood."[74]

The commissioners' encouragement of Indian interest in education and agriculture did not always accord with Ottawa's interpretation of the same question. Still, the Canadian government and its commissioners, in no hurry to encourage Indian settlement because there were no settler pressures forcing the issue, probably saw no purpose in making cut-and-dried provisions. If government actions were as directed by Indian pressures as some historians have suggested, perhaps officialdom would have been more susceptible to continued pressures to act on these measures.[75] They were not. Once the treaties were signed, the government proved reluctant to survey reserves and to confirm them officially. Casually phrased treaty terms that irrationally promised agricultural assistance "for every family *actually* cultivating" were narrowly interpreted so that Indians who required aid to *begin* farming could not easily acquire the means to do so. Education was given serious consideration only in 1879 with the commissioning of the Davin Report, and the recommended system of residential and industrial schools, premised on the assimilation of a race, was almost certainly not the way the Indians had envisaged the education program they had sought during treaty negotiations.[76] As in the timetable for treaty making itself, the government was moved to a response admittedly more quickly than it otherwise would have done, but it is difficult to imagine that there was not a framework for future policy on the model already in place in Ontario.

Pressures that apparently forced the government to concede on terms in the field proved ineffective when applied to the fulfillment of those terms. The explanation may reside in the different bodies responsible for the negotiation and implementation of treaties. The treaty commissioners in the field, notably Alexander Morris, agreed to an expansion of the terms being offered. The government in Ottawa accepted these terms by ratifying the treaties, but implementation was in the hands of Indian Affairs, which was considerably more rigid and less open to influence from the Indians. Perhaps Indian pressure could only be effective in the field, where even a vaguely receptive bureaucrat could see the sense in their demands. The decision makers in Ottawa, on the other hand, seldom if ever ventured west to visit their charges and thus could remain impervious to their appeals.

Again circumstances intruded as the critical factor. For the United States, the very real threat of Indian extinction made a civilization program imperative. It was recognized that civilization was an expensive process, but the Americans had a convincing rationalization for that lament in the refrain that it was "cheaper to feed them than fight them." For those who objected to feeding people who willfully would not provide for themselves, the energetically embraced civilization program offered at least a time limit for what detractors considered unwarranted generosity.

If what Canada had could be called a timetable, then it was operating at a different speed than that of the United States. Again, money was a factor in Canada in all things. There was no push to get Indians to reserves, and priorities lay more clearly with avoiding any premature financial obligations. Canada's commitment does look doubtful and puny in comparison to the American terms, but Canada's civilization measures had never been expressed in treaties. In central Canada, civilization legislation had followed treaties for land extinguishment. Expansion in the West had begun with the thoughtless application of the treaty process there, and so it is hard to imagine that Canadian policymakers envisaged any other course for future civilization policies than the one pursued elsewhere in the country.

The United States did not have this alternative. Until 1871 Congress was not empowered to legislate for the Indians beyond commerce. The United States put detailed measures of civilization into the treaties in a deliberate expansion of the functions of the questionable practice of treaty making as it had previously existed. Canada had no need to do so, and its treaties remained, except under pressures that resulted in vague declarations of intent, more narrowly defined.

In the 1860s and 1870s, Indian relations on the American Plains were in a state of crisis, characterized by vicious and expensive wars that demanded redress at once. The Americans, afflicted with the contradictory impulses both to expand without restraint but also to preserve the Indian race, had to resort to immediate and radical solutions. Their response was to reconstitute and formalize the reservation system, which had been in operation in that nation throughout the century, and to inaugurate a wide-ranging civilization program to gain a long-term solution to a persistent national problem. The central components of that program were Christianity, education, and agriculture, and the treaties of 1867 and 1868 demonstrated American zeal at least for the latter two as remedies to the Indian problem. The extensive nature of the provisions relating to these two items in the treaties with the plains peoples indicated not only American commitment to such things, but also the pressing necessity for a solution. In the American West, conflict between the races threatened either the extinction or extermination of one of the contenders. The government and its treaty commissioners perceived that if they did not act soon in offering a comprehensive means to avert a disaster, then it was foreordained. There were, in other words, considerable pressures and incentives for the Americans to take drastic action to recreate the Indians in their own image, the only acceptable "alternative to extinction" the Americans bothered to devise. In 1867 and 1868 the only means the government had of dealing with the Indian was through treaties. It was a natural evolution, therefore, especially with challenges to the treaty-making system in its traditional role of extinguishing land title, to expand these documents to incorporate the now vital elements of American Indian policy—reservations and civilization.

Canada was under no such pressures. The conflict in the West that goaded the Americans to action was absent north of the forty-ninth parallel. This permitted the Canadian government to assume, or delude itself into believing, that there was no crisis on the prairies, although evidence from traders, officials, travelers, and Indians themselves indicated an imminent food crisis. Canada's first tentative ventures in the West operated under the general intentions inherited from British policy, specifically the necessity to treat for land rights first and afterward to introduce a program to "civilize" the Indians.

Intentions, however, were not plans. Unlike the United States, Canada failed to recognize, or willfully ignored, all signs of the crisis brewing in its own backyard. A conviction of national superiority, stemming from differences in circumstance over which the government exercised no control, permitted Canadians to deceive themselves. There was no acknowledgment of problems that did not assume the same form as those confronting the Americans. This led, in the first instance, to different attitudes and a different pace in the implementation of policies meant to address the Indian situation in the West. The Americans pressed ahead with their plans. Canada held back. The advantages of doing so—and in the eyes of administrators there were many—were immediate. Unfortunately, they were of only short-term duration.

8 Buffalo Preservation, Hunting Rights, and Subsistence

Agriculture was not just a means of "civilization," it also offered a pragmatic solution to the vexing question of how the Indians were to survive after the demise of the buffalo. This animal was an important influence at treaty negotiations in both the United States and Canada, although the species merited mention only in American documents. Still, how the nations dealt with the buffalo, especially as manifested in concerns for its preservation, and in treaty terms relating to hunting rights and food provisions for the Indians, reflects the commitment to "civilization" by each nation.

The idea of the "vanishing Indian" animated many aspects of Canadian and American Indian relations, but the image of the "vanishing buffalo" was also frequently evoked.[1] There was more reliable evidence on the extinction of the buffalo. As early as 1846 the American superintendent of Indian affairs was remarking on the decline of this animal.[2] On the Canadian prairies Capt. John Palliser recorded impressions of the "scarcity of the buffalo" in 1857, while the Plains Crees, who were severely affected early on, were advocating restrictive hunting measures in 1859.[3] By the late 1860s predictions about the dissipation of this plains staple animal were common in both countries. Because of the erratic course of this journey to extinction, there has been much confusion about when and where the buffalo faded. Generally, though, the buffalo had disappeared from the southern American Plains by 1878, the Canadian prairies by 1879, and the northern American Plains by 1883. Long before those dates the buffalo had receded from great pockets of territory. It had faded from the north-central prairie homeland of the Crees by the beginning of the 1870s, although it remained in other areas, including Blackfoot territory and the Cypress Hills, until the last years of that decade. The longevity of the species determined in large part the outlook of the Indians involved at the various treaty gatherings.

The United States Indian peace commissioners went to treaty talks in 1867 and 1868 armed with the conviction of the vanishing buffalo. During the course of treaty negotiations, the American officials repeatedly impressed this fact on their Indian audiences. "Formerly you could find all the game you needed but now the buffalo have entirely disappeared from a large portion of your country," Commissioner Taylor told the Sioux at Fort Laramie in 1867.[4] At Medicine Lodge Creek Senator Henderson told the Comanches that "the buffalo would not last forever. They were disappearing, and the Indians must know it."[5] References of this kind littered the conversations of the government's commissioners. With such invocations they stressed the immediacy of the problem and offered a solution in the form of agriculture: "The sooner you give up your ideas about living by hunting, the better it will be for you all. The buffalo is fast disappearing. In the course of a few years they will all be gone and you must look forward to that time when you must live by agriculture or die."[6]

At Medicine Lodge Creek and the various sites where discussions took place for the Fort Laramie Treaty, the disappearance of the buffalo was a hard sell. On the southern plains the Cheyennes and Arapahos found buffalo enough in the vicinity of the treaty grounds that they did not have to avail themselves of the beef supplies the Americans offered.[7] The peoples assembled to discuss terms, invariably expressing little interest in any of the accoutrements of "civilization" beyond rifles offered by the commissioners, were more sanguine about the future of their staple food. In response to the repeated warnings of doom and the promised salvation of reservation life, Spotted Tail of the Brulé Sioux replied, "We want a reservation on the White River, and when the buffaloes are gone, we will go upon it. . . . Now we want to live as our fathers have lived, on the buffalo and the deer that we find on our hunting grounds. We love to roam over the plains. . . . We love to hunt. We do not want to live like the white man. The Indian cannot be a white man."[8] Kiowa leader Satanta put the Indian response more bluntly: "It is time enough to build us houses when the buffalo are all gone, but do tell the great Father that there is plenty of buffalo yet, and when the buffalo are all gone, I will tell him."[9] The closest the American Plains Indians came to demanding preservation measures for the buffalo was to insist on the inviolability of their hunting territories. Spotted Tail spoke for many of the Sioux, Northern Cheyennes, and Northern Arapahos when he declared: "we do object to the Powder River road and the road on the Smoky Hill Route. The country in which we live is cut up by the white men who drive away all the game. That is the cause of our troubles."[10]

The Plains Indians were wise not to seek assistance in methods to preserve the buffalo, for the United States was not interested in offering any. One historian has suggested that some army officers decried the intensive annihilation of the buffalo because of the impact this would have on Indian lives.[11] But many Americans in a position to care either did not think about it or actively encouraged the animal's destruction. General Sherman saw the buffalo, as much as the railroad, as an important factor in the solution of the Indian problem. "I think it would be wise to invite all the sportsmen of England and America there for a Great Buffalo hunt . . . and make one grand swap of them all," he suggested in May 1868.[12] In this he had the support of another senior military officer, Gen. Phil Sheridan, who a few years later would applaud the buffalo hunters of the Texas plains, for "these men have done more in the last two years, and will do more in the next year, to settle the vexed Indian question . . . than the entire regular army has done in the last thirty years. They are destroying the Indians' commissary."[13] Secretary of the Interior Columbus Delano captured this attitude in an official statement in 1874, reporting, "I regard the destruction of such game [buffalo] . . . as facilitating the policy of the Government, of destroying their hunting habits, coercing them on reservations, and compelling them to begin to adopt the habits of civilization."[14] The single measure passed by Congress to address the preservation of the buffalo was pocket-vetoed by President Grant.[15] Americans therefore not only observed the decline of the buffalo, accelerated it by overhunting, encouraged it through the extension of the railroad and the development of a new tanning process, but also applauded it.

Still, Indian obstinacy in recognizing what the Americans so confidently predicted forced treaty concessions incompatible with American goals during the negotiations. At Medicine Lodge Creek it became apparent that the Indians found nothing of value in the extensive civilization provisions offered. In response to one of Senator Henderson's long-winded speeches on the benefits being offered, Buffalo Chief of the Cheyenne responded, "We don't want any houses; we prefer living on the prairie instead of houses and civilization."[16] The incompatibility of the desires of both parties created a stumbling block at each of the major treaty negotiations.

At length the civilian commissioners relented. The Kiowas and Comanches were acknowledged in the right to continue to hunt in the territory they had been assigned under the Treaty of the Little Arkansas in 1865, and which they were now surrendering.[17] Under the terms of the treaty they signed at Medicine Lodge, the Southern Cheyennes and Southern Arapahos were granted exactly the same rights as those accorded the Kiowas and Comanches, although at the talks themselves Commissioner Henderson had promised more. The 1867 treaty confirmed their right to hunt only south of the Arkansas River on territory that had been designated a Cheyenne and Arapaho reservation in 1865 and from which they would now be removed. Yet in a confidential bargaining session, made necessary by the stalemate in negotiations, Henderson had restored all the hunting rights promised in the 1865 treaty, including the assurance that the Cheyennes and Arapahos might hunt north of the Arkansas as far as the Platte Rivers, on lands they had previously claimed and ceded in Kansas.[18] In the case of the Sioux, other circumstances surrounding the Powder River road controversy resulted in a completely unprecedented concession in American Indian treaties. Along with the right to hunt "off reserve" in ceded territory, the Sioux were to enjoy the Powder River country as "unceded Indian territory" from which the United States withdrew without conditions (Article 11).

As the military commissioners pointed out, such concessions, by perpetuating roaming, effectively defeated the provisions for peace, the establishment of reservations, and the civilization measures. Their civilian colleagues had counterarguments. They were convinced that without these provisions, the Indians would likely not have signed the treaties as there was little else of immediate appeal to them.[19] Of equal importance were the qualifying parts of the terms. In each case was added the clause "so long as the buffalo may range thereon in such numbers as to justify the chase." As everyone, except perhaps the Indians, conceded that the buffalo's time was running short, it could be argued that this right was distinctly finite. Furthermore, the most troublesome of the concessions, those to the Cheyennes and the Arapahos, were granted under the terms of the Treaty of the Little Arkansas of 1865, which specifically provided that the Indian "parties hereto . . . will not . . . encamp by day or night within ten miles of any of the main traveled routes or roads through the country to which they go, or of the military posts, towns, or villages therein."[20] Given the development of white settlement in this region, it was already difficult, if not yet impossible, for the Cheyennes and Arapahos to hunt there and yet comply with the treaty. Whatever the rationalizations, the military men suspected such arrangements would still end in violence. Sherman insisted that the rights given to the southern Indians be extended to the Sioux in the Fort Laramie Treaty, adding, "But I would let them understand, clearly and distinctly, that the moment they pass beyond the prescribed limits they become liable to fall in with parties of our miners and travelers and to involve themselves in trouble."[21] He also issued a general order confirming the hunting rights of the Cheyennes and Arapahos north of the Arkansas River, honoring Senator Henderson's impromptu promise, although the ratified treaty was not amended to reflect it.[22] The practical effect of the hunting provisions was to annul the concept of reservations, or at least to inhibit it severely, for under the treaty terms of 1867 and 1868 the reservations were not yet compulsory.

Believing food to be the central issue for the Indians and convinced, as was the *New York Times*, that the Indians could hardly resist their liberal terms, the commissioners extended an even more generous incentive in the Fort Laramie Treaty with the Sioux by offering daily rations. The Americans were not reluctant to employ food in this way. When violence flared up on the southern plains in the fall of 1868, despite the great efforts at Medicine Lodge Creek only a year before, it was the military that called for an extension of the food allowances not specifically included in the Medicine Lodge Treaties to all those actually on reservations.[23] Congress apparently had no objections to such a move, for in debates on the Indian appropriations bill for 1871 an amendment providing for daily rations for all those with whom treaties were made at Medicine Lodge in 1867 was passed without challenge.[24]

The hunting provisions served other purposes. They may well have induced the Indians to sign the treaties, but by doing so they also provided the United States with a powerful weapon. The military commissioners had agitated for compulsory reservations and had failed to obtain them. However, when violence erupted again for the usual reasons, since the source of conflict still had not been eradicated, the military could take action. In the fall of 1868, amid renewed fighting on the southern plains, the Great Peace Commission met for a final time. With the military in control, the members suggested to Congress "that existing treaties shall be maintained and respected, until their violation by the Indians themselves shall justify the Government in abrogating them severally" and coupled this with a recommendation for a compulsory reservation policy.[25] It would take the U.S. Army more than a decade to enforce this policy, but it could claim the treaties of 1867 and 1868, and the violation of the terms therein, as the legitimate basis for its work. Thus the impediment to civilization conceded to the Indians by the commissioners had eventually proved to be a useful tool, first in winning Indian assent to the treaties and then in providing a justification for the implementation of a coercive reservation and civilization policy.

Developments in Canada unfolded in a different direction. At treaty talks in the 1870s, the commissioners did not often employ the specter of the vanishing buffalo. As with all other issues except land title, this subject was raised by the Indians, especially by the Plains Crees of Treaty 6 and the Blackfoot of Treaty 7, peoples for whom the buffalo was a vital commodity. Confronted by these concerns, Lieutenant Governors Morris and Laird each responded in the same way, with an assurance of a buffalo preservation measure that, it was hoped, would reduce pressure on the Indians to conform immediately to a new way of life. They expected this at the same time to delay the implementation of any treaty term except for the all-important surrender of land title to the Crown.[26] It was not in the best fiscal interests of the Canadian government to rush the Indians to settlement, so instead Ottawa softened the revolutionary suggestion of the relinquishment of the land with the guarantee of continued use of that very same territory. As long as the Indians continued to hunt, they would not require either government assistance in agriculture or government subsistence, items that might include a hefty price tag. The Canadian government was so committed to this strategy that it declined to make plans for immediate and meaningful agricultural aid. This contrasted sharply with the American approach, which embraced such measures, at least in the short run, in order to establish the reservation system.

What Canada wanted was land title, and in the uncertain circumstances of the 1870s, the Indians were reluctant to surrender their one asset—the land—without meaningful compensation. This discussion was particularly acute in the Treaty 6 negotiations at Fort Carlton. The commissioners, notably Alexander Morris, countered Indian fears by offering two things: a guaranteed right to the use of the land surrendered (subject to certain restrictions and identical to hunting provisions in each of the previous treaties) and agricultural assistance (at the insistence of the Indians) when they were "actually settled."

It is hard to believe that the successive lieutenant governors of the

Northwest Territory, Alexander Morris and David Laird, were not sincere in their assurances for and commitment to the Indians' future. Literally every treaty began with an assertion that the Indians might rest assured in "Her Majesty's bounty and benevolence." Morris responded to the appeals of Poundmaker at Fort Carlton for assistance with the assurance that "What I have offered does not take away your living, you will have it then as you have now, and what I offer now is put on top of it. This I can tell you, the Queen's Government will always take a deep interest in your living."[27] Morris's correspondence during five years as lieutenant governor of Manitoba and the Northwest Territory indicates a level of concern for the subjects in his charge, not echoed in Ottawa, for making and keeping honorable terms, for addressing Indian grievances, and for conceding to demands he could clearly see arose from legitimate circumstances.[28] Laird, too, exhibited the same kind of concern on those occasions when he had personal contact with the Indians involved. His 1874 journey to the West and interviews with the aggrieved signatories of Treaties 1 and 2 prompted the final resolution of the Outside Promises fiasco.[29] In his capacity as lieutenant governor of the Northwest Territory, Laird sponsored the buffalo preservation measure long demanded by the Plains Crees.[30] Laird also insisted that the peoples of Treaty 4 receive the annual one-thousand-dollar agricultural assistance granted for three years under Treaty 6, and he fought a vituperative if unsuccessful battle with Minister of the Interior David Mills over agricultural supplies and instruction for the plains people starving on the Saskatchewan in 1878–79.[31] It is more difficult to give Ottawa the benefit of the doubt.

In the United States it was agreed that hunting rights were the turning point in winning Indian adhesion to the treaties. In Canada, the critical feature was a different matter. The deadlock of Treaty 3 was broken by Morris's unprecedented official concession of agricultural assistance. The grievances leveled by the Treaty 1 and 2 Indians revolved around the Outside Promises, which dealt with the same issue. But the fullest discussions, or the fullest record of such discussions, were those at Treaty 6, in which Morris identified the resolution of the food question as the crucial element. Thus, while Indians in the American West turned aside government offers of assistance, which they felt were not needed, Canadian Indians demanded such assistance, which the government did not offer.

At Fort Carlton in 1876, Morris flatly turned down any suggestion of Canada supplying daily rations to the Indians, and in doing so he invoked the two rationalizations that inhibited all impulses of generosity on the part of the government: "you are many, and if we were to try to do it, it would take a great deal of money, and some of you would never do anything for yourselves."[32] According to Morris's account, the two sides then came to a meeting of minds on the central point. The Indians apparently wanted a promise of assistance in developing agriculture as a new means of subsistence and an assurance of a government-sponsored "security net" for the feared rocky passage on this route. Both were reasonable expectations of the new relationship being established between the Crown and the plains peoples.

If Morris believed that the Indians were unduly apprehensive about the fate of the buffalo, he nevertheless recognized the real fear they had for a future without it and made concessions accordingly. These included a broadening of the agricultural implements supplied (although still limited in comparison to those offered by the United States), a one thousand-dollar fund for three years to provide assistance in farming, and a "famine relief" clause.[33] In the context of the treaty talks themselves, these clauses addressed the Indians' fears and promised, in Morris's view at least, nothing more than what Canada and the Hudson's Bay Company had always done in the way of famine relief or what the government intended to do by way of agriculture.[34] These terms came under fire from Ottawa, where criticisms characterizing such concessions as "onerous" and likely to predispose the Indians to "idleness" amplified the rationalizations Morris had expressed more tactfully at Fort Carlton.[35]

In short, the official position of the Canadian government on subsisting the Indians was a concerted unwillingness to do so on a daily basis or even to record an obligation to do so under the direst circumstances. The Indians were not to be encouraged to a dependence on the government, and food was not to be used as an inducement to take up reserve lands, as was the case in the United States, even if, as Lieutenant Governor Laird warned, the government's options were "to help the Indian to farm and raise stock, to feed them, or to fight them."[36]

The signal indifference of the Canadian government, in contrast to the earnest interventionary attitude of the Americans, was apparent in the Canadian response to agitation over measures to preserve the buffalo. In the years leading up to the treaty talks, there was no shortage of warnings on the precarious state of this beast and no dearth of plans suggesting an amelioration of the situation.[37] The Indians themselves had discussed action as early as 1859 and made concerted appeals of various sorts in the 1870s. All of these reports would have passed Morris's desk, yet he did not seem moved to action until 1876 when, on the North Saskatchewan, he was personally confronted with several pleas for aid. Morris's responsiveness to the Indians grew with his exposure to them. It may be that he did not take the reports seriously until he came face to face with the problem. At the Fort Carlton and Fort Pitt negotiations, he promised to press Ottawa on the question of aid and did so in subsequent official reports and correspondence.[38] However, by late 1876 he had jurisdiction over Manitoba only and would soon no longer be a lieutenant governor at all. Lieutenant Governor Laird of the Northwest Territory took up Morris's battle and continued pressing the Dominion government. In Parliament, during one of the very few extended discussions of any sort about Indians, John Christian Schultz led the struggle for legislation to preserve the buffalo by restricting the hunt, and he found support among the other members from Manitoba as well. Minister of the Interior Mills put them all off, acknowledging the problem but claiming "it had better be left to be dealt with by the Government of the North-West rather than by Parliament here."[39] Under Laird's stewardship, the North-West Council did pass a preservation bill in 1877, just in time to reassure the Blackfoot at the Treaty 7 negotiations, although the measure was repealed the following year.[40]

Canada's lethargic approach to the application of its reserve and civilization policy in the West found reflection in its official attitude toward subsisting the Indians. Enthusiasm was expressed only for hunting, the single means by which the Indians could continue to fend for themselves at no cost to the government, while support for agriculture was grudgingly approved, belatedly given, or denied altogether. This attitude persisted in the face of reports from a number of sources, including two lieutenant governors whose own personal observations revealed to them the reality on the plains, but resulted only in unsatisfactory guarantees and limited commitments to the Indians' vital concerns. Throughout the treaty process Canada remained consistent in its interpretation of the treaty-making function as it had been practiced in British North America. The national government's exclusive focus was the extinguishment of land title, admitting revision only under pressure and as pecuniary considerations allowed. The United States had diverged significantly from the original treaty-making purpose, inspired both by the need to fit an available instrument to new functions and a sincere missionary zeal that combined genuine humanitarianism with a single-minded self-interest.

In the end the two nations came away with signed treaties, although concessions were made in both instances that pleased neither, and the expected measures of persuasion in both countries proved less effective than anticipated. The treaties had achieved the goals set out in their instructions, although the Numbered Treaties, in their limited aspirations of securing land title, proved the more enduring. The Medicine Lodge and Fort Laramie Treaties had a more uneven record. They had created the required reservations and established the framework for a comprehensive policy of civilization on the plains meant to bring an end to the Indian problem once and for all. But even before Red Cloud signed the Fort Laramie Treaty in November 1868, the southern peoples were again in conflict with the United States, and the voluntary nature of the reservation and civilization policies was under fire. The perceived effectiveness of the treaties in gaining their ends was a significant issue in the ratification struggles that followed.

9 Ratification, Indian Status, and Treaty Making

Ratification of the Great Plains Indian peace treaties was a deceptively simple process in the United States and almost a matter of form for the Numbered Treaties in Canada. The actions of the Senate and the Governor-General-in-Council—the entities responsible for ratification in each country—gave little hint of potential dissent, although it did take the Senate almost a year to act on each of the treaties concluded by the Great Peace Commission.

Constitutionally, and as reiterated in the July 20 Act itself, Senate ratification was all that was necessary to make the work of the Great Peace Commission law. But to carry out the provisions of these treaties required a vast increase in expenditures, and the treasury was the stronghold of the House of Representatives, which took the opportunity in raucous debates on the Indian appropriations bills between 1868 and 1871 to change the course of U.S. Indian relations and bring an end to the treaty-making system.

Canada experienced nothing like this. With the exception of some grumbling over the "onerous" terms of Treaty 6, the Numbered Treaties were accepted with almost congratulatory self-satisfaction by the government. Little attention was paid to anything more than the fact that the agreements had secured their purpose—the extinguishment of Indian land title—and had done so rather economically and very peacefully.

The final stage of treaty making thus drew to a close, as had each previous step, with bitter and furious consideration in the United States and continued thoughtless neglect in Canada. Problems the two nations believed they were solving when they put the treaties behind them in the 1870s would return to haunt them decades later precisely because of the decisions made in the last days of these treaty-making sessions.

Indian treaty making had long been a contentious issue by the time debate on the Indian appropriations bill for 1870 came up in Congress. Because the Senate had failed to ratify the 1867 Medicine Lodge Treaties until July 1868, the appropriations required under them were not included in that year's budget so no annuities were paid. This may have been one of the causes for the eruption of violence on the southern plains at the end of 1868.[1] The ratification of the Fort Laramie Treaties in February 1869 did make it possible to include their terms in the financial arrangements for the upcoming year. The two significant works of the Great Peace Commission finally came together under the Indian appropriations bill for the year ending in June 1870.

Technically, and under the Constitution, the treaties of 1867 and 1868 had been ratified by Senate approval, and debate should have ended there. But the House of Representatives believed it had good reason to challenge these documents, and deliberations for the 1870 appropriations bill, for which the House was responsible, provided an opportunity. The price tag of the treaties was the catalyst, although not the cause or even the main issue, which sparked renewed conflict over the question of Indian treaties. Wrangling over money continued, but this was not the most troublesome of the questions that surfaced during this debate. These revolved around the more sensitive matters of perceived transgressions on the constitutional responsibilities vested in each house — joint control of the disposition of public lands, House control of the public purse, and the Senate treaty ratification function. Although not directly related to any of these questions, the dilemma of Indian status proved the key to the conflict.

Each house of Congress was jealous of its prerogatives, but because of the nature of the Indian treaties in American law, House responsibilities were vulnerable to being undermined by the treaty-making process. In 1867 Secretary of State William Seward had closed a seven-million-dollar deal to purchase Alaska — a controversial and doubtful achievement at the time dubbed "Seward's folly" — but because it had been accomplished by treaty with Russia, the House had no choice but to surrender the required funds. In 1870 there were rumblings of absorbing San Domingo into the Union in the same way and for a substantial price that aggravated House sensibilities once more.[2] These matters involved treaties with unquestionably sovereign nations, and the House eventually retreated from the constitutional conflicts that fiscal opposition might have incurred. But the ramifications of objecting to Indian treaties were less complicated, and a challenge to them more likely to succeed, especially given the post–Civil War attitudes toward Indians. The treaties of 1867 and 1868 provided the House considerable ammunition in this battle.

Although the Act of July 20 had acknowledged the Senate's constitutional authority as the proper body for ratification of the work of the Great Peace Commission, the legislation also called for congressional approval of the reservation lands chosen. This provision was never honored. The House seized on this omission as evidence of encroachment on its powers, for this failure not only violated the act itself but also the Constitution, which in Article 4, section 3, put regulation of U.S. territory under the authority of Congress rather than the Senate alone. Congressmen thus could and did protest the incursion. The size of reservations assigned was one sore point, with members objecting to handing over to the Indians state-sized territories. Particularly exasperating was Article 16 of the Sioux treaty, which established, as one uncomprehending congressman pointed out, a zone encompassing "a third or a half of the Territory of Wyoming" in the Bighorn Mountains as "unceded Indian territory" in addition to reservations lands that constituted literally half of South Dakota.[3] To those who could not grasp or specifically objected to the deliberately gradualist program for civilization set out in the treaties, such grants of land were absurd.[4]

The question of large or small reservations was a contentious one. But the principle at issue was the blatant disregard for House authority. A simultaneous dispute in Congress involved a treaty with the Osage Indians of Kansas, whereby lands surrendered by the Osages were handed over directly to railroad interests, violating the long-term practice of Indian lands entering first into the public domain, where they could be distributed to ordinary Americans pursuing the American dream rather than to corporate interests.[5] The clause in the Sioux treaty, leaving what had been Indian territory in Indian hands, hardly seems comparable to the questionable machinations of the Osage treaty, but the House pushed the parallel to highlight the perceived encroachment on its rights. This point, along with the extraordinary level of expenditures, gave congressmen cause to believe that the Senate would ratify almost anything identified as a treaty, leaving the more responsible House with no room to object and yet saddled with paying the bill.

Indian treaties were already under fire as documents of questionable legitimacy, and they now were burdened with charges of circumventing congressional authority and exceeding all reasonable financial limits.

The Senate's alleged irresponsibility in treaty matters, combined with these criticisms, led to a renewed challenge by the House of the Indian treaty system in what was actually an attempt to safeguard the rights of the House of Representatives.

Under the Constitution, financial bills originated in the House and thus control of the treasury resided there. But treaties were recognized, by tradition and Supreme Court decisions, to be the supreme law of the land, and so the House was in theory, and had been in practice, bound to accept Senate amendments to Indian appropriations bills, however much representatives might have disagreed with them. The widespread dissatisfaction with the 1867 and 1868 treaties, however, led the junior body to make a stand on the status of Indians in the United States. The House, although disgruntled over the deals for Alaska and San Domingo, focused its battle on Indian treaties alone.

Contemporary perceptions of Indian status cloud this issue. The Marshall decisions of the 1830s had defined Indian status in a unique way as "domestic dependent nations." This differentiated them from foreign nations like England and Russia in that only the United States could legitimately engage in official relations with them. As far as external nations were concerned, the Indians were an exclusively American responsibility. From the narrower national perspective of United States–Indian relations, however, the difference between official dealings with Indian nations, on the one hand, and England, on the other, were not so significant. Indian nations were collectively held responsible for the actions of individual nationals, and treaties, a tool employed only in international relations, were the accepted means of establishing a relationship. As one House member pointed out, "treating them as foreign nations gives them the right as such to make war. If an Indian agent breaks a treaty, according to the principles of international law they have a right to make war upon us to obtain their remedy." [6]

If the perception had prevailed that Indians constituted independent nations, as England and Russia clearly did, then the treaty-making function might have gone unquestioned. But few in Congress or outside its chambers were convinced by 1869 that they did. If Indian nations were not independent foreign nations, then the House saw no reason why it should continue to be excluded from a role in guiding relations with what were essentially other portions of the American population. All the old arguments about treaties were resurrected—including charges of corruption and inefficiency—but increasingly the critical issue resolved itself into a reconsideration of the status of Indians themselves.

The House refused to back down before Senate vitriol on its right to make and ratify treaties. As a result the Indian appropriations bill for 1870 bounced back and forth between House and Senate within their Indian affairs committees, with the Senate repeatedly adding the terms for the 1867–68 treaties and the House diligently removing them. Facing the end of the congressional session for 1870 without having passed the critical bill, the two chambers concluded an uneasy compromise. The House, proving that it objected to the form rather than the cost of the obligations incurred under these treaties, voted a two-million-dollar general appropriation for the Plains Indians and put it in the hands of the president to spend as he saw fit, even if he chose to use it to the ends stipulated in the objectionable treaties. In doing so the House specifically stated that such a move was not to be construed in any way as House ratification or acceptance of the 1867–68 treaties.[7] Defenses of the Senate's legitimate treaty-making power went hand in hand in this decision with general unease at giving a single individual such an enormous amount of money to be used at his discretion, even if that person was the president. In making known his objection, Congressman James Garfield declared, "We might as well appropriate $300,000,000 and put it into the hands of the President and authorize him to run the Government with it as he pleases."[8] The Senate, anxious to ensure that the programs established under the treaties would in fact receive funding and perhaps ameliorate or remove cause for conflict on the plains, accepted the compromise, if uncomfortably, and the issue was put to rest for another year.

The subsequent Congress, however, refused to let the matter go unresolved, and the Indian appropriations bill for 1871 brought the matter to a head. Once more the House offered the temporary solution of voting a blanket appropriation to the president, but the Senate refused to concede. Both houses acknowledged the potential for damaging and perhaps lethal consequences for Indian and white alike on the plains in the event that another year should pass without adequate appropriations, but neither chamber would back down. U.S. Indian relations and the treaty system, which for almost a century had served as its backbone, were at a crisis point brought on by the Treaties of Medicine Lodge and Fort Laramie.

No such crisis prevailed in Canada. The only evidence of dissension over the treaties in that nation was the disgruntled response to the costly terms of Treaty 6. Otherwise, ratification of the Numbered Treaties elicited little more than a simple report and formal endorsement under the auspices of the Privy Council. A report of the Privy Council on Treaty 4 specified the terms undertaken and concluded with the remarks:

> Mr. Mackenzie states that the Treaties [4 and supplementary] appear to him to be satisfactory and he, therefore, recommends that they be approved by Your Excellency in Council.
>
> He further submits that the satisfactory conclusion of the Treaties is mainly due to the patience, firmness, tact and ability displayed by the Commissioners in the conduct of the negotiations. The Committee concur in the foregoing Report and recommend and advise that the Treaties be approved and accepted and enrolled in the usual manner.[9]

The governor general simply signed, and the treaties were official.

Even in the case of Treaty 6 the dissatisfaction, such as it was, was almost negligible for practical purposes. David Mills, the recently appointed minister of the interior in 1876, voiced his displeasure, reporting, "The stipulations with respect relating to agricultural implements are somewhat more onerous, too, than in previous treaties." His response to the "famine relief" clause, which he described as a "wholly new provision," was somewhat more heated: "This stipulation the undersigned regards as *extremely objectionable*, tending, as it will, to predispose the Indians to idleness, since they will regard the provision as guaranteeing them protection against want, and they will not be inclined to make proper exertions to supply themselves with food and clothing, thereby largely to increasing the expenditure imposed upon the country in the management of the Indian Affairs."[10] Despite this, Mills could not bring himself to recommend rejecting the treaty. "Although the undersigned considers the terms of the Treaty to be very onerous, some of the provisions being exceedingly objectionable and such as ought not to have been made with any race of savages, he nevertheless thinks it proper to recommend the same for the ratification of Your Excellency, as the mischiefs which might result from refusing to ratify it might produce discontent and dissatisfaction, which in the end would prove more detrimental to the country, than the ratification of the objectionable provisions referred to."[11] Mills's devotion to economy warred between "feeding or fighting," suggesting perhaps more dissension in the cabinet on this issue than is apparent from the minimal documentation available. Though reluctant to do either, the government in the end came down at least in theory on the side of feeding the Indians. This attitude was somewhat different from the American situation, wherein members of Congress, both House and Senate, were by 1871 willing to risk the wrath of the Plains Indians rather than retreat from a principled stand.

Official disgruntlement, expressed by David Mills and repeated almost word for word in both the "Report of the Privy Council to the Governor General" and in the "Speech from the Throne" of 1877 to Parliament, did not impede ratification. The apathy of the Canadian government toward the treaties and their terms, despite the magnitude of their central focus—the land—is as striking as the furor raised in the United States over the treaties the House refused to accept, for the consequences were at least as significant for Canada as for its southern neighbor. To resolve its conflict over the 1867–68 treaties, Congress wrought what it thought was a significant and definitive change in the relationship of the United States to its indigenous inhabitants. Canada blithely ratified the Numbered Treaties without a thought as to how they might have affected Indian relations. The misconceptions inherent in the attitudes that led to these decisions set the stage for a new phase in Indian treaty relations in both countries, although they would lie dormant in both places for several decades.

In the United States, treaty making had affirmed and maintained an almost century-old practice of nation-to-nation relationships in Indian affairs. The constitutional interpretation of Indian tribes as equivalent to foreign nations and the 1830s Marshall decisions had established the various Indian peoples as nations in American law and practice. Despite the considerable criticism of the validity of this status before 1867, the treaties of that and the subsequent year confirmed that status once again by perpetuating this nation-to-nation relationship.

The 1867 and 1868 treaties were, in essence, peace treaties. Under these agreements the Indians did not become citizens of the United States nor did they even become subject to its jurisdiction. The terms establishing reservations obviously moved Indians from lands they had claimed and restricted their movement to others, but these set-aside territories remained beyond the reach of American law. The Indians were obliged therein only to cooperate with American legal authorities in dealing with Indian violators outside the reservations and were encouraged to seek redress for their own grievances in Washington. There is no denying the emphasis on the civilization program in the treaties, but these clauses were perceived as inducements to the Indian, however much they also served American purposes, and were neither compulsory nor imposed, at least initially.

The only duties the treaties required of the Indians were those relating to war and peace and other behaviors that fell into the realm of national obligations. The first article of each treaty declared an end to war and pledged both the United States and the relevant Indians to peace. A subsequent article listed a series of other stipulations that reinforced the view that the American treaty commissioners were dealing with people they considered as representatives of foreign nations. Other elements supported this. Article 1 also made clear that the Indian people as a whole would be held responsible for the acts of individuals, with American victims compensated from the annuities of the entire tribe, unlike the consistent Canadian policy (until 1885) of dealing with violators on an individual basis. Article 11 also differed from similar terms in the Numbered Treaties in which promises not to molest travelers or to interfere with government works were identified as "pledges," suggesting a different kind of relationship. (See table 5.)

In return for the Indian commitment to peace, the United States promised a variety of things. Among them were guaranteed reservation lands and an alternate way of life, neither of which appealed to the Indians and so failed to persuade them to sign. There was also the more overt inducement — bribes, as General Pope would have it — in the form of annuities. These were offered for a limited term — the lifetime of the treaty — and to all individuals without differentiating on the basis of an individual's status (for example, a chief). Although the hunting provisions and the Powder River road concession likely won Indian cooperation, these were not American ideas and were not part of the original quid pro quo of peace for benefits. The surrender of American claims on the Powder River, and the designation of the area as "unceded Indian territory" in particular, resembled a concession that might be made in treaties with foreign nations. While the treaties did involve a land cession, this grant was a legal formality buried in the text because of its insignificance in these documents. (See table 6.)

The structure of the documents, the pride of place given to the subjects of war and peace, and the clear exchange of peace and good behavior on the part of the Indians for various benefits — both planned and unplanned by the United States — attests to the characterization of the

Table 5: National obligations of Indians in American and Canadian treaties

TREATIES OF MEDICINE LODGE CREEK AND FORT LARAMIE	NUMBERED TREATIES
Article 1	**Opening preamble**
War: to cease	Identification of participants
Peace: pledged by both parties	Statement of purpose, including the
Individual violators, Indian or white, to be dealt with by U.S. law	Queen's wishes and assurances
Indian complaints to be forwarded through agents to commissioner of Indian Affairs	
Indian violators to be handed over or else victims to be compensated from treaty annuities	
Article 11. Other stipulations on Indians	**Pledges**
Will not object to a railroad through the Smoky Hills or railroads being built on the plains	To observe treaty
Will allow the peaceful building of a railroad that doesn't cross their reservations	To be loyal subjects
Will not molest wagon trains, people, or cattle belonging to the United States	To obey the laws
Will not carry off white women	To keep the peace
Will not kill or scalp white men or hurt them	Not to molest people or property in the ceded tracts
Will withdraw all opposition to the railroad being built along the Platte Road	Not to bother travelers
Will not obstruct any U.S. facilities (i.e., mail, roads, etc.)	To assist in justice
If such things interfere with Indian lands a commission of three, including a "chief or headman of the tribes," will determine the compensation for damages	
Will withdraw all opposition to U.S. military posts being built in western territories	

Note: Terms have been summarized. Quotation marks indicate exact wording. See appendix 1 for a complete chart comparing American and Canadian treaty terms.

Table 6: Summary of terms for annuities and land provisions in the Medicine Lodge Creek and Fort Laramie Treaties

TREATIES OF MEDICINE LODGE CREEK	TREATY OF FORT LARAMIE (WITH THE SIOUX)
Article 10	**Article 10**
Annuities	*Annuities*
To be delivered to the agency house on the reservation.	To be delivered to the agency house on the reservation.
To be delivered on October 15 "for thirty years."	To be delivered on October 15 "for thirty years."
To include:	To include:
for males 14 and older: 1 good suit of woolen clothing; for females 12 and older: 1 skirt or cloth, hose, and other material; for all children: clothes.	for males 14 and older: 1 good suit of woolen clothing; for females 12 and older: 1 skirt or cloth, hose, and other material; for all children: clothes.
Other necessities	*Other provisions*
$25,000 will be provided each year for 30 years to be spent by the secretary of the interior, at the commissioner of Indian Affairs's recommendation, on necessities (unspecified) for Indians.	Persons who continue to roam and hunt will receive $10.00 per year for 30 years.
Congress may change the purpose of the appropriation but cannot change the amount of or withdraw the appropriation for 30 years.	Persons engaged in farming will receive $20.00 per year for 30 years.
	The money will be used by the secretary of the interior to purchase articles deemed to be of necessity for the Indians.
	If during the 30 years it is found money can be better spent on the Indians in some other way, Congress may change the purpose of the appropriation but cannot change the amount of or withdraw the appropriation for 30 years.
	An army officer will be appointed to inspect goods and supervise their delivery.
	Food provisions
	Every Indian over 4 years of age who has settled permanently on a reservation and adhered to the treaty will be provided with 1 pound of meat and

Table 6: *continued*

1 pound of flour per day for 4 years if they cannot furnish their own subsistence at an earlier date.

Cows and Oxen

The United States will give each family (lodge) who has settled to farm "1 good American cow and 1 good well-broken pair of American oxen" within 60 days of their settlement.

Article 11	***Article 11***
Relinquishing lands	*Relinquishing lands*
Indians party to this agreement will "relinquish all rights to occupy permanently the territory outside their reservation."	Indians party to this agreement will "relinquish all rights to occupy permanently the territory outside their reservations."
Right to hunt	*Right to hunt*
Indians retain the right to hunt on any lands south of the Arkansas River "so long as the buffalo may range thereon in such numbers as to justify the chase."	Indians retain the right to hunt on any lands north of the North Platte River and on the Republican fork of the Smoky Hill River "so long as the buffalo may range thereon in such numbers as to justify the chase."

Article 16

Unceded territory

"The United States hereby agrees and stipulates that the country north of the North Platte River and east of the summits of the Big Horn Mountains shall be held and considered to be unceded Indian territory, and also stipulates and agrees that no white person or persons shall be permitted to settle upon or occupy any portion of the same."

Indian permission is needed for any person to pass through this land.

Within 90 days of peace being concluded with the Sioux Nation, the military posts in this territory and the road leading to them and to Montana shall be closed.

Note: Terms have been summarized. Quotation marks indicate exact wording.

relationship involved therein as nation to nation. Had the treaties actually achieved their purpose in winning peace on the plains, the treaty system itself might not have fallen. However, the Indians no more wanted to change their ways than the Americans wanted to restrain their own advance. As dissenting congressmen made clear, it was not necessarily the program in the treaties or the cost involved, but the treaties themselves that elicited their opposition because the documents perpetuated an outdated, unrealistic, and to some unfair relationship between the United States and the Indian peoples.

It was the general consensus on the latter point that put an end to the treaty-making system in 1871, though under the auspices of a battle over constitutional prerogatives in Congress. At the final meeting of the Great Peace Commission in October 1868, the now military-dominated board recommended "that henceforth, the Government shall cease to recognize the Indian tribes as domestic dependent nations, except so far as it may be absolutely required to so recognize them by existing treaties. . . . That, hereafter no treaties shall be made with any Indian tribe but that their rights of person and properties and duties of the Government toward them shall be defined by statute law." [12] Indian reformers and humanitarians had at last found an issue on which they could agree with the army. Long-time Indian advocate Bishop Henry Whipple of Minnesota, who had championed the Indians' cause after the massacre of 1862—a heroically unpopular stand—added his voice to the growing chorus of calls for a change in Indian relations. He noted a fundamental hypocrisy in the process: "We recognize them as nations, we pledge them our faith, we enter on solemn treaties and these treaties are ratified, as with all foreign powers, by the highest authority in the nation." But such an approach was, he declared, "a shameless lie," and the treaties "often conceived in fraud and made solely to put money in some white man's pocket." [13] More scathing still was the attack by Felix Brunot, chair of the Board of Indian Commissioners, a semiautonomous body of noted philanthropists appointed by the president to share oversight of Indian affairs with the secretary of the interior. Brunot declared:

> The United States first creates the fiction that a few thousand savages stand in the position of equality in capacity, power, and right of negotiation with a civilized nation. They next proceed to impress upon the savages, with all the form of treaty and the solemnity of parchment, signatures and seal, the preposterous idea that they

were the owners in fee of the fabulous tracts of country over which their nomadic habits have led them or their ancestors to roam. The title being thus settled, they purchase and promise payment for a portion of the territory, and further bind themselves in the most solemn manner to protect and defend the Indians in the possession of some immense remainder defined by boundary in the treaty, thus becoming, as it were, *particps criminis* with the savage in resisting the "encroachments" of civilisation and the progressive movement of the age. Having entered into this last-named impractical obligation, the fact of its non-performance becomes the occasion of disgraceful and expensive war to subdue their victims to the point of submission to another treaty. And so the tragedy of war and the farce of treaty have been enacted again and again, each time with increasing shame to the nation.[14]

These views were supported by the serving commissioner of Indian Affairs, Ely S. Parker, himself a Seneca Indian, and by many voices in Congress.[15]

A further spur to a reconsideration of Indian status came in a constitutional form in 1868. The Fourteenth Amendment declared, "All persons born or naturalized in the United States and subject to the jurisdiction thereof, are citizens of the United States and of the State wherein they reside." For many in Congress, the legal possibility of concluding further treaties with Indians seemed now irrelevant. In recognition at least of the dilemma, President Grant withdrew from Senate consideration Indian treaties that had been concluded in the latter half of 1868.[16]

A stumbling block remained. There were those members of Congress, especially in the Senate, who resisted a change in Indian status, putting the pressure to do so down to a mean "might is right" sentiment—that is, when the Indians were strong, it was politic to make treaties with them, but now that they were weak, the United States could do as it liked.[17] But some cogent arguments were offered to justify acceptance of a change in status. Remarking on how Indian status had been transformed over the past century, one member pointed out that Texas had once been an entity with which the United States had seen fit to make treaties, but no one objected to the impossibility of doing so after 1845.[18] What proved the greatest sticking point, however, was what to do about the treaties that had been negotiated and duly ratified before the current crisis.

The logical course of action in 1871 would have been to abolish the treaties altogether. Few could countenance this, though. Even the military faction of the Great Peace Commission had been obliged to temper its recommendations on Indian status by recognizing existing treaties. The constitutional argument against Indian treaties suffered a setback with the Senate Judiciary Committee's examination of the Fourteenth Amendment. The committee reviewed both the jurisdiction and intent of the amendment, which had been created to address the citizenship of liberated slaves, and found that it did not apply to Indians. This decision was validated by the Supreme Court several years later.[19]

Once again national honor was a factor. To change the rules was one matter, but to discard the past was something few could face, particularly in the Senate, which its members considered the guardian of Indian best interests. Only when the House and the Senate could reach a satisfactory compromise on this problem could the appropriations bill impasse, which had wrought the crisis in the treaty system, be resolved. At length it was. Attached to the appropriations bill for 1871 was a resolution that effectively ended the treaty-making system in the United States but failed, as had the treaties of 1867 and 1868 themselves, to eliminate the contradictions of U.S. Indian relations. It read: "*Provided*, That hereafter no Indian nation or tribe within the territory of the United States shall be acknowledged or recognized as an independent nation, tribe, or power with whom the United States may contract by treaty. *Provided further*, That nothing herein contained shall be construed to invalidate or impair the obligation of any treaty heretofore lawfully made and ratified with any such nation or tribe."[20]

This removed the obstruction to the Indian appropriations bill for 1871, which subsequently passed. It also cleared the way for the United States to legislate for the Indians as the legislatures in British North America had been doing for decades. The Indians thus became "wards of the state" in official terms. Though this development emerged from a battle over the Plains Indians and the treaties made with them in 1867 and 1868, it applied henceforth to all American Indians.

The immediate problem had been surmounted to the satisfaction of all but the most ardent reformers, who continued to lament the tribal relationship that existing treaties perpetuated. But the compromise did not solve what Francis Prucha has called the "anomaly" of Indian treaties. Indians had lost their distinctive status as "domestic dependent nations" and become subject to government authority under legislation just like American citizens. But congressional reluctance to abolish existing Indian treaties, or to ignore their terms, coupled with official confirmation that Indians yet remained outside American citizenship meant that Indians were still not like other Americans. This failure to clarify the status of Indians in American society would return to haunt the United States in the next century when courts would find new purpose for Indian treaties.

The 1867–68 treaties in the United States were premised on a concept of Indian relations that Americans no longer found useful and was the root of the conflict that erupted over the ratification of those treaties. In Canada the Numbered Treaties established a new and direct relationship between the Indians of the Prairie West and the Dominion. But Canada did not seem to realize, either in the 1870s or for almost a century thereafter, that this change had occurred or, even more, that there was a relationship at all.

Canada and the United States embraced the practice of treaty making from their British roots without stopping to examine the nature of treaties themselves. Perhaps the British were to blame, for the Proclamation of 1763, the kernel of the system, was itself a document of expediency that came to mean far more in practice than British policymakers had originally intended. The Americans had adopted and emphasized the nation-to-nation aspect that, while expedient in the early days of the Republic, gave them increasing degrees of grief as the decades passed. Canada, on the other hand, like the British before them, embraced a much narrower definition of treaties. In British North America after the War of 1812, treaties were used exclusively as a tool to secure the extinguishment of Indian land title, and though the term "treaties" was used, there was no indication that, in British understanding at least, this made Indians the equivalent of France or Russia. The fact that the British government, and subsequently the colonial and Canadian legislatures, saw no contradiction between making treaties *and* legislating for the Indians illustrates this ambivalence.

The indifference that Canada displayed toward the opinions of the indigenous inhabitants in the takeover of Rupert's Land and toward the repeated admonitions on the state of the buffalo arose also in a manifest disregard for the format in which the massive land transfers and the very minor tangible benefits conferred for them were transacted. Although one minister of the interior, more than one treaty commissioner, and every treaty affirmed that by such means the Dominion was establishing a formal relationship with the Indians with obligations and advantages to each party, this appeared to have escaped the notice of the Canadian government.

The acknowledgment of a relationship was made explicit in the preamble of each of the Numbered Treaties, wherein each document was identified, as in Treaty 3, as "Articles of a Treaty made and concluded . . . between Her Most Gracious Majesty the Queen of Great Britain and Ireland, by her Commissioners . . . of the one part; and the Saulteaux tribe of the Ojibbeway Indians . . . of the other part."[21] The role of the Crown was a vital one. In his dealings with the Indians on any matter, Alexander Morris knew it to be of critical importance to maintain the connection to the Crown.[22] The queen, or "Great Mother" as she was designated by her officials, was invoked at every turn as the partner with whom the Indians were dealing. The treaty terms were advanced as the wishes of the "Great Queen Mother," or the intentions of "Her Majesty."

An understanding of the nature of that relationship emerges from an examination of a variety of sources, including remarks by different government officers as well as from the treaty deliberations themselves. From these it can be discerned that at least some elements in the government recognized that the relationship being established was one that entailed an exchange of services and an acknowledgment of mutual obligations, all of permanent duration.

By treaty, the Indians in the Canadian West had entered into a special relationship with the Crown, but shortly thereafter they found themselves wards of the state and under the authority of the 1876 Indian Act, which effectively blotted out any practical impact of the relationship established by treaty. Yet the fact that this association was to be an enduring one was emphasized often during the negotiations, as the commissioners frequently employed the words "forever" and "as long as the sun shall shine."[23] Morris made it more overt when he told the Indians of Treaty 3: "I think you are forgetting one thing, that what I offer is to be while the water flows and the sun rises. You know that in the United States they only pay the Indian for twenty years."[24] The comparison does not really clarify the difference between the two nations. Like the promises of "forever" when reserve holdings were concerned, it was not necessarily a contradiction for the commissioners to invoke "forever" when they understood that "civilization" and assimilation would eventually eradicate the Indians as distinct entities.

Government officials may have labored under the delusion of the eventual assimilation of the Indians, but this does not absolve them of the consequences of their actions any more than the original intent of the 1763 Proclamation mars its subsequent application as an affirmation of the recognition of Indian peoples as nations. Canadian officials freely invoked the format and language of a more serious, permanent relationship than one to which they perhaps were committed. Their terminology was as definitive as their formal instruments. Morris wrote of treaty-making efforts in the West as "securing the alliance of the Indian tribes" and held out as the fruition of healthy treaty relationships the prospect of "seeing the Indians, faithful allies of the Crown."[25] When Americans spoke of Indians of the future, they employed the term "citizen." Morris, who could be expected to know the meaning of formal terms like "citizen" and "subject," chose the word "allies."

The nature of the relationship as one with mutual and long-term obligations was implied in the treaties themselves by a list of additional duties required of the Indian signatories. These obligations contrast in intent with the list of similar requirements made in the American treaties. (See table 5.) Canadian Indians were enjoined to adhere to these obligations "as good and loyal subjects of Her Majesty the Queen."[26] Conversely, the Americans demanded these, not on the basis of the relationship established, but "in consideration of the advantages and benefits conferred by this treaty."[27] The American obligations addressed specific problems arising from the immediate difficulties with the Indians. Canadian treaties included similar terms, but also involved various responsibilities regarding law, loyalty, and justice, which bespoke a closer association.

It may well be that Canadian officials, like the British before them, envisaged the treaties as "the formalization and elaboration of the relationship which already existed between the crown as landowners and the Indians as occupants."[28] But the Indians appear in many cases to have understood more, a conclusion particularly apparent in the context of the negotiations for Treaty 6, in which both sides clearly appreciated the intangible nature of the bond formed — most evident in the resolution of the "food question."[29] That the Indians could somehow have absorbed "the belief that they were establishing a special relationship with the Canadian government consisting of two equal parties who stood to benefit mutually from the agreement" was natural.[30] Officials of the Canadian government said as much themselves in words of their own choosing in their own language. Surprisingly, Canadian officials exhibited a disinclination, deliberately or thoughtlessly, to recognize what they themselves had wrought. This failure to provide a frank statement of their true intentions and beliefs, clouded instead in a veil of language that implied and sometimes overtly stated something distinctly different, would, like the American failure to clarify the civil status of Indians, return to plague the Canadian government in the next century when courts took the government to task for what was said rather than assumed in the treaties and their negotiations during the 1870s.

In the late twentieth century, both nations belatedly have come to recognize that documents of treaty status are not to be brushed aside so lightly. Under the Indian Claims Commission in the United States, a body created to adjudicate Indian grievances of treaty violations, the treaties of 1867 and 1868 have proven effective weapons in Indian hands. In just one example, the American absorption of the Black Hills of South Dakota by "arrangement" in 1876 was shown to be in violation of Article 12 of the Treaty of Fort Laramie with the Sioux, which prohibited further land cessions without the approval of three-fourths of all adult male Indians, and was therefore an illegal seizure. The Sioux were awarded a multimillion-dollar settlement in compensation, an unsatisfactory judgment that they initially refused, desiring instead the return of the land.[31]

Canada, unlike the United States, had done its best to avoid clearly delineated commitments in the treaties. This did serve government interests in sidestepping the pitfalls the Americans faced with specific provisions, but it has not eliminated controversy. Canada's treaties established a relationship embedded in these documents and understood by those who negotiated them. The government and the commissioners were not perhaps insincere but simply unable to envisage, in their fixed ideas about the imminent disappearance one way or another of the Indians, of that relationship having any long-term consequences. Controversy has mounted in the twentieth century over the spirit and intent of the Numbered Treaties, challenging the narrowly or vaguely defined terms regarding agricultural assistance (job creation), schools (education), and a medicine chest (health care). Particularly important to such interpretations are the exchanges recorded between the lieutenant governor and the Crees during the Treaty 6 negotiations, which support a broader interpretation of the relationship than was conveyed in the stingy terms. If the commissioner spoke out of turn and made commitments the government did not wish to undertake, then the opportunity to reject that action came at the point of ratification. But Canada's lethargic and indifferent approach to Indian relations prevailed there too, binding the nation, in its own word, "forever."

Both Canada and the United States would have been more astute to have paid attention to the pronouncements of U.S. Supreme Court Justice John Marshall, whose 1830s decisions continue to cast a shadow over Indian relations in the two countries. It was a contemporary argument that the Indians could hardly be expected to understand what they were signing, and humanitarians and critics of the treaty system alike lamented this failing.[32] This view continues to have adherents today among some Indian groups and among historians seeking explanations.[33]

But the governments, which in the twentieth century have been confronted by the obligations they undertook in nineteenth-century treaties, can not claim ignorance as an excuse. "The words 'treaty' and 'nation' are words of our own language," John Marshall wrote in 1833, "selected in our diplomatic and legislative proceedings, by ourselves, having each a definite and well understood meaning. We have applied them to Indians, as we have applied them to the other nations of the earth. They are all applied in the same sense."[34]

10 "Humane, Just, and Christian"

Historians may have largely neglected a comparative approach to Canadian and American Indian policy, but contemporaries were keenly aware of the other's existence and commented frequently on the differences between the two nations. Canadian smugness in the realm of Indian policy, based firmly on a widespread disdain for the way Americans managed their affairs, was present from Confederation. In parliamentary discussions on the absorption of Rupert's Land, William McDougall said: "the system pursued in the United States had led to border wars of greater or lesser magnitude. But the system which Canada had hitherto pursued had been very successful, and under that which was proposed for the Government of the territory, there need be no fear of disturbances."[1] This sentiment, reinforced by a decade of American Indian wars during which the Canadian West remained serene, was reiterated in the House of Commons in 1877. Albert Smith observed, "The Americans, of course, had many such wars, but the action of the Canadian Government towards the Indians had been very different to that of the United States under similar circumstances."[2] The manifest arrogance of the Canadians was further exemplified in the annual report of Minister of the Interior David Mills later that same year: "The conclusion of this treaty with these warlike and intractable tribes, at a time when the Indian tribes immediately across the border were engaged in open hostilities with the United States troops, is certainly a conclusive proof of the just policy of the Government of Canada toward the aboriginal population."[3]

It is difficult to overlook the note of haughty superiority affected toward the situation in the United States, most acute in 1877 with the American military debacle at the hands of the Sioux at the Little Bighorn still clear in the minds of contemporaries. What is particularly striking is the willingness of Canadian officials to attribute the difference between the two nations to policy, a deliberate system applied by the Canadian government. The only indication of modesty lies in the implication that this approach had imperial, or at least pre-Confederation, antecedents. More remarkable even than the assertion of a positive policy is the absence of acknowledgment of other factors. Nowhere is there any suggestion that external events, and perhaps even the Indians themselves, may have had some influence on the different national experiences.

The Americans were not always so generous in their assessment of Canadian success. In a country where national honor and international opinion carried significant weight, particularly where Indian relations were concerned, this animosity may have arisen in part because of the frequent invocation by many Americans of the alleged superiority of the Canadian "system." "Why is it," Congressman John Pruyn demanded of his colleagues, "that we have failed so utterly in doing our duty to these Indian tribes? Why is it that the English Government, the Canadian Government has always succeeded in maintaining an almost unbroken peace with them?"[4] It was a common lament in Congress, especially among detractors of the treaty system. Rep. Benjamin Butler, a persistent critic, painted a stark picture of the contrast between the two nations: "There runs through this continent an invisible line separating the British dominions from the United States. That almost trackless wilderness is full of Indians, as many on one side of the line as upon the other. Yet, sir, on one side of that line, in the British dominions, there has not been an Indian war for sixty years, while on the other side, within the limits of the United States, we have had upon our hands perpetual Indian wars."[5] Despair at the inadequacies of the American system concerned not only humanitarian issues, but also pecuniary ones. As Sen. William Stewart informed his colleagues, "It would bankrupt this New Dominion, or Old Dominion, or whatever it is called, to make the appropriations that we are lavishing every year upon the Indians."[6]

Canadian politicians would have been gratified by this celebration of their frugality, but not all Americans were so impressed. In response to repeated criticism extolling the superiority of the Canadian approach to that of the United States, an exasperated Sen. James Harlan declared: "We often hear it said that the policy of the United States toward the Indian tribes is wrong, because we have Indian wars while the people of Great Britain in the Canadas live in peace with their Indians. Sir, the Indian policy in the United States is the English policy, established here before our Government was formed, and only modified as circumstances and the changed condition of the Indian tribes required it."[7]

Reasons for the success of Canadian policy were given far more consideration in the United States than in the Dominion itself and taxed politicians, bureaucrats, military men, and the press alike to explain the anomaly.[8] An astute analysis was offered in an examination of U.S. Indian policy in 1879 by Gen. Nelson A. Miles, soon to be the highest ranking soldier in the U.S. Army and a man who made his reputation in the Indian wars of the post–Civil War era. He posed the perennial question as to why peace reigned in the Dominion and not on the American Plains and concluded: "Their system is permanent, decided, and just. The tide of immigration in Canada has not been as great as along our frontier; they allow the Indians to live as Indians, and do not attempt to force upon the natives the customs which to them are distasteful."[9] Miles had put his finger on the two critical elements that self-congratulatory Canadian policymakers chose to overlook or misrepresent: emigration and civilization policy.

The pressures of emigration forced the Americans to treaty making in 1867 and 1868 in order to address problems of security, humanity, and, as always, economy. Confronted with the prospect of expensive plains-wide Indian wars, brought on by the collision of land-hungry settlers with the resisting indigenous inhabitants, the American government was impelled to act. The tide of settlement not only necessitated the treaty process but also influenced the direction that process took. The reservation and civilization policies arose as a direct result of the population crisis, for it was widely acknowledged that unless the Indians were "civilized," they would face certain extinction, perhaps by extermination.

The absence of such pressures in Canada simplified matters significantly. There was no violent conflict between peoples precipitated by uncontrolled emigration to prompt negotiations for security purposes. Because the Indians were not threatened with extinction from the same source, neither was there a humanitarian impulse to solve an "Indian problem" through a concerted policy of civilization.

Canada could afford not only a leisurely pace in expansion but also a dilatory application of its existing Indian policy. A commitment to deal justly with the Indians, understood to involve treaties, initially took no tangible form. When Canada came to make treaties in the 1870s, external forces precipitated action in every case. Negotiations for Treaty 3 arose from the exigencies of the Red River Rebellion. Five of the Numbered Treaties resulted from Indian pressures. The Blackfoot treaty was prompted by an American Indian war and the Sioux attempt to create an alliance with the Blackfoot. In every instance, Canada reacted to circumstances rather than initiate its own policy. This indifferent and sluggish approach to Indian treaty-making policy characterized treaty terms as well as implementation. Canadian authorities envisaged treaties as narrowly defined documents with the single purpose of extinguishing Indian land title. Attempts to broaden the meaning were resisted as much as possible.

In form, the changes that were made, particularly those dealing with agriculture, resembled terms in American treaties. But in the American context such items were offered at the initiative of the government and were framed in a precise program of civilization. The Americans were not interested, in the first instance, in providing the Indians with an alternate means of subsistence. The threat to American Indians, and indeed to Americans, came from the conflict of the races, not the extinction of the buffalo. Treaty commissioners used the very real decline of the buffalo population to persuade the Indians of the benefits of a "white man's existence," but their major concern was to inaugurate a program to transform the Indian and thus "save" the race. Agriculture was only one element in this struggle. In Canada it was the Indians who demanded these terms, and there were no difficult overtones of racial absorption. What the Americans saw as instruments of civilization, Canadian officials viewed, in the short term, as unnecessary expenses.

Canada did embrace the form of a projected agricultural existence for the Indians by calculating reserves on the basis of individual farm size, but there was little substance to this effort. Reserves were calculated but only reluctantly surveyed. Agricultural implements were even more grudgingly forthcoming. There was no well-plotted, deliberately gradualist policy in Canada to which the subsequent peaceful expansion in the West might be attributed. By the same token, neither was there a gaping void that inspired makeshift, stopgap measures when events on the prairies finally pushed Ottawa to take action. The Dominion government had an established reserve and civilization policy based largely on earlier implementation in Upper Canada and the united colony during the pre-Confederation era. When the nation confronted the Indians of western Canada after 1870, however, other concerns, coupled with an overwhelming lack of interest, ensured that this Indian policy was not immediately applied, and a dilatory approach prevailed. Under pressure mainly from the Indians, the government undertook the negotiation of treaties. This it was not necessarily averse to doing, for the extinguishment of Indian land title accorded with the exigencies of John A. Macdonald's national policy. In the process, government negotiators also proved receptive to demands made by the Indians that reflected elements of the policy already in place elsewhere in the country, particularly with regard to agriculture and education. But these changes were not made at the government's initiative. Canada wanted nothing beyond land title and made no objectionable demands for the immediate and irreversible reformation of the Plains Indian cultures. In the Canadian West the Indians did not meet with the transformationist zeal exhibited by American treaty commissioners, who confronted the Indians there with a comprehensive plan to alter every aspect of Plains Indian life.

The absence of such a program in the Canadian treaties goes a long way to explaining a second critical aspect in the difference between the American and Canadian frontiers. Emigration, or lack of it, established a general context for Indian relations in the two countries. But Indian policy, as expressed in the 1867–68 and Numbered Treaties, was at least as significant a factor in the contrasting levels of violence that governed the Plains and Prairie West in each nation.

The United States treaties at Medicine Lodge and Fort Laramie were explicitly "reformist documents." The bulk of each dealt with measures "most likely to insure the civilization of the Indians," as directed in the July 20 Act. The treaties—in specific provisions for education, agriculture, reservations, and even citizenship—were directed to the transformation of the Indians, not only from nomadic hunters to "Jeffersonian yeoman farmers" but also from Indian to white. These documents contained an explicit program to remake one race in the image of another. The impact of this plan on the Plains Indians was recognized by at least one U.S. senator, who objected to the proposed creation of the Great Peace Commission on this basis: "It will be saying to them in very plain terms: 'We . . . will compel you to resort to agriculture to raise your bread and thus feed and subsist yourselves. We will compel you to become educated. We will compel you to become voters. We intend to coerce you to give up your old habits, your old customs, to abandon all your old traditions, your old ideas, as old as the continent. We intend to compel you to abandon all this and to become citizens of the United States, educated men, and Christians. . . . ' Will not the mere announcement that such is our policy make them still more unfriendly, more irreconcilable to us?" [10]

These prophetic words were not heeded. Instead, treaty commissioners were at pains to explain the very transformation they had in mind to the Indians they met in 1867 and 1868. They did this so effectively at Medicine Lodge that their promises of houses, hospitals, and farms were emphatically rejected by the buffalo-hunting plains peoples. Indeed, only the promise of continued hunting rights won Indian favor to the treaties.

The Indian peoples of the American Plains faced circumstances every bit as compelling as those that drove the Americans. When the American civilization and reservation policies became coercive, as they shortly did, these peoples recognized that they were in a fight for their lives — confronted by the threat of extinction by assimilation. The strong military culture of the plains buffalo hunters militated against a passive or resigned response to such a policy, and warfare continued across the American Plains for a decade after the great peace treaties were signed.

The American misfortunes were sparked in the first instance by uncontrolled emigration, but to a large extent, the violence of the 1870s was the result of an active interventionist policy aimed at the salvation of the Indians by an elaborate federal policy, the object of which was assimilation. To the dismay of the often humanitarian, if decidedly ethnocentric, sponsors of that policy, the Plains Indians not only objected to a cultural death but also had the means and willingness to resist it violently, if only for a time.

The situation in Canada was drastically different (no thanks to the smug Canadian officials who took credit for it). The absence of emigration meant that the pressures that aggravated the American situation did not exist. The reactive nature of the Canadian government also permitted the narrowest application of treaty making with, consequently, almost no practical consideration of the future of Indians within the Dominion.

General Miles had suggested that Canada's success lay in part with the fact that Canadians "allow the Indians to live as Indians." To some extent, at least in 1879, this was true. The civilization components of the Numbered Treaties were minimal compared to those in the American treaties, and both schools and agricultural tools were promised only when the Indians "settled down," something that was understood, by the government, not to be an immediate concern.

Miles's use of the word "allow" implied that tolerance of the continued existence of Indian cultures on the prairies after the treaties were signed was a deliberate decision by the Canadian government. In reality it was yet another manifestation of Canadian indifference. Transformation and an interventionist policy required interest, attention, and financial support. Canada was willing to offer none of these, hence the reluctance of the government to survey reserves or distribute agricultural equipment even when administrators on the spot and the Indians themselves demanded fulfillment of these treaty provisions. In the short term, this hands-off approach did achieve something the Americans proved chronically unable to manage—a peaceful Indian frontier. But Canadian restraint was not due to wisdom but rather to indifference and lethargy.

The lack of a coercive policy of civilization meant that Canadian Indians, unlike their American counterparts, did not necessarily read into the adoption of agriculture an attack on their culture. In the Canadian West the Indians themselves viewed agriculture as a potential solution to an Indian problem rather than as an assault on their existence from outside. Thus the second element that impelled American Indians to violence— a coercive, perceived assault on the aboriginal way of life—was also absent in Canada. This was a significant factor for future Canadian Indian policy and the Canadian self-image in this field.

Those aspects of a civilization policy contained in the Numbered Treaties were there at Indian insistence, not Canadian. Because they originated with the Indians, these accoutrements of "civilization" carried none of the ominous overtones of cultural obliteration that the same terms conveyed in the American context. Canadian Indians also faced a fight for their lives in the 1870s, but their enemy was starvation, not assimilation, and they saw agriculture as a means of salvation.

Canadian indifference thus worked in favor of the government in mitigating violence, at least in the short term. But the limited virtues of a "policy" of indifference and neglect, manifested in a lack of concern over the demise of the buffalo and in a reluctance to provide promised agricultural assistance, returned to haunt the Dominion in 1885. During that year a conflict, in which the much-taxed Indians played only a minimal part, erupted on the prairies and gave Canada an excuse to abandon its pattern of indifference for a concerted policy of coercion, much more in keeping with the efforts of the Americans. A subtle difference remained, however. In the 1870s the United States warred with the Indians on the plains in an effort to enforce the treaties of 1867 and 1868. In Canada, prompted by a growing Indian movement in the years prior to 1885 to revise the treaties and address Indian needs more adequately, the post-1885 repression involved a violation not only of the spirit in which the

Numbered Treaties were negotiated, but also of specific terms contained therein.

The 1877 Speech from the Throne had characterized Canadian policy as "humane, just, and Christian" in implicit contrast with the approach taken south of the forty-ninth parallel. An examination of treaty making in a comparative framework suggests, however, that this is a more apt characterization of American policy, although it would be necessary to add the terms "ethnocentric" and "self-interested" to that list of descriptors as well. A more appropriate and accurate assessment of Canadian efforts in regard to the Indians in the 1870s would be "cheap, indifferent, and reactive," reflecting the government's greatest concern, its general attitude, and the major motivating factor impelling negotiations in that decade.

The Treaties of Medicine Lodge and Fort Laramie and the Numbered Treaties were meant to address particular problems of Indian relations in both countries. In this the American treaties were probably less effective, for despite the provisions for peace and a permanent solution to the Indian question, warfare continued for more than a decade, and the Indians violently resisted the humanitarian solutions of reservations and civilization. Canada at least gained title to the land it sought, although the Numbered Treaties did not close the Indian question in that nation either. In the 1867–68 and 1870s negotiations, the two governments thought they were concluding a chapter on Indian relations. But the means that they chose — treaties — in both cases ensured a rebirth for the very peoples they had sought to absorb, this time around in courts of law and firmly based on the legal instruments nineteenth-century governments had sought to employ to their own advantage.

Appendix 1
Comparison of Terms
in American and Canadian Treaties

UNITED STATES	CANADA
Treaties of Medicine Lodge Creek, 1867 (with the Kiowas and Comanches, and Southern Cheyennes and Southern Arapahos) Treaties of Fort Laramie, 1868 (with the Sioux and Arapahos and the Northern Cheyennes and Northern Arapahos)[1]	*Numbered Treaties Treaty 1, 1871 Treaty 2, 1871 Treaty 3, 1873 Treaty 4, 1874 Treaty 5, 1875* Treaty 6, 1876 Treaty 7, 1877
Official preamble* Identification of participants and naming of the members of the Great Peace Commission and specific Indian peoples	**Official preamble** Identification of participants and establishment of the treaty as one between the queen and specific Indian peoples
No equivalent Expresses the desire for land and assurances of the queen's benevolence	**Formal statement of purpose**
Acknowledgment of authority of chiefs to negotiate* Validation of the chiefs' legitimacy	**Acknowledgment of authority of chiefs to negotiate** Identification of the chiefs and headmen and validation of their legitimacy
Peace War to cease* Peace to be maintained*	**Peace** Pledge to maintain peace
No equivalent	**Assurance of reciprocal obligations**
Detailed description of lands *to be reserved*	**Detailed description of lands *to be ceded***
Additional lands To be acquired if reservations do not contain enough arable land	**No equivalent**
Buildings for Indian use Government to provide several on reservations	**No equivalent**
No equivalent	**Buildings for public use** Government may appropriate reserve land for public works or buildings but must compensate Indians with land or money

Agents	**No equivalent**
To live on reservations	
To deal with complaints by and about the Indians	

Lands for farming	**Lands for farming**
To be taken from reservation lands	Measure which determines size of reserve lands
Up to 320 acres per head of family	160 acres per family of 5, adjusted for smaller or larger families (Treaties 1, 2, 5)
Up to 80 acres for any man or woman over 18	
Personal acreages registered in Land Book and removed from common holdings	640 acres per family of 5, adjusted for smaller or larger families (Treaties 3, 4, 6, 7)

Reservation lands	**Reserve lands**
Large territories to be held in common	Determined by the number of Indians and the amount of land (160 or 640 acres) assigned to each family
Specifically designated in detail	Lands designated in general terms but not immediately surveyed (Treaties 1, 2, 5, 7)
	Lands to be laid out later (Treaties 3, 4, 6)

Education*	**Education**
Necessary "to insure the civilization of the tribes"	Schools provided on each reserve when Indians desire them (Treaties 1, 2, 3, 5, 6)
Children ages 6–16 compelled to attend school	Schools provided on each reserve when Indians are "settled and prepared" (Treaty 4)
Indian agent responsible for the children's attendance	Teachers' salaries to be paid when deemed advisable and Indians are settled (Treaty 7)
An "English education" to be provided	
Teachers, schools, and teachers' houses provided by the U.S. government	
Teachers hired by the U.S. Government	
1 teacher for every 30 children	
These provisions to last "not less than 20 years"	

Agricultural assistance*

Provided once a family or an individual has selected lands for farming

Up to $100 worth of seeds and implements (unspecified) for the first year of agricultural activity

Up to $25 worth of seeds and implements (unspecified) for the next 3 years

Instruction from a farmer employed by the U.S. Government

1 cow and 1 pair of oxen to each family (lodge) who has settled (Treaties of Fort Laramie only)

Agricultural assistance

Itemized list of farm implements, varying among the treaties, distributed to individual families, shared by a number of families, or given to chiefs for use by their bands

"Enough" wheat, barley, potatoes, and oats to plant the land actually broken up (Treaties 3, 4, 6, 7)

Specification that all aid is given "once for all"

1 bull, 1 cow, 1 boar, 1 sow, and "a male and female of each kind of animal raised by farmers" (outside promises of Treaties 1 and 2)

1 yoke of oxen, 1 bull, and 4 cows per band (Treaties 3 and 4)

4 oxen, 1 bull, 6 cows, 1 boar, 2 sows per band (Treaty 6)

2 cows per family of 5; 3 cows per family of 6–9; 4 cows per family of 10 + (Treaty 7)

Personnel provided

1 blacksmith (equipped) for every 100 persons cultivating

1 carpenter

1 engineer

1 miller

1 physician

1 farmer

Equivalents

1 chest of ordinary carpenter's tools per chief for use of the band (Treaties 3, 4, 6, 7)

1 handmill when sufficient amount of grain produced (Treaty 6)

1 medicine chest to be kept at the home of the Indian agent (Treaty 6)

Compensation for withdrawn personnel

Any of the above personnel may be withdrawn after 10 years, but the government must compensate the Indians with $10,000 for "educational and moral improvement"

Agricultural assistance—financial

$1000 per year for 3 years to parties of both Fort Carlton and Fort Pitt (Treaty 6)

Annuities*

To be delivered at the agency house on the reservation

To be delivered on October 15 or September 1

To continue for 30 years

To include each year for males 14 and older 1 good suit of woolen clothing

To include each year for females 12 and older 1 skirt or cloth, hose, and other material

To include clothes for children each year

$10.00 per person who continues to roam and hunt

$20.00 per person settled and farming

Money to be used at the discretion of the secretary of the interior to purchase "other necessities" (Treaties of Fort Laramie)

$25,000 per year for 30 years to be used at the discretion of the secretary of the interior to purchase necessities (Treaties of Medicine Lodge Creek)

An army officer to inspect all goods and to supervise their delivery

Annuities

To be delivered at a mutually agreed upon location

To be delivered at an agreed upon date

To be delivered every year (unlimited term)

$5.00 per man, woman, or child

$25.00 per chief

$15.00 per headman/councillor (Treaties 1 and 2: in goods [at cost in Montreal] or in cash; Treaties 3, 4, 5, 6, 7: in cash)

1 good suit of clothing per chief and headmen every 3 years

$1500 per year for ammunition and twine (Treaty 3)

$750 per year for powder, shot, ball, and twine (Treaty 4)

$500 per year for ammunition and twine (Treaty 5)

$1500 per year for ammunition and twine, or other things at the government's discretion (Treaty 6)

$2000 per year for ammunition, or other things at the government's discretion and with the Indians' consent (Treaty 7)

Food*

1 pound of meat and 1 pound of flour daily for four years for every Indian over 4 years of age who has settled on the reservation (Treaties of Fort Laramie)

Famine relief clause

Assistance in the event of a general famine or pestilence, certified as such by the resident Indian agents (Treaty 6)

Presents for signing treaties

Distributed, but not designated in the treaties

Presents for signing treaties

$3.00 per person (Treaties 1, 2)

$12.00 per person (Treaties 3, 4, 6, 7)

Medals for chiefs (Treaties 3, 4, 6, 7)

Flags for chiefs (Treaties 3, 4, 6, 7)

1 Winchester rifle per chief (Treaty 7)

1 horse, wagon, and harness per chief (Treaty 6)

Extinguishment of land rights*

Indians relinquish all rights to occupy permanently the territory outside the reserve

Extinguishment of land rights

Indians cede rights, privileges, and titles to lands specified forever

Indians cede rights to any other lands in the Dominion to which claims may be made (Treaties 5, 6, 7)

Right to hunt

Indians retain right to hunt on designated tracts of lands surrendered "so long as the buffalo may range thereon in such numbers as to justify the chase"

Rights to hunt, fish, and trap

Indians retain the right to hunt and fish on ceded lands within government regulations and so long as such activity does not interfere with other government uses of the land (e.g. settling, mining, lumbering) (Treaties 3, 4, 5, 6, 7)

Trapping rights (Treaty 4)

Census*

Taken annually to assist the agent in delivering the proper amount of annuities

Census

Taken as soon as possible to assist in the designation of reserves

Other requirements of Indians

Will not object to railroads passing through specific areas (e.g. Smoky Hill, North Platte)

Will allow the peaceful construction of railroads outside their reservations

Will not molest wagon trains, people, or cattle belonging to the United States

Will not abduct white women or children

Will not kill, scalp, or otherwise hurt white men

Will not obstruct U.S. facilities (e.g. U.S. mail)

Will not oppose the establishment of U.S. military forts in western territories

If the construction of railroads or U.S. facilities interferes with Indian lands, compensation for damages will be assessed by a commission of 3, including a chief or headman

Other requirements of Indians

Will observe the treaty

Will be loyal subjects

Will obey Canadian laws

Will maintain peace with other Indians and with other subjects

Will not molest people or property in the ceded territory

Will not bother persons traveling through the ceded tracts

Will assist in bringing to justice any Indian who violates either the law or treaty

Cession of lands	**Cession of lands**
Land can be ceded only if three quarters of all adult males agree Such a cession cannot infringe on the rights of any Indian who has chosen an individual tract of land without his/her consent	Government may sell, lease, or dispose of reserve lands for the Indians' benefit with the Indians' consent (Treaties 3, 4, 5, 6)
Personnel hiring	**No equivalent**
With equal qualifications, preference to be given to hiring Indians (Medicine Lodge Creek Treaties)	
Reward for crops*	**No equivalent**
$500 per year to 10 best agricultural producers	
Unceded territory	**Additional reserved territory**
Territory north of the North Platte River and east of the Big Horn Mountains (i.e., the Powder River country) is considered "unceded Indian territory," and white settlement there is prohibited Indian permission is required to enter U.S. military posts and travel routes through the area are to be abandoned within 90 days of signing (Treaty of Fort Laramie with the Sioux)	Belt of land on the south side of the Bow and South Saskatchewan Rivers restricted for 10 years to Indian use only (Treaty 7)
Effect of this Treaty	**No equivalent**
To abrogate all previous treaties with the same peoples (Fort Laramie Treaties)	
No equivalent	**Liquor** Prohibited on reserves
No equivalent	**Explanation** Statement that the treaty has been read and explained to Indian participants and witnessed Includes the identification of the interpreters involved

Note: Unless otherwise noted, the treaty terms are identical in all of the treaties signed by that country. Terms have been summarized. Quotation marks indicate exact wording.

1. The Treaty of Fort Laramie with the Northern Cheyennes and Arapahos, 1868, is an abbreviated document sharing only the terms marked with an asterisk (*).

Appendix 2
Comparison of Terms
in the Numbered Treaties

SUMMARY

TERM DESCRIPTION	Treaty 1	Treaty 2	Treaty 3	Treaty 4	Treaty 5	Treaty 6	Treaty 7
Identification of participants	List of the participating commissioners and Indians (generally)						
Statement of purpose	Expression of the desire for land and assurances of the queen's benevolence						
Acknowledgment of authority of chiefs to negotiate	Certification of the chiefs and headmen to negotiate						
Naming of Indian representatives	Identification of the chiefs and headmen						
Cession of rights	Statement of the extinguishment or cession of rights, privileges, and titles to lands forever						
Land cession	Detailed description of lands to be ceded						
Relinquishment of land rights				Relinquishment of rights to any other lands in the Dominion outside of these, which are claimed.			
Land ceded (in square miles)			55,000		100,000	120,000	

	Treaty 1	Treaty 2	Treaty 3	Treaty 4	Treaty 5	Treaty 6	Treaty 7
Reserves	Commitment to establish reserves				Commitment establish reserves, acknowledging lands already cultivated	Commitment to establish to reserves	
Reserve location	Designation of area where reserves are to be established for specific bands		Selection of area by government officers "after conference with the Indians" Selection to occur next summer or as soon as practicable	Selection of area by government officers "after conference with each band"	Designation of area where reserves are to be established for specific bands	Selection of area by Chief Superintendent of Indian Affairs appointee "after consulting with the Indians"	Designation of area where reserves are to be established for specific bands
Farm acreage (per family of 5)	160 acres prorated for larger or smaller families		640 acres (1 square mile) prorated for larger or smaller families		160 acres prorated for larger or smaller families	640 acres (1 square mile) prorated for larger or smaller families	
Reserve Holdings	One 25-square-mile band around Yellow Quill's reserve		To include "farming land" and "other"		"other"	To include "farming land" and	

	Treaty 1	Treaty 2	Treaty 3	Treaty 4	Treaty 5	Treaty 6	Treaty 7
Presents	$3 per man, woman, and child Adjusted by the memo on "Outside Promises"* 1 set of clothing per chief and per headman (2 headmen per chief) every 3 years 1 buggy per chief (except to Yellow Quill) and per headman	$3 per man, woman, and child Adjusted by the memo on "Outside Promises"* 1 set of clothing per chief and per headman (2 headmen per chief) every 3 years 1 buggy per chief and per headman	$12 per man, woman, and child 1 flag and 1 medal per chief upon signing the treaty 1 set of clothing per chief and per headman (3 headmen per chief) every 3 years	$12 per man, woman, and child Per chief: $25 1 Queen's silver medal 1 flag $15 per headman (4 per band) 1 coat per chief and per headman Powder, shot, blankets, calicoes, etc. to those assembled	$5 per man, woman, and child 1 flag and 1 medal per chief upon signing the treaty	$12 per man, woman, and child Per chief: 1 suitable flag 1 medal 1 horse 1 wagon 1 harness Fort Carlton chiefs to receive 2 carts with iron bushings and tires instead of wagons	$12 per man, woman, and child Per chief: 1 suitable medal 1 suitable flag 1 Winchester rifle (as soon as is convenient) 1 Winchester rifle per minor chief and Stony chief
Schools	Provided on each reserve when Indians desire them			Provided on each reserve as soon as Indians are settled and prepared for a teacher	Provided on each reserve when Indians desire them	Provided on each reserve when Indians desire them	Teachers salaries to be paid when Indians are settled and desire teachers

	Treaty 1	Treaty 2	Treaty 3	Treaty 4	Treaty 5	Treaty 6	Treaty 7
Liquor	Liquor prohibited on reserves						
Census	Census to be taken as soon as possible						
Annuities (per year)	$15 per family of 5 (prorated) in goods, at cost in Montreal, or in cash Adjusted by memo on "Outside Promises" to $5 per man, woman, and child and $25 per chief		$5 per man, woman, and child to be paid in cash to each individual $25 per chief $15 per headman 1 suit of clothing per chief and headman every 3 years	$5 per man, woman, and child to be paid to heads of families $25 per chief $15 per headman (no more than 4 headmen per band) 1 suit of clothing per chief and headman every 3 years	$5 per man, woman, and child $25 per chief $15 per headman (no more than 3 headmen per band) 1 suit of clothing per chief and headman every 3 years	$5 per man, woman, and child $25 per chief $15 per headman (no more than 4 headmen per band) 1 suit of clothing per chief and headman every 3 years	$5 per man, woman, and child to be paid to heads of families $25 per chief $15 per headman 1 suit of clothing per chief and headman every 3 years
Extra provisions (per year)			$1500 for ammunition and twine	$750 for powder, shot, ball, and twine	$500 for ammunition and twine	$1500 for ammunition and twine, or other things, at the government's discretion	$2000 for ammunition, or other things, at the government's discretion, with the consent of the Indians

	Treaty 1	Treaty 2	Treaty 3	Treaty 4	Treaty 5	Treaty 6	Treaty 7
Sale of lands				Indians may not sell or alienate reserve lands			
Agricultural aid	Provided in the memo on "Outside Promises" For each settler cultivating the ground: 1 plough 1 harrow 1 bull per reserve 1 boar per reserve 1 cow per chief 1 sow per chief "a male and female of each animal raised by farmers"		To every family "actually cultivating": 2 hoes 1 spade 1 scythe 1 plough per 10 families 5 harrows per 20 families Per band: 1 axe 1 crosscut saw 1 handsaw 1 pitsaw the necessary files 1 grindstone 1 auger 1 chest of ordinary	"To every family "actually cultivating": 2 hoes 1 spade 1 scythe 1 axe 1 plough per 10 families 2 harrows per 10 families Per chief for the band's use: 1 crosscut saw 5 handsaws 1 pitsaw the necessary files 1 grindstone 5 augers 1 chest of	To every family "actually cultivating": 2 hoes 1 spade 1 scythe 1 axe 1 plough per 10 families 5 harrows per 20 families Per band: 1 crosscut saw 1 handsaw 1 pitsaw the necessary files 1 grindstone 1 auger 1 chest of ordinary	"To every family "actually cultivating": 4 hoes 2 spades 2 scythes 1 whetstone 2 hayforks 2 reaping hooks 1 plough per 3 families 1 harrow per 3 families Per band: 2 axes 1 crosscut saw 1 handsaw 1 pitsaw the necessary files	"For each chief, minor chief, and Stony chief, for use of their bands: 1 bull 10 axes 5 handsaws 5 augers 1 grindstone the necessary files and whetstones 2 cows per family of 5 or less 3 cows per family of 6 to 9 4 cows per family of 10 or more For those who

Treaty 1	Treaty 2	Treaty 3	Treaty 4	Treaty 5	Treaty 6	Treaty 7
		carpenter's tools per chief for use of the band	ordinary carpenter's tools per chief for use of the band	carpenter's tools per chief for use of the band	1 grindstone 1 auger 1 chest of ordinary carpenter's tools per chief for use of the band	want to cultivate (per family): 1 less cow than above BUT ALSO 2 hoes 1 spade 1 scythe 2 hay forks 1 plough per 3 families 1 harrow per 3 families
		"enough" wheat, barley, potatoes, and oats per band to plant the land "actually broken up"	"enough" seed, oats, wheat, barley, and potatoes to plant the land "actually broken up"	"enough" wheat, barley, potatoes, and oats to plant the land "actually broken up"	"enough" wheat, barley, potatoes, and oats to plant the land "actually broken up"	"enough" potatoes, barley, oats, and wheat (if suitable) for the land "actually broken up"
		Per band: 1 yoke of oxen 1 bull 4 cows	Per chief for the band's use: 1 yoke of oxen 1 bull 4 cows	1 yoke of oxen 1 bull 4 cows	Per band: 4 oxen 1 bull 6 cows 1 boar 2 sows 1 handmill when the amount of grain warrants it	Specification that all aid is given "once and for all"
		Specification that all aid is given "once and for all	Specification that all aid is given "once and for all"	Specification that all given "once for all"	Specification that all aid is given "once and for all"	

	Treaty 1	Treaty 2	Treaty 3	Treaty 4	Treaty 5	Treaty 6	Treaty 7
Extra agricultural aid						$1000 per year for 3 years for both the Fort Carlton and Fort Pitt signatory bands	
Other supplies						Medicine chest to be kept at the house of the Indian agent	
Famine relief clause						Assistance in the event of a general famine or pestilence, certified as such by the resident Indian agent	
Additional reserve territory							Portion of land reserved for 10 years

	Treaty 1	Treaty 2	Treaty 3	Treaty 4	Treaty 5	Treaty 6	Treaty 7
Indian pledges	To observe the treaty	To observe the treaty	To observe the treaty	To observe the treaty			
	To keep the peace	To be loyal subjects	To be loyal subjects	To be loyal subjects			
	Not to molest white subjects	To keep the peace	To obey Canadian laws	To obey Canadian laws			
		Not to molest those on ceded tracts	To keep the peace	To keep the peace			
		Not to bother persons traveling through ceded tracts	Not to molest those on ceded tracts	Not to molest people or property on ceded tracts			
		To assist in bringing to justice Indians who violate the law or treaty	Not to bother persons traveling through ceded tracts	Not to bother persons traveling through ceded tracts			
			To assist in bringing to justice Indians who violate the law or treaty	To assist in bringing to justice Indians who violate the law or treaty			
Government land rights			Government may sell, lease, or dispose of reserve lands, for the Indians' benefit, with the Indians' consent				

	Treaty 1	Treaty 2	Treaty 3	Treaty 4	Treaty 5	Treaty 6	Treaty 7
Government use of reserves			Government may appropriate reserve lands for public works and buildings but must compensate the Indians	Government may appropriate reserve lands for public works and buildings but must compensate the Indians with land or money	Government may appropriate reserve lands for public works and buildings but must compensate the Indians		
Hunting and fishing rights			Hunting and fishing permitted on ceded lands To be government regulated Lands subject to other uses by the government	Hunting, fishing, and trapping permitted on ceded lands To be government regulated Lands subject to other uses by the government	Hunting and fishing permitted on ceded lands To be government regulated Lands subject to other uses by the government		Hunting permitted on ceded lands To be government regulated Lands subject to other uses by the government
Closing statement	Statement that the treaty has been read and explained and witnessed; includes the signatures of the main participants						

Note: The treaty terms have been summarized. Quotation marks indicate exact wording.

*"Memorandum of things outside of the Treaty which were promised at the Treaty at the Stone Fort, signed August 3, 1871, as validated by an Order in Council dated April 30, 1875, and applied to Treaties No. 1 and 2," RG 10, NAC, vol. 3571, file 124 (pt. 2), reel C-10101.

Source: The treaty terms have been summarized from Morris, *The Treaties of Canada with the Indians.*

Appendix 3
Summary of Terms in Treaties Signed
at Medicine Lodge Creek (1867)
and Fort Laramie (1868)

TERM DESCRIPTION	TREATY WITH THE KIOWAS AND COMANCHES, MEDICINE LODGE CREEK, OCT. 21, 1867 / TREATY WITH THE SOUTHERN CHEYENNES AND SOUTHERN ARAPAHOS, MEDICINE LODGE CREEK, OCT. 28, 1867*	TREATY WITH THE SIOUX AND ARAPAHOS, FORT LARAMIE, APR. 29, 1868**	TREATY WITH THE NORTHERN CHEYENNES AND NORTHERN ARAPAHOS, FORT LARAMIE, MAY 19, 1868
War	*(Article 1)* War to cease		
Peace	*(Article 1)* Both parties pledged to keep peace Individual violators, Indian or white, to be dealt with by U.S. law Indian complaints to be forwarded through agents to the commissioner of Indian Affairs (CIA) Indian violators to be handed over to the government or victims to be compensated from Indian annuities		
Reservation boundaries	*(Article 2)* Laid out in detail, by rivers, longitude, and latitude Inviolate except to those on government business "For the absolute and undisturbed use" of these Indians, unless they agree to accept other tribes or individual Indians among them		*(Article 2)* Indians agree to accept for their permanent home a piece of the reservation assigned to either the Southern Cheyennes and Southern Arapahos by the Medicine Lodge Treaty or part of the reservation assigned to the Sioux in the Fort Laramie Treaty of April 1868 Given a choice of reservations

	(Article 3)	(Article 6)	(Article 3)
Additional land	Additional land to be purchased by U.S. government if the reservation does not contain enough arable land to allow all authorized Indians 160 acres of tillable soil		
Buildings on the reservation	*(Article 4)* The U.S. government to provide at its own expense all general buildings (i.e., agency storeroom, physician's office, and 5 others); the amount to be spent on the buildings is specified in the treaty The government to provide a schoolhouse or mission building "so soon as a sufficient number of children can be induced by the agent to attend school"		
Agent's residence and duties	*(Article 5)* Agent to live on the reservation Responsible for handling complaints by and about Indians		
Lands for farming	*(Article 6)* Heads of family can select a piece of reservation land that does not exceed 320 acres to start farming; upon doing so, this piece of land will cease to be held in common Land to be held by the individual as long as it is cultivated Any man or woman over 18 can choose up to 80 acres of land These transactions are to be recorded in the Land Book The status of the land is not fee simple but may be made so at the president's discretion	*(Article 6)* Heads of family can select a piece of reservation land that does not exceed 320 acres to start farming; upon doing so, this piece of land will cease to be held in common Land to be held by the individual as long as it is cultivated Any man or woman over 18 can choose up to 80 acres of land These transactions are to be recorded in the Land Book The status of the land is not fee simple but may be made so at the president's discretion	*(Article 3)* Heads of family can select a piece of reservation land that does not exceed 320 acres to start farming; upon doing so, this piece of land will cease to be held in common Land to be held by the individual as long as it is cultivated Any man or woman over 18 can choose up to 80 acres of land These transactions are to be recorded in the Land Book The status of the land is not fee simple but may be made so at the president's discretion

The United States can make laws on the alienation of this type of property and other matters relating to it

The United States can make laws on the alienation of this type of property and other matters relating to it

Any male Indian over 18 who shall occupy a piece of land *outside* the reservation that shall not be mineral lands or any other reserved for use by the United States, and who has made improvements of more than $200 in value and occupied this land for 3 years continuously, shall be entitled to receive a U.S. patent for 160 acres, including his improved land

After providing written application and proof of 2 disinterested witnesses, the Indian can register this land at the General Land Office and hold it as long as he continues to live there

Citizenship

Any Indian receiving a patent under the above rules may become a citizen of the United States and be entitled to all the rights of citizenship and shall "at the same time retain all his rights to benefits accruing to Indians under this treaty"

The United States can make laws on the alienation of this type of property and other matters relating to it

	(Article 7)	(Article 4)
Civilization and education	"In order to insure the civilization of the tribes . . . the necessity of education is admitted"	"In order to insure the civilization of the tribes . . . the necessity of education is admitted"
	Children (ages 6–16) will be compelled to attend school	Children (ages 6–16) will be compelled to attend school
	For every 30 children, the U.S. government will supply teacher housing and a teacher "competent to teach elementary branches of an English education"	For every 30 children, the U.S. government will supply teacher housing and a teacher "competent to teach elementary branches of an English education"
	This article is to continue "for not less than 20 years"	This article is to continue "for not less than 20 years"

	(Article 8)	(Article 5)
Agriculture	Once an Indian selects lands for farming, he/she is entitled to:	Once an Indian selects lands for farming, he/she is entitled to:
	—up to $100 worth of seeds and implements (unspecified) for the first year and up to $25.00 worth for the next 3 years	—up to $100 worth of seeds and implements (unspecified) for the first year and up to $25.00 worth for the next 3 years
	—farming instruction by a farmer provided by the United States	—farming instruction by a farmer provided by the United States
	For every 100 persons cultivating, a blacksmith will be provided, as well as iron, steel, and other materials	For every 100 persons cultivating, a blacksmith will be provided, as well as iron, steel, and other materials

	(Article 9)	
Withdrawing personnel	After 10 years, the United States may withdraw the physician, farmer, blacksmith, carpenter, engineer, and miller provided by the treaty but shall compensate the Indians with $10,000 per annum to be devoted to education The expenditure of such money will be decided by the commissioner of Indian Affairs, who will direct the money toward that which will "best promote the educational & moral improvement" of these Indians	
	(Article 10)	(Article 6)
Annuities	To be delivered to the agency house on the reservation To be delivered on October 15 "for thirty years" To include: —for all males 14 and older: 1 good suit of woolen clothing —for all females 12 and older: 1 skirt or cloth, hose, and other material —for all children: clothes	To be delivered to the agency house on the reservation To be delivered on October 15 "for thirty years" To include: —for all males 14 and older: 1 good suit of woolen clothing —for all females 12 and older: 1 skirt or cloth, hose, and other material —for all children: clothes
	(Article 10)	(Article 6)
Census	Census to be taken annually	Census to be taken annually

Other necessities

(Article 10)

$25,000 each year for 30 years to be spent by the secretary of the interior, at the CIA's recommendation, on necessities (unspecified) for the Indians ($20,000 in the Treaty with the Southern Cheyennes and Southern Arapahos)

If during the 30 years it is found the money can be better spent on the Indians in some other way, Congress may change the purpose of the appropriation but may not change the amount of or withdraw the appropriation for 30 years

An army officer to be appointed to inspect goods and supervise their delivery

(Article 10)

Persons who continue to roam and hunt to receive $10.00 per year for 30 years

Persons engaged in farming to receive $20.00 per year for 30 years

The money is to be used by the secretary of the interior to purchase articles deemed to be of necessity for the Indians

If during the 30 years it is found the money can be better spent on the Indians in some other way, Congress may change the purpose of the appropriation but may not change the amount of or withdraw the appropriation for 30 years

An army officer to be appointed to inspect goods and supervise their delivery

Food Provisions

Every Indian over 4 years of age who has settled permanently on a reservation and adhered to the treaty is to be provided with 1 pound of meat and 1 pound of flour per day for 4 years if they cannot furnish their own subsistence at an earlier date

(Article 6)

Persons who continue to roam and hunt to receive $10.00 per year for 30 years

Persons engaged in farming to receive $20.00 per year for 30 years

The money is to be used by the secretary of the interior to purchase articles deemed to be of necessity for the Indians

If during the 30 years it is found the money can be better spent on the Indians in some other way, Congress may change the purpose of the appropriation but may not change the amount of or withdraw the appropriation for 30 years

An army officer to be appointed to inspect goods and supervise their delivery

Food Provisions

Every Indian over 4 years of age who has settled permanently on a reservation and adhered to the treaty is to be provided with 1 pound of meat and 1 pound of flour per day for 4 years if they cannot furnish their own subsistence at an earlier date

	Cows and oxen	**Cows and oxen**
	The United States will give each family (lodge) who has settled to farm "1 good American cow and 1 good well-broken pair of American oxen" within 60 days of their settlement	The United States will give each family (lodge) who has settled to farm "1 good American cow and 1 good well-broken pair of American oxen" within 60 days of their settlement
Relinquishing lands	*(Article 11)* Indians party to this agreement will "relinquish all right to occupy permanently the territory outside their reservation"	*(Article 2)* "And the Northern Cheyenne and Arapahoe Indians do hereby relinquish, release, and surrender to the United States, all right, claim, and interest in and to all territory outside the two reservations above mentioned."
Right to hunt	*(Article 11)* Indians retain the right to hunt on any lands south of the Arkansas River "so long as the buffalo may range thereon in such numbers as to justify the chase" No white settlers are to be allowed on any part of the old reservations as defined in the Treaty of Little Arkansas (1865) for three years *(Article 11)* Indians retain the right to hunt on any lands north of the North Platte River and on the Republican fork of the Smoky Hill River "so long as buffalo may range thereon in such numbers as to justify the chase"	*(Article 2)* Indians retain the right "to roam and hunt while game shall be found in sufficient quantities to justify the chase"
Other stipulations on the Indians	*(Article 11)* Will not object to a railroad through the Smoky Hills Will withdraw objections to railroads being built on the plains	

	(Article 12)	(Article 8)
	Will allow the peaceful construction of railroads that do not cross reservation territory	Will allow the peaceful construction of railroads that do not cross reservation territory
	Will not molest wagon trains, people, or cattle belonging to the United States	Will not attack wagon trains, travelers, etc.
	Will not abduct white women and children	Will not abduct white women and children
	Will not kill, scalp, or otherwise hurt white men	Will not kill, scalp, or otherwise hurt white men
	Will withdraw all objections to the railroad being built along the Platte Road	Will withdraw all opposition to the railroad being built along the Platte Road
	Will not obstruct any U.S. facilities (i.e., mail, roads, etc.)	A commission of 3, including a chief or headmen of the tribes, will determine the compensation for damages of any government works that touch the Indians' lands
	If such things interfere with Indian lands, a commission of 3, including a chief or headmen of the tribes, will determine the compensation for damages	Will withdraw opposition to the U.S. military post being built south of the North Platte River
	Will withdraw opposition to U.S. military posts being built in the western territories	
Validity of cessions	(Article 12)	(Article 8)
	Reservation lands cannot be ceded validly "unless executed and signed by at least three fourths of all the adult male Indians occupying the same"	Reservation lands cannot be ceded validly "unless executed and signed by at least a majority of all adult male Indians occupying the same"
	The cession will not be valid without the consent of any Indian who is deprived of his selected tract of land	

Personnel— hiring	(Article 13) When hiring a farmer, blacksmith, miller, etc., "qualifications being equal, [the agent] shall give preference to Indians"		
Personnel to be provided	(Article 14) The United States will hire a physician, teachers, a carpenter, a miller, an engineer, a farmer, and blacksmiths and provide money to pay them	(Article 13) The United States will hire a physician, teachers, a carpenter, a miller, an engineer, a farmer, and blacksmiths and provide money to pay them	(Article 7) The United States will hire a physician, teachers, a carpenter, a miller, an engineer, a farmer, and blacksmiths and provide money to pay them
House for Toshewa	(Article 15) A specific appropriation for a particular Indian's house (Toshewa expressed his wish to settle immediately)		
Reward for crops	(Article 15) $500 to be awarded annually to the 10 best agricultural producers	(Article 14) $500 to be awarded annually to the 10 best agricultural producers	(Article 9) $500 to be awarded annual to the 10 best agricultural producers
Permanent homes	(Article 16) Once buildings are constructed, Indians will make the reservations their permanent homes and have no other "But they shall have the right to hunt on the lands south of the Arkansas River . . . subject to the modifications named in this treaty"	(Article 15) Once buildings are constructed, Indians will make the reservations their permanent homes and have no other "But they shall have the right, subject to the conditions and modifications of this treaty, to hunt, as stipulated in Article 11 hereof"	(Article 2) Once they have moved to the reservation, that will be their permanent home and they will have no other

Unceded territory	*(Article 16)* "The United States hereby agrees and stipulates that the country north of the North Platte River and east of the summits of the Big Horn Mountains shall be held and considered to be unceded Indian territory, and also stipulates and agrees that no white person or persons shall be permitted to settle upon or occupy any portion of the same" Indian permission is needed to pass through this land Within 90 days of peace being concluded with the Sioux Nation, the military posts in this territory and the road leading to them and to Montana, shall be abandoned
Effect of this treaty on other treaties	*(Article 17)* This treaty eliminates all agreements, annuities, provisions, etc. made in previous treaties with these people

Note: Terms have been summarized. Quotation marks indicate exact wording.

*Treaty with the Southern Cheyennes and Southern Arapahos, signed October 28 1867 at Medicine Lodge Creek, is identical to the Treaty with the Comanches, Kiowas, and Kiowa-Apaches, with the exception of Articles 13 and 15.

**The Sioux signing this treaty include the Brulés, Oglalas, Miniconjous, Yanktonais, Hunkpapas, Blackfeet, Two Kettles, Sans Arcs, and Santees.

Source: Treaty terms summarized from Kappler, *Indian Treaties, 1778–1883.*

Notes

INTRODUCTION

1. Speech from the Throne, in House of Commons, *Debates*, February 8, 1877, p. 3.

2. Miller, *Skyscrapers Hide the Heavens*, p. 162.

3. Washburn, "Indian Removal Policy," p. 276.

4. Utley, *Indian Frontier*, p. 271.

5. Utley, *Indian Frontier*, p. 270.

6. Wooster, *The Military and United States Indian Policy*, pp. 59–60.

7. Bolt, *American Indian Policy and American Reform*, p. 70.

8. Miller, *Skyscrapers Hide the Heavens*, p. 163.

9. Dickason, *Canada's First Nations*, p. 275.

10. White-Harvey, "Reservation Geography," 587, 593, map, 594, map.

11. Stanley, *Birth of Western Canada*, pp. xxv–xxvi.

12. Utley, *Indian Frontier*, p. 122.

13. The Great Peace Commission of 1867–68, which concluded these treaties, had a broad mandate that extended beyond the Great Plains to include negotiations with the Navajos, Crows, Bannocks, and Shoshones.

14. Nichols, *Indians in the United States and Canada*. See also Samek, *Blackfoot Confederacy*; Gulig, "In Whose Interest?"; Baker, "Color, Culture, and Power," pp. 3–20; and Allen, *His Majesty's Indian Allies*.

15. See Satz, *American Indian Policy in the Jacksonian Era*; Trennert, *Alternative to Extinction*; Danziger, *Indians and Bureaucrats*; and Priest, *Uncle Sam's Stepchildren*. See also Ellis, *General Pope and U.S. Indian Policy*; Bailey, *Pacifying the Plains*; Mardock, *Reformers and the American Indian*; and Prucha, *American Indian Policy in Crisis*.

16. Prucha, *American Indian Treaties*. The only book-length work on the treaties examined herein is Jones, *Treaty of Medicine Lodge*. Articles include Jones, "Medicine Lodge Revisited," pp. 130–42; and two older studies, Taylor, "Medicine Lodge Peace Council," pp. 98–118; and Connelly, "Treaty Held at Medicine Lodge," pp. 601–6. An additional study is Parrish, "Indian Peace Commission of 1867."

17. On Indian policy see Leighton, "Federal Indian Policy in Canada"; Tay-

lor, "Indian Policy for the Canadian Northwest"; and Tobias, "Protection, Civilization, Assimilation." Studies of treaties include Hall, "'A Serene Atmosphere'?"; Friesen, "Magnificent Gifts"; Tobias, "Subjugation of the Plains Cree"; McKay, "Fighting for Survival"; and John L. Taylor, "Two Views of the Meaning of Treaties 6 and 7," in Price, *Alberta Indian Treaties*.

18. One exception is Jennings, "North West Mounted Police and Indian Policy."

19. The most commonly used sources for Indian voices in treaty-making negotiations are published accounts of the records made by the Canadian and American governments. These are Morris, *Treaties of Canada with the Indians* and *Proceedings of the Great Peace Commission*. As helpful as these works are in conveying the speeches made by Indian statesmen, in translation they do not provide the whole picture. Thus, other sources have emerged as important elements of the entire story. An account by Métis interpreter Peter Erasmus, for example, sheds considerable light on Indian perspectives of the Treaty 6 negotiations, offering a glimpse of Indian councils that took place away from the official talks with Canadian representatives. See Erasmus, *Buffalo Days and Nights*. In recent years, oral history testimony has been employed to offer an Indian point of view derived from aboriginal sources as a counterbalance to the official records.

1. TREATY-MAKING PRECEDENTS AND PROGRESS

1. "The Royal Proclamation, October 7, 1763," *Revised Statutes of Canada, 1970—Appendices*, pp. 127–28.

2. Sosin, *Revolutionary Frontier*, pp. 10–11; Tucker and Hendrickson, *Fall of the First British Empire*, p. 91.

3. Tucker and Hendrickson, *Fall of the First British Empire*, p. 92.

4. B. D. Bargar, *Lord Dartmouth and the American Revolution*, pp. 39, 68; Sosin, *Revolutionary Frontier*, p. 11.

5. Tucker and Hendrickson, *Fall of the First British Empire*, pp. 57, 392; Christie and Labaree, *Empire or Independence*, pp. 193, 196.

6. Greene, *Colonies to Nation*, p. 428. Maryland, a small state fearing domination by larger states within the Union, had refused to accept the Articles of Confederation in 1781 until the states with western boundaries conceded their western claims. The details for the formation of new states out of these lands and their admission to the Union were laid out in 1787 in the Northwest Ordinance. Greene, *Colonies to Nation*, pp. 469–74.

7. Nichols, *Indians in the United States and Canada*, p. 166; and Miller, *Skyscrapers Hide the Heavens*, pp. 92–93.

8. Noel Dyck, *What is the Indian "Problem,"* p. 49. See also Miller, *Skyscrapers Hide the Heavens*, p. 100.

9. Dickason, *Canada's First Nations*, p. 273.

10. Thomas Jefferson's views are stated in his "Special Message to Cong.," January 18, 1803, and "Second Inaugural Address," March 4, 1805, in Richardson, *Compilation of Messages and Papers of the Presidents*, 1:352, 380. See also Berkhofer, *White Man's Indian*, pp. 149, 157.

11. Marshall's decisions were elaborated in *Johnson and Graham's Lessee v. McIntosh* (1823), *Cherokee Nation v. Georgia* (1831), and *Worcester v. Georgia* (1832). For a thorough discussion of the influence of the Marshall Court on Indian policy, see Monikowski, "'The Actual State of Things.'"

12. Gov. George Gilmer (1829–31) quoted in Utley, *Indian Frontier*, p. 36.

13. Andrew Jackson, "Farewell Address," March 4, 1837, in Richardson, *Compilation of the Messages and Papers of the Presidents*, 3:294.

14. Trennert, *Alternative to Extinction*, p. 7; Prucha. *The Great Father*, 1:272.

15. Mardock, *Reformers and the American Indian*, p. 86.

16. Ellis, *General Pope and U.S. Indian Policy*, p. 32.

2. TREATY-MAKING PROBLEMS

1. Prucha, *American Indian Treaties*, p. 209.

2. Prucha, *The Great Father*, 1:57.

3. Sen. William Stewart, *Congressional Globe*, 40th Cong., 2d sess., July 16, 1868, vol. 39, p. 4120. See also Sen. John Sherman, *Congressional Globe*, 39th Cong., 2d sess., February 23, 1867, vol. 37, p. 1798.

4. Sen. John Sherman, *Congressional Globe*, 39th Cong., 1st sess., April 18, 1866, vol. 36, p. 2010. See also Sen. Samuel Pomeroy, *Congressional Globe*, 41st Cong., 1st sess., March 6, 1869, vol. 41, p. 23; and Sen. William Stewart, *Congressional Globe*, 41st Cong., 2d sess., June 2, 1870, vol. 42, p. 4006.

5. Prucha, *American Indian Treaties*, p. 209.

6. Sen. William Stewart, *Congressional Globe*, 39th Cong., 1st sess., April 18, 1866, vol. 36, p. 2014.

7. Gen. John Pope quoted by Rep. John Kasson, *Congressional Globe*, 39th Cong., 1st sess., July 16, 1866, vol. 36, p. 3846.

8. Sen. James Doolittle, *Congressional Globe*, 39th Cong., 2d sess., January 26, 1867, vol. 37, p. 762. See also Prucha, *The Great Father*, 1:486.

9. Sen. James McDougall, *Congressional Globe*, 39th Cong., 1st sess., April 18, 1866, vol. 36, p. 2010.

10. Sen. John Sherman, *Congressional Globe*, 39th Cong., 2d sess., February 23, 1867, vol. 37, p. 1801, and *Congressional Globe*, 40th Cong., 1st sess., July 17, 1867, vol. 38, p. 680.

11. Sen. Jacob Howard, *Congressional Globe*, 40th Cong., 1st sess., July 17, 1867, vol. 38, p. 684.

12. Sen. James Doolittle, *Congressional Globe*, 39th Cong., 1st sess., April 18, 1866, vol. 36, p. 2012.

13. Sen. William Stewart, *Congressional Globe*, 41st Cong., 2d sess., July 14, 1870, vol. 42, p. 5585.

14. See for example, Sen. John Sherman, *Congressional Globe*, 40th Cong., 1st sess., March 27, 1867, vol. 38, p. 379; Rep. Benjamin Butler, *Congressional Globe*, 40th Cong., 2d sess., May 27, 1868, vol. 39, p. 2615; and Sen. William Stewart, *Congressional Globe*, 41st Cong., 3d sess., February 10, 1871, vol. 43, p. 1112.

15. Sen. Alexander Ramsey, *Congressional Globe*, 40th Cong., 1st sess., March 27, 1867, vol. 38, p. 379.

16. Rep. Walter Burleigh, *Congressional Globe*, 39th Cong., 1st sess., June 9, 1866, vol. 36, p. 3056. See also Hyde, *Spotted Tail's Folk*, p. 107; and Utley, *Indian Frontier*, p. 96.

17. Sen. Samuel Pomeroy, *Congressional Globe*, 39th Cong., 1st sess., April 18, 1866, vol. 36, p. 2014.

18. Lawrence Vankoughnet, Department of the Interior memorandum, December 2, 1876, Department of Indian Affairs Central Registry Files, RG 10, National Archives of Canada (hereafter NAC), vol. 3638, file 7253, reel C-10112.

19. See remarks by Sen. James Doolittle, *Congressional Globe*, 39th Cong., 2d sess., January 26, 1867, vol. 37, p. 763; "Report by Commissioner of Indian Affairs" quoted by Sen. John Henderson, *Congressional Globe*, 40th Cong., 1st sess., July 13, 1867, vol. 38, p. 624; and Sen. Samuel Pomeroy, *Congressional Globe*, 40th Cong., 1st sess., July 17, 1867, vol. 38, p. 681.

20. See remarks by Sen. James Doolittle, *Congressional Globe*, 39th Cong., 1st sess., June 30, 1866, vol. 36, p. 3507; and Sen. Samuel Pomeroy, *Congressional Globe*, 39th Cong., 2d sess., February 20, 1867, vol. 37, p. 1624.

21. U.S. Senate, "Report of Gen. N. B. Buford, Special Commissioner, to E. M. Stanton, Secretary of War," *Information Touching the Origin and Progress of Indian Hostilities on Frontier*, 40th Cong., 1st sess., 1868, S. Doc. 13, serial 1308, p. 60; and U.S. Senate, "Report of General John Sanborn, Special Indian Commissioner," *Information Touching the Origin and Progress of Indian Hostilities on Frontier*, 40th Cong., 1st sess., 1868, S. Doc. 13, serial 1308, pp. 66–67.

22. Sen. James Doolittle, *Congressional Globe*, 39th Cong., 2d sess., January 26, 1867, vol. 37, p. 763.

23. Gen. William T. Sherman quoted by Sen. John Henderson, *Congressional Globe*, 40th Cong., 1st sess., July 16, 1867, vol. 38, p. 669; and General Sherman to Senator Sherman, December 30, 1866, *The Sherman Letters*, p. 287.

24. See Sen. John Sherman, *Congressional Globe*, 39th Cong., 1st sess., June 30, 1866, vol. 36, p. 3506.

25. U.S. Department of War, *Report of the Secretary of War* (November 20, 1868), *Congressional Globe*, 40th Cong., 3d sess., 1869, vol. 40, "Appendix,"

p. 10; Sen. John Sherman, *Congressional Globe*, 39th Cong., 1st sess., June 30, 1866, vol. 36, pp. 3506–7.

26. Sen. Thomas Hendricks, *Congressional Globe*, 39th Cong., 1st sess., July 3, 1866, vol. 36, p. 3553.

27. Ellis, "Humanitarian Generals," pp. 172, 175–76.

28. General Pope quoted by Rep. John Kasson, *Congressional Globe*, 39th Cong., 1st sess., July 16, 1866, vol. 36, p. 3846. See also Sen. B. Gratz Brown, *Congressional Globe*, 39th Cong., 2d sess., February 21, 1867, vol. 37, p. 1680.

29. Leighton, "Federal Indian Policy in Canada," p. 289.

30. House of Commons, *Debates*, November 29, 1867, p. 159.

31. "British North America Act," sect. 6, art. 91(24), *Revised Statutes of Canada, 1870—Appendices*, p. 215.

32. Adams Archibald to John A. Macdonald, October 7, 1871, Macdonald Papers, NAC, vol. 187, reel C-1587.

33. Jennings, "North West Mounted Police and Indian Policy," p. 57.

34. See, for example, Alexander Morris to Minister of the Interior, October 24, 1876, General Correspondence, Morris Papers, NAC, reel M-69, p. 3; and memorandum by Charles Houtzky (Horetzky), November 27, 1873, RG 10, NAC, vol. 3605, file 2912, reel RC-10105, pp. 3–4, 10. See also Beal and Macleod, *Prairie Fire*, p. 52.

35. February 2, 1871, in "Report of the Indian Branch of the Department of the Secretary of State," *Sessional Papers*, 1871, no. 23, vol. 5, p. 6; and report by William Spragge, deputy superintendent of Indian Affairs, March 18, 1874, in "Report of the Indian Branch of the Department of the Minister of the Interior," *Sessional Papers*, 1874, no. 17, vol. 6, p. 6.

36. Charles Bell, March 23, 1874, RG 10, NAC, vol. 3609, file 3229, reel C-10106. See also Carter, *Lost Harvests*, p. 51. Treaty 1 negotiations were reported in *The Manitoban*, published at Winnipeg, reprinted in Hall, "'A Serene Atmosphere'?" pp. 126–48. An account of the proceedings at Fort Qu'Appelle, Treaty 4, is F. L. Hunt, "Notes on the Qu'Appelle Treaty." The Toronto *Globe* carried an account of Treaty 7 negotiations, reprinted in Alexander Morris, *Treaties of Canada with the Indians*, pp. 263–75.

37. Adams Archibald to Joseph Howe, July 20, 1871, in "Report of the Indian Branch," *Sessional Papers*, 1872, no. 22, vol. 7, p. 14.

3. THE CONTEXT OF TREATY MAKING

1. See letter from Gen. John Pope to Gen. U. S. Grant, January 25, 1867, in U.S. House of Representatives, *Report of Colonel Parker on Indian Affairs*, 39th Cong., 2d sess., 1867, H. Doc. 37, serial 1302, p. 11; "Indian Movements on the Plains," *The New York Times*, April 9, 1867, p. 5; and "Report of the Sec-

retary of War *ad interim* and General, United States Army, (November, 1867)," *Congressional Globe*, 40th Cong., 2d sess., 1868, vol. 39, "Appendix," p. 14.

2. "Letter from John Evans, Governor of Colorado Territory and Supt. of Indian Affairs, to Commissioner of Indian Affairs," October 15, 1864, in U.S. Department of the Interior, *Report of the Commissioner of Indian Affairs for the Year 1864*, p. 216; and K2 Proclamation by Governor Evans [n.d.], U.S. Department of the Interior, *Report of the Commissioner of Indian Affairs for the Year 1864*, p. 230.

3. The Sand Creek Massacre was the Indian wars' equivalent of the My Lai Massacre during the Vietnam War a century later. It remains a controversial event and the historiography is vast. At least two hundred Cheyenne Indians, most of them women and children, were brutally slain while encamped under both a U.S. flag and a flag of truce. Eastern revulsion stemmed in large part from the extensive and appalling mutilation of the dead. The hundred-day enlistment of the perpetrators ran out before a court-martial could be mustered, and the culprits escaped judgment for their actions. For a succinct account of the massacre, see Berthrong, *Southern Cheyennes*, pp. 195-223. See also Leckie, *Military Conquest of the Southern Plains*, pp. 23-24; and Utley, *Indian Frontier*, pp. 92-93.

4. Berthrong, *Southern Cheyennes*, p. 224.

5. Utley, *Indian Frontier*, p. 96.

6. Utley, *Indian Frontier*, p. 97.

7. Robert Utley, *Frontiersmen in Blue*, pp. 336, 337 n.63.

8. This exact phrase was repeated frequently in Congress. See, for example, remarks by Sen. Samuel Pomeroy, *Congressional Globe*, 40th Cong., 1st sess., July 18, 1867, vol. 38, p. 709; Rep. Benjamin Butler, 40th Cong., 3d sess., January 28, 1869, vol. 40, p. 683; and Rep. Aaron Sargent, 41st Cong., 2d sess., February 25, 1870, vol. 42, p. 1576.

9. See Rep. Benjamin Butler, *Congressional Globe*, 40th Cong., 3d sess., January 28, 1869, vol. 40, p. 683; Sen. William Stewart, 41st Cong., 2d sess., June 2, 1870, vol. 42, p. 4005; and Rep. Sargent, 41st Cong., 2d sess., March 2, 1870, vol. 42 p. 1639.

10. Sen. Samuel Pomeroy, *Congressional Globe*, 40th Cong., 1st sess., July 18, 1867, vol. 38, p. 709.

11. Joint Committee on the Conduct of the War, *Massacre of the Cheyenne Indians*, 38th Cong., 2d sess., 1865, S. Rept. 142, serial 1214; U.S. Senate, *Proceedings of a Military Commission convened by Special Orders No. 23 . . . in the case of Colonel J. M. Chivington*, 1867, S. Doc. 26, serial 1277; U.S. Senate, *The Chivington Massacre*, 1867, S. Rept. 156, serial 1279, pp. 26-98; and U.S. Senate, *Information Touching the Origin and Progress of Indian Hostilities*, 40th Cong., 1st sess., 1868, S. Doc. 13, serial, 1308.

12. "Governor and Superintendent of Indian Affairs Newton Edmunds to

William P. Dole," September 20, 1864, in U.S. Department of the Interior, *Report of the Commissioner of Indian Affairs for the Year 1864*, p. 260.

13. Sen. John Sherman queried this maneuver in the Senate and elicited an explanation from Sen. James Doolittle, *Congressional Globe*, 39th Cong., 1st sess., April 18, 1866, vol. 36, p. 2012.

14. Gen. John Pope to Gen. W. T. Sherman, August 11, 1866, in U.S. Department of War, *Annual Report of the Secretary of War*, 1866, p.23.

15. Hyde, *Spotted Tail's Folk*, p. 107; Larson, *Red Cloud*, p. 88.

16. Grinnell, *The Fighting Cheyennes*, pp. 245–46.

17. Hagan, *United States-Comanche Relations*, p. 21; Leckie, *Military Conquest of the Southern Plains*, p. 26.

18. "Report of the Secretary of War *ad interim* and General United States Army, November, 1867," *Congressional Globe*, 40th Cong., 2d sess., 1868, "Appendix," p. 14; "Indian Outrages and Indian Wrongs," *The New York Times*, April 28, 1867, p. 4. See also Hagan, *United States-Comanche Relations*, p. 2.

19. Chaput, "Generals, Indian Agents, Politicians," pp. 271–72.

20. Report of the Joint Special Committee, *Condition of the Indian Tribes*, 39th Cong., 2d sess., 1867, S. Rept. 156, serial 1279, pp. 3–4, 5, 6.

21. U.S. Senate, *Information Touching the Origin and Progress of Indian Hostilities*, 40th Cong., 1st sess., 1868, S. Doc. 13, serial, 1308, pp. 66–67.

22. In 1867, under the restrictions of the Radical Republicans' Reconstruction program, representatives from former Confederate states in the South did not sit in Congress. Thus the battle over Indian policy, between humanitarian and exterminationist, was a sectional battle fought between the Northeast and the West without a southern voice.

23. *Proceedings of the Great Peace Commission*, pp. 10–28.

24. The first invocation of this image was by Puritan leader John Winthrop in a speech delivered on the *Arbella* just before landing in Massachusetts in 1630. John Winthrop, "A Model of Christian Charity," in Heimert and Delbanco, *Puritans in America*, p. 91.

25. Sen. Willard Warner, *Congressional Globe*, 40th Cong., 3d sess., December 10, 1868, vol. 40, p. 42.

26. Mardock, *Reformers and the American Indian*, p. 5.

27. Rep. Walter Burleigh, *Congressional Globe*, 40th Cong., 2d sess., July 21, 1868, vol. 39, "Appendix," p. 461.

28. See for example Sen. John Henderson, 40th Cong., 1st sess., July 16, 1867, vol. 38, p. 669; and Sen. James Doolittle, *Congressional Globe*, 40th Cong., 2d sess., July 16, 1868, vol. 39, p. 4116; U.S. House, *Report of Colonel Parker*, H. Doc. 37, p. 5.

29. Sen. Reverdy Johnson, *Congressional Globe*, 40th Cong., 1st sess., July 18, 1867, vol. 38, p. 715.

30. Sen. John Henderson, *Congressional Globe*, 40th Cong., 1st sess., July 16, 1867, vol. 38, pp. 667–68.

31. "Our Indian Troubles—How to Meet Them," *The New York Times*, July 19, 1867, p. 4.

32. General Sherman, who as Commander of the Department of the Missouri in 1867 was in a position to know as well or better than Senator Henderson, disputed these figures in private correspondence. Letter from General Sherman to Senator Sherman, July 15, 1867, *The Sherman Letters*, p. 291.

33. See, for example, Sen. James Doolittle, *Congressional Globe*, 40th Cong., 2d sess., July 16, 1868, vol. 39, p. 4116; Rep. Walter Burleigh, *Congressional Globe*, 40th Cong., 3d sess., February 27, 1869, vol. 40, p. 1702; and "Extract from the Report of the Secretary of the Interior Relative to the Report of the Commissioner of Indian Affairs for 1865," in Department of the Interior, *Report of the Commissioner of Indian Affairs for 1865*, p. iii.

34. Rep. Walter Burleigh, *Congressional Globe*, 40th Cong., 2d sess., July 21, 1868, vol. 39, "Appendix," p. 461.

35. Utley, *Indian Frontier*, p. 109.

36. William Henry Chipman, *Debates of the House of Commons*, 1st Parliament, 1st sess., December 4, 1867, p. 187. A Liberal member of Parliament representing the constituency of King's, Nova Scotia, Mr. Chipman had been among those who had opposed Confederation.

37. James A. Grant, House of Commons, *Debates*, May 28 1869, p. 498.

38. S. J. Dawson, "Report on the Line of Route between Lake Superior and the Red River Settlement," *Sessional Papers*, 1869, no. 42, vol. 5, pp. 20–21.

39. Mawedopenais quoted in Morris, *Treaties of Canada with the Indians*, p.62. Emphasis in the original.

40. Adams Archibald to Joseph Howe, July 19, 1871, *Sessional Papers*, 1872, no. 22, vol. 7, p. 10.

41. Sweetgrass to Adams Archibald, 1871, in Morris, *Treaties of Canada with the Indians*, pp. 170–71.

42. Morris, *Treaties of Canada with the Indians*, p. 106.

43. See G. McMicken to Sir John A. Macdonald, June 22, 1872, Macdonald Papers, NAC, vol. 246, reel C-1670; petitions from Sweetgrass, Kihewin, and Kis-ki-on, 1871, in Morris, *Treaties of Canada with the Indians*, pp. 170–71; and James Seenum to Alexander Morris, June 7, 1876, RG 10, NAC, vol. 3632, file 6352, reel C-10111. On the obstruction of the telegraph line and geological survey see G. A. French, NWMP, to the Minister of Justice, August 6, 1875, RG 10, NAC, vol. 3624, file 5152, reel C-10109.

44. Report from Indian Commissioner J. A. N. Provencher to the minister of the interior, December 31, 1873, in "Report of the Deputy Superintendent General of Indian Affairs," *Sessional Papers*, 1875, no. 8, vol. 7, p. 56.

45. See for example Sen. James Doolittle, *Congressional Globe*, 39th Cong., 1st sess., April 18, 1866, vol. 36, p. 2014; Sen. James Harlan, *Congressional Globe*, 41st Cong., 1st sess., April 1, 1869, vol. 41, pp. 421-22; and Sen. Lot M. Morrill of Maine, *Congressional Globe*, 41st Cong., 2d sess., July 2, 1870, vol. 42, p. 5111.

46. Morris, *Treaties of Canada with the Indians*, pp. 331 (Treaty 4), 344 (Treaty 5), 352 (Treaty 6), and 369 (Treaty 7).

47. Kappler, *Indian Treaties*, pp. 980 (Kiowa and Comanche Treaty), 988 (Cheyenne and Arapaho Treaty), 1002 (Sioux Treaty), and 1012 (Northern Cheyenne and Northern Arapaho Treaty). Emphasis added.

48. See, for example, the 1871 messages of the Cree chiefs of the plains to Lieutenant Governor Archibald in Morris, *Treaties of Canada with the Indians*, pp. 170-71; the extensive list of demands presented to the commissioners during the Treaty 1 negotiations, discussed in Hall, "'A Serene Atmosphere'?" p. 117; and the list of terms presented to Morris by the Plains Cree at Fort Carlton in Morris, *Treaties of Canada with the Indians*, p. 215.

49. Petition from Sweetgrass, in Morris, *Treaties of Canada with the Indians*, pp. 170-71.

50. Copy of memorandum of "Outside Promises" signed by Adams Archibald, James McKay, W. M. Simpson, and Molyneux St. John, August 3, 1871, RG 10, NAC, vol. 3571, file 124 (pt. 2), reel C-10101.

51. Morris, *Treaties of Canada with the Indians*, p. 70.

52. William McDougall, House of Commons, *Debates*, December 4, 1867, p. 181.

53. Leighton, "Federal Indian Policy in Canada," pp. 115, 208; Tobias, "Protection, Civilization, Assimilation," pp. 132-33.

54. "Report of the Department of the Interior for 1875," *Sessional Papers*, 1876, no. 9, vol. 7, p. xiii.

55. Alexander Morris to the secretary of state, July 11, 1876, Morris Papers, NAC, reel M-69, p. 2.

56. Morris to secretary of state, July 11, 1876, p. 4.

57. Dempsey, *Red Crow*, p. 114.

58. Tough, *"As Their Natural Resources Fail,"* p. 89.

59. "Report of the Department of the Interior for 1875," p. viii.

60. Miller, *Skyscrapers Hide the Heavens*, p. 162.

61. Alexander Mackenzie to Alexander Morris, December 6, 26, 1873, Morris Papers, NAC, vol. 541, reel M-70.

4. MEDICINE LODGE, FORT LARAMIE, AND NUMBERED TREATIES

1. "An Act to establish Peace with certain Hostile Indian Tribes," *Congressional Globe*, 40th Cong., 1st sess., July 19, 1867, vol. 38, "Appendix," pp. 44-45.

2. Rep. Aaron Sargent, *Congressional Globe*, 41st Cong., 2d sess., July 14, 1870, vol. 42, p. 5608.

3. "An Act to establish Peace . . . ," *Congressional Globe*, 40th Cong., 1st sess., vol. 38, "Appendix," p. 44.

4. "Report by the Indian Peace Commission," January 7, 1868, in U.S. Department of the Interior, *Annual Report of the Commissioner of Indian Affairs for 1868*, p. 27.

5. See, for example, Rep. Cavanaugh, *Congressional Globe*, 41st Cong., 2d sess., March 2, 1870, vol. 42, p. 1644; and Rep. James Beck, 41st Cong., 3d sess., January 26, 1871, vol. 43, p. 765.

6. Instructions from Joseph Howe, secretary of state, to W. M. Simpson, S. J. Dawson, and Robert Pither, May 6, 1871, in "Report of the Indian Branch," *Sessional Papers*, 1872, no. 22, vol. 7, p.6. About the amount of annuities to be offered in Treaty 3, see also Alexander Campbell to Alexander Morris, July 31, August 5, and August 14, 1873, Morris Papers, NAC, vol. 528, reel M-70. For Treaty 4 instructions, see Minute 1332, November 4, 1874, Privy Council Minutes, RG 2, NAC, ser. 1, vol. 101, reel C-3310.

7. Howe to Simpson, Dawson, and Pither, May 6, 1871, *Sessional Papers*, 1872, no. 22, vol. 7, p. 6.

8. Memorandum from Alexander Campbell, Minute 962, 1873, Privy Council Minutes, RG 2, NAC, ser. 1, vol. 83, reel C-3303.

9. Alexander Campbell to Alexander Morris, October 28, 1873, Morris Papers, NAC, vol. 528, reel M-70, p. 2.

10. See Campbell to Morris, October 28, 1873, p. 2. By the same terms, disapproval was expressed when the commissioners failed to make terms acceptable to the tight-fisted government. See Department of the Interior memorandum, February 12, 1877; and Minister of the Interior David Mills (unsigned) to Alexander Morris, March 1, 1877, RG 10, NAC, vol. 3636, file 6694–2, reel C-10111.

11. Alexander Mackenzie to Alexander Morris, December 6, 26, 1873, Morris Papers, NAC, vol. 541, reel M-70, p. 1; David Laird to Alexander Morris, May 29, 1874, Morris Papers, vol. 535, reel M-70.

12. David Laird to Alexander Morris, July 15, 1876, RG 10, NAC, vol. 3636, file 6694–1, reel C-10111.

13. David Laird to Alexander Morris, April 27, 1875, Morris Papers, NAC, reel M-70; David Laird (unsigned) to Morris, July 7, 1875, RG 10, NAC, vol. 3621, file 4767, reel C-10108.

14. See "Copy of a Report of a Committee of the Honourable the Privy Council," February 10, 1877; Department of the Interior memorandum by the minister of the interior, January 31, 1877; Department of the Interior memorandum by L. Vankoughnet, February 12, 1877; and David Mills (unsigned) to

Alexander Morris, March 1, 1877. For responses to the criticism contained in these three documents, see Alexander Morris to the minister of the interior, March 27, 1877, and James McKay to Alexander Morris, March 28, 1877, RG 10, NAC, vol. 3636, file 6694–2, reel C-10111.

15. Alexander Morris to David Mills, minister of the interior, March 27, 1877, Morris Papers, NAC, reel M-69, p. 5.

16. For example, see remarks by Sen. Lot M. Morrill, *Congressional Globe*, 41st Cong., 2d sess., July 2, 1870, vol. 42, p. 5112; and Rep. James A. Garfield, *Congressional Globe*, 41st Cong., 2d sess., July 14, 1870, vol. 42, p. 5607, and July 15, 1870, p. 5638. See also Secretary of the Interior J. D. Cox to Pres. Ulysses S. Grant, March 7, 1870, in U.S. Senate, *President's Message on Appropriations to Carry Out Indian Treaties made by Peace Commission*, 41st Cong., 2d sess., 1870, S. Doc. 57, serial 1406, p. 5.

17. "An Act to establish Peace . . . ," p. 44.

18. "Samuel Tappan," in Thrapp, *Encyclopedia of Frontier Biography*, 3:1401–02; Bailey, *Pacifying the Plains*, p. 30.

19. See account of the final meeting of the commission, in *Proceedings of the Great Peace Commission*, pp. 158–60.

20. For an example of some of Sen. John Sherman's remarks on this subject, see *Congressional Globe*, 39th Cong., 1st sess., April 18, 1866, vol. 36, pp. 2010, 2013.

21. "Christopher Augur," in Thrapp, *Encyclopedia of Frontier Biography*, 1:44; "William Harney," 2:618; and "Alfred Terry," 3:1410–11.

22. Bailey, *Pacifying the Plains*, p. 31.

23. Molyneux St. John to William Spragge, February 24, 1873, RG 10, NAC, vol. 3598, file 1447, reel C-10104

24. Leighton, "Federal Indian Policy in Canada," p. 288.

25. Negotiations were the responsibility of the main treaty commissioners, but a number of other men secured adhesions to the treaties from Indians either not present or not willing to sign at the time of negotiations. These men included J. Lestock Reid (Treaty 4), Thomas Howard (Treaties 3 and 5), and M. G. Dickieson (Treaties 4 and 6).

26. S. J. Dawson, "Report on the Line of Route," *Sessional Papers*, 1869, no. 42, vol. 5, p. 20.

27. Irene Spry, "William Christie," in *Dictionary of Canadian Biography*, 12:194.

28. Morris, *Treaties of Canada with the Indians*, p. 273.

29. For example, see Adams Archibald to the secretary of state, July 19, 1871, *Sessional Papers*, 1872, no. 22, vol. 7, p. 10; and Alexander Morris to the minister of the interior, February 18, 1876, Morris Papers, NAC, reel M-69, pp. 4–6.

30. Adams Archibald to Joseph Howe, secretary of state, February 12, 1872, in "Copies of all Communications to Indians or others in Manitoba . . . ," *Sessional Papers*, 1873, no. 23, vol. 5, p. 2; Alexander Morris to Sir John A. Macdonald, October 26, 1872, Macdonald Papers, NAC, vol. 252, reel C-1673.

31. At a meeting with the Brulé Sioux on September 19, 1867, General Sherman issued a general invitation to any of the assembled Indians to make such a trip for this purpose. *Proceedings of the Great Peace Commission*, p. 62.

32. Taylor, "Indian Policy for the North-West," p. 79.

33. Parrish, "Indian Peace Commission of 1867," p. 36.

34. Dempsey, *Crowfoot*, pp. 93–94.

35. Mistawasis to Alexander Morris, January 16, 1875, and Alexander Morris to the Secretary of State, February 22, 1875, RG 10, NAC, vol. 3616, file 4490, reel C-10107, p. 3.

36. Alexander Morris to Sir John A. Macdonald, November 4, 1875, Macdonald Papers, NAC, vol. 252A, reel C-1673; Alexander Morris to Alexander Mackenzie, January 22, 1877, Mackenzie Papers, NAC, reel M-199.

37. Utley, *Indian Frontier*, p. 116.

38. "Report of the Indian Peace Commission," January 7, 1868, in U.S. Department of the Interior, *Annual Report of the Commissioner of Indian Affairs for the Year 1868*, p. 29.

39. See Sen. James Doolittle, *Congressional Record*, 39th Cong., 1st sess., April 18, 1866, vol. 36, p. 2014; and Rep. J. Francesco Chaves, 39th Cong., 2d sess., February 19, 1866, vol. 35, p. 1344.

40. For example, see Alexander Campbell to Alexander Morris, August 14, 1873, Morris Papers, NAC, reel M-70, p. 3; Alexander Morris to minister of the interior, September 20, 1873, Morris Papers, NAC, reel M-70; and Department of the Interior memorandum from E. A. Meredith, August 24, 1875, RG 10, NAC, vol. 3624, file 5152, reel C-10109.

41. Wemyss Simpson to William Spragge, deputy superintendent of Indian Affairs, September 27, 1872, RG 10, NAC, vol. 3576, file 378, reel C-10101.

5. THE ROLE OF "OTHERS"

1. Robert Utley, quoted in Jones, *Treaty of Medicine Lodge*, p. 104.

2. "Charles Bent" and "George Bent," Thrapp, *Encyclopedia of Frontier Biography*, 1:96–98; "Edmund Guerrier," 2:596–97; and "John Simpson Smith," 3:1333.

3. Douglas Jones discusses the problem of Kiowa interpretation in some detail but found no evidence to prove that any of the interpreters spoke the language. Jones, *Treaty of Medicine Lodge*, p. 106. Entries in the *Encyclopedia of Frontier Biography* on Comanche interpreter Philip McCusker and Arapaho interpreter Mrs. Fitzpatrick (Adams) make firmer assertions as to their fluency in Kiowa, but the evidence is not conclusive. "Mrs. Margaret Fitzpatrick," in

Thrapp, *Encyclopedia of Frontier Biography*, 1:495; and "Philip McCusker," 2:896.

4. "Philip McCusker," in Thrapp, *Encyclopedia of Frontier Biography*, 2:896-97.

5. Satanta, quoted in *Proceedings of the Great Peace Commission*, p. 69.

6. Satanta, quoted in *Proceedings of the Great Peace Commission*, p. 74.

7. "Joseph Bissonette," in Thrapp, *Encyclopedia of Frontier Biography*, 1:117; "Antoine Janis" and "Nicholas Janis," 2:722; and "Leon Pallarday," 3:1104. The other interpreters listed were Charles E. Guern, Lefroy Jott, and Franc. Laframboise.

8. For remarks by various Sioux spokesmen, see *Proceedings of the Great Peace Commission*, pp. 33, 64, 111, 119-20, 137-38.

9. For examples of Senator Henderson's speeches, see *Proceedings of the Great Peace Commission*, pp. 69, 73, 80.

10. See remarks by General Sanborn, *Proceedings of the Great Peace Commission*, pp. 101, 106-7, 116, 136-37.

11. "Account of Red Cloud Signing the Treaty," November 20, 1868, *Proceedings of the Great Peace Commission*, pp. 173-74.

12. *The Manitoban*, cited in Hall, "'A Serene Atmosphere'?" p. 127.

13. Frits Pannekoek, "Charles Pratt," in *Dictionary of Canadian Biography*, 11:712.

14. Morris, *Treaties of Canada with the Indians*, p. 158.

15. Memorandum of August 3, 1871, RG 10, NAC, vol. 3571, file 124 (pt. 2), reel C-10101.

16. Morris, *Treaties of Canada with the Indians*, p. 140.

17. Morris, *Treaties of Canada with the Indians*, p. 48.

18. Erasmus, *Buffalo Days and Nights*, p. 241.

19. Morris, *Treaties of Canada with the Indians*, p. 178.

20. Chief Mistawasis quoted in Erasmus, *Buffalo Days and Nights*, p. 238.

21. Morris, *Treaties of Canada with the Indians*, p. 196.

22. David Laird, ["Dispatch"], in Morris, *Treaties of Canada with the Indians*, p. 261.

23. Laird, ["Dispatch"], in Morris, *Treaties of Canada with the Indians*, p. 261. See also Dempsey, *Crowfoot*, p. 83 n. 8.

24. Laird, ["Dispatch"], in Morris, *Treaties of Canada with the Indians*, p. 256.

25. Laird, ["Dispatch"], in Morris, *Treaties of Canada with the Indians*, p. 262.

26. Laird, ["Dispatch"], in Morris, *Treaties of Canada with the Indians*, pp. 267-69, 271.

27. For remarks by various Blackfoot leaders, see Morris, *Treaties of Canada with the Indians*, pp. 270-73.

28. Grant, *Moon of Wintertime*, p. 149.

29. Gerald M. Hutchinson, "James Evans," in *Dictionary of Canadian Biography*, 7:277.

30. Choquette, *The Oblate Assault*, p. 37.

31. Hall, "'A Serene Atmosphere'?" p. 149, n. 4, n. 5.

32. *The Manitoban*, in Hall, "'A Serene Atmosphere'?" p. 147.

33. *The Manitoban*, in Hall, "'A Serene Atmosphere'?" p. 148.

34. Tough, *"As Their Natural Resources Fail,"* p. 93.

35. Molyneux St. John to William Spragge, February 24, 1873, RG 10, NAC, vol. 3598, file 1447, reel C-10104.

36. Morris, *Treaties of Canada with the Indians*, pp. 158, 164.

37. Wemyss Simpson to William Spragge, September 27, 1872, RG 10, NAC, vol. 3576, file 378, reel C-10101.

38. See Alexander Morris to Alexander Campbell, minister of the interior, August 4, 1873, Morris Papers, NAC, reel M-70, no. 48N, pp. 1–2; George McDougall to Alexander Morris, October 23, 1875, RG 10, NAC, vol. 3624, file 5152, reel C-10109; and Alexander Morris to minister of the interior, October 24, 1876, Morris Papers, NAC, reel M-69, p. 2.

39. McDougall to Morris, October 23, 1875.

40. Morris to minister of the interior, October 24, 1876, p. 4.

41. "Report of Rev. George McDougall in *Wesleyan Missionary Notices*" (vol. 23, pp. 357–58), May 1874, RG- 0, NAC, vol. 3609, file 3229, reel C-10106; George McDougall to the Honourable D. A. Smith, January 8, 1874, RG 10, NAC, vol. 3609, file 3278, reel C-10106.

42. Dempsey, *Red Crow*, pp. 110–11.

43. Alexander Morris to Alexander Mackenzie, August 20, 1875, Morris Papers, NAC, vol. 553, reel M-70, pp. 3–4.

44. Morris, *Treaties of Canada with the Indians*, p. 175.

45. "Bishop Henry Whipple," in Thrapp, *Encyclopedia of Frontier Biography*, 3:1547.

46. Mattison, "Indian Missions and Missionaries," p. 145.

47. Joseph Schafer, "Pierre-Jean De Smet," in Johnson and Malone, *Dictionary of American Biography*, 3:256. See also *Proceedings of the Great Peace Commission*, p. 1.

48. *Proceedings of the Great Peace Commission*, p. 10.

49. *Proceedings of the Great Peace Commission*, p. 31. See also Jones, *Treaty of Medicine Lodge*, pp. 49, 74–75, 76.

50. Prucha, *American Indian Policy in Crisis*, pp. 31–32, 48, 52.

51. *Proceedings of the Great Peace Commission*, p. 30.

52. Jones, *Treaty of Medicine Lodge*, pp. 38–39.

53. Jones, *Treaty of Medicine Lodge*, p. 80.

54. References to the assistance provided by the Hudson's Bay Company

are numerous. For example, see Joseph Howe to Simpson, Dawson, and Pither, May 6, 1871, *Sessional Papers*, 1872, no. 22, vol. 7, p. 6; Simpson to Howe, November 3, 1871, in Morris, *Treaties of Canada with the Indians*, p. 43; and the numerous acknowledgments by Morris himself, in Morris, *Treaties of Canada with the Indians*, pp. 83, 151, 152, 181, 196.

55. Wemyss Simpson, November 3, 1871, in "Report of the Indian Branch," *Sessional Papers*, 1872, no. 22, vol. 7, p. 28; Morris, *Treaties of Canada with the Indians*, p. 52.

56. Alexander Morris to Sir John A. Macdonald, September 22, 1873, Macdonald Papers, NAC, vol. 252A, reel C-1673.

57. Alexander Morris to Sir John A. Macdonald, September 20, 1873, Macdonald Papers, NAC, vol. 252A, reel C-1673.

58. Colonel Robertson-Ross to minister of the militia and defense, August 12, 1873, Minute 1051(b), Privy Council Minutes, RG 2, NAC, ser. 1, vol. 83, reel C-3305.

59. Morris, *Treaties of Canada with the Indians*, p. 82.

60. Erasmus, *Buffalo Days and Nights*, p. 239.

61. Erasmus, *Buffalo Days and Nights*, p. 248.

62. Laird, ["Dispatch"], in Morris, *Treaties of Canada with the Indians*, p. 262.

63. Mardock, *Reformers and the American Indian*, pp. 34–35; and Jones, *Treaty of Medicine Lodge*, p. 133.

64. The only woman interpreter noted in any accounts was Mrs. Margaret Fitzpatrick Adams, who translated for the Arapaho at Medicine Lodge. See Jones, *Treaty of Medicine Lodge*, pp. 107–8; and "Mrs. Margaret Fitzpatrick," in Thrapp, *Encyclopedia of Frontier Biography*, 1:496.

65. *Proceedings of the Great Peace Commission*, p. 115.

66. General Sanborn quoted in *Proceedings of the Great Peace Commission*, p. 116.

67. Wemyss Simpson quoted in Morris, *Treaties of Canada with the Indians*, p. 41.

68. Morris, *Treaties of Canada with the Indians*, pp. 69, 123, 222.

69. Morris, *Treaties of Canada with the Indians*, p. 222.

70. Morris, *Treaties of Canada with the Indians*, p. 195.

71. Adams Archibald to Sir John A. Macdonald, December 6, 1870, Macdonald Papers, NAC, vol. 187, reel C-1587.

72. See remarks by Wemyss Simpson and Alexander Morris in Morris, *Treaties of Canada with the Indians*, pp. 43, 138, 148, 152, 195.

73. Morris, *Treaties of Canada with the Indians*, p. 74.

74. Morris, *Treaties of Canada with the Indians*, p. 69.

75. David T. McNab, "Nicholas Chatelain," in *Dictionary of Canadian Biography*, 12:187.

76. Morris, *Treaties of Canada with the Indians*, p. 51.

77. Friesen, "Magnificent Gifts," p. 47.

78. The Earl of Dufferin quoted in Morris, *Treaties of Canada with the Indians*, p. 294.

6. RESERVES

1. Dickason, *Canada's First Nations*, p. 233; Trennert, *Alternative to Extinction*, p. 3.

2. Trennert, *Alternative to Extinction*, p. 2.

3. Francis Bond Head, "Memorandum on the Aborigines of North America," November 20, 1836, in *The Native Imprint*, vol. 2, pp. 4–5, 10.

4. Miller, *Skyscrapers Hide the Heavens*, pp. 103–4.

5. Carter, *Lost Harvests*, p. 24; Tobias, "Protection, Civilization, Assimilation," pp. 129–30.

6. Prucha, *The Great Father*, 1:348; Priest, *Uncle Sam's Stepchildren*, pp. 177–78.

7. Prucha, *The Great Father*, 1:325.

8. Trennert, *Alternative to Extinction*, p. 195; Tobias, "Protection, Civilization, Assimilation," p. 131.

9. Carter, *Lost Harvests*, p. 24; and Tobias, "Protection, Civilization, Assimilation," pp. 131 and 133.

10. Tobias, "Protection, Civilization, Assimilation," p. 133.

11. Miles, "The Indian Problem," p. 42. See also Carter, *Lost Harvests*, pp. 18, 24.

12. For example, see remarks by General Sanborn at Fort Rice, July 2, 1868, *Proceedings of the Great Peace Commission*, p. 135.

13. Morris, *Treaties of Canada with the Indians*, pp. 314 (Treaty 1), 318 (Treaty 2), 322 (Treaty 3), 331 (Treaty 4), 344 (Treaty 5), 352 (Treaty 6), 369 (Treaty 7).

14. See comparative maps of reservation size in White-Harvey, "Reservation Geography," pp. 593, 594.

15. See article 2 of each of the treaties with the Kiowa and Comanche, the Cheyenne and Arapaho, and the Sioux for the lands reserved to these peoples, and Article 2 of the Treaty with the Northern Cheyenne and Northern Arapaho for the provisions requiring them to choose a reservation on the lands allotted to the other nations. Kappler, *Indian Treaties*, pp. 977–78, 985, 998–99, 1012–13.

16. See remarks by Secretary of the Interior J. D. Cox quoted in Prucha, *American Indian Policy in Crisis*, p. 103.

17. Treaties 1, 2, and 5 allowed for only 160 acres per family of five. In Treaties 3, 4, 6, and 7, 640 acres per family of five was the basis of the calculation.

18. Adams Archibald quoted in *The Manitoban*, reprinted in Hall, "'A Serene Atmosphere'?" p. 129.

19. McKay, "Fighting for Survival," pp. 76–77; Tough, *"As Their Natural Resources Fail,"* p. 91.

20. Report by William Spragge, deputy superintendent of Indian Affairs, July 27, 1872, RG 10, NAC, vol. 724, reel C-13413, pp. 43–48. See also Stanley, *Birth of Western Canada*, p. 210.

21. Morris, *Treaties of Canada with the Indians*, p. 288.

22. Article 13 of the Gradual Enfranchisement Act, in De Brou and Waiser, *Documenting Canada*, p. 28.

23. Article 94 of the Indian Act, 1876, in De Brou and Waiser, *Documenting Canada*, p. 102.

24. See remarks by Adams Archibald in *The Manitoban*, reprinted in Hall, "'A Serene Atmosphere'?" pp. 128–29.

25. Morris, *Treaties of Canada with the Indians*, pp. 29, 287.

26. Morris, *Treaties of Canada with the Indians*, p. 205.

27. Hagan, "The Reservation Policy," p. 164; Hagan, *United States-Comanche Relations*, p. 7; Prucha, *Indians in American Society*, p. 46.

28. "An Act to establish Peace with certain Hostile Indian Tribes," *Congressional Globe*, 40th Cong., 1st sess., July 19, 1867, vol. 38, "Appendix," p. 44.

29. Utley, *Indian Frontier*, p. 116.

30. Article 16 of Treaty with the Sioux, in Kappler, *Indian Treaties*, pp. 1002–3.

31. See remarks by Sen. James Harlan, *Congressional Globe*, 40th Cong., 1st sess., July 17, 1867, vol. 38, p. 678; and July 18, 1867, p. 713.

32. Jones, *Treaty of Medicine Lodge*, p. 145.

33. Utley, *Last Days of the Sioux*, p. 41.

34. Treaties 1, 2, 5, and 7 included general designations of areas where reserves would be established. See text of treaties in Morris, *Treaties of Canada with the Indians*, pp. 315, 318–19, 344–45, 369–70. Reserves in Treaties 3, 4, and 6 were to be laid out "after conference with the Indians." See Morris, *Treaties of Canada with the Indians*, pp. 322, 331, 353.

35. Carter, *Lost Harvests*, p. 60.

36. Alexander Morris to the minister of the interior, January 19, 1877, pp. 1–2; Morris to the minister of the interior and the secretary of state, February 19, 1877, Morris Papers, NAC, reel M-69.

37. Carter, *Lost Harvests*, p. 60.

38. See remarks by Sen. John Sherman, *Congressional Globe*, 40th Cong., 1st sess., July 17, 1867, vol. 38, p. 680; and by Sen. Timothy Howe, 40th Cong., 1st sess., July 17, 1867, vol. 38, p. 682.

39. Rep. Benjamin Butler, *Congressional Globe*, 40th Cong., 3d sess., February 27, 1869, vol. 40, p. 1699.

40. David Mills, minister of the interior, to David Laird, lieutenant governor of the Northwest Territory, August 1, 1877, RG 10, NAC, vol. 3650, file 8347, reel C-10114.

41. See remarks by Sen. James Harlan, *Congressional Globe*, 40th Cong., 1st sess., July 17, 1867, vol. 38, p. 678; and Sen. Jacob Howard, *Congressional Globe*, 40th Cong., 1st sess., July 17, 1867, vol. 38, p. 684.

42. E. A. Meredith, deputy of the minister of the interior, to J. A. N. Provencher, acting Indian superintendent, July 6, 1876, RG 10, NAC, vol. 3677, file 11 528, reel C-10119.

43. Beal and Macleod, *Prairie Fire*, p. 57.

44. Tobias, "Subjugation of the Plains Cree," pp. 156, 157, 159.

45. Dempsey, *Crowfoot*, pp. 104, 110.

46. Morris, *Treaties of Canada with the Indians*, p. 288.

47. Morris, *Treaties of Canada with the Indians*, p. 288.

48. Carter, *Lost Harvests*, pp. 209–10.

49. "The Indian Peace Commission," *The New York Times*, October 16, 1867, p. 4; and "Indian Peace Treaties," October 29, 1867, p. 4.

50. Prucha, *The Great Father*, 1: 493. Emphasis added.

51. White-Harvey, "Reservation Geography," p. 587.

7. CIVILIZATION

1. Miller, *Shingwauk's Vision*, p. 39; Miller, *Skyscrapers Hide the Heavens*, pp. 33–34.

2. Leighton, "Federal Indian Policy in Canada," p. iii; and Taylor, "Indian Policy for the Canadian North-West," p. 20.

3. Prucha, *The Great Father*, 1:11.

4. Miller, *Skyscrapers Hide the Heavens*, p. 104.

5. Carter, *Lost Harvests*, p. 23; and Samek, *Blackfoot Confederacy*, p. 17.

6. Leighton, "Federal Indian Policy in Canada," pp. 48, 81, 87.

7. Miller, *Shingwauk's Vision*, pp. 81, 84.

8. Mattison, "Indian Missions and Missionaries," p. 128.

9. Nichols, *Indians in the United States and Canada*, p. 201.

10. The United States first offered agricultural assistance in the form of equipment, cattle, and instruction in the Treaty with the Chippewa of 1820 (Kappler, *Indian Treaties*, p. 186). In the 1822 Treaty with the Osage, both agricultural aid and a teacher were promised (Kappler, *Indian Treaties*, p. 200). A later treaty with the Osage in 1825 extended these provisions and added a further clause assisting the missionary settlement among them, "so long as said Missions shall be usefully employed in teaching, civilizing, and improving the said Indians." (Kappler, *Indian Treaties*, p. 220). Except for some peace and friendship treaties in addition to those strictly focused on removal, most

U.S. Indian treaties after 1825 included provisions of some sort for education and agriculture.

11. Report of the Joint Special Committee, *Condition of the Indian Tribes*, 39th Cong., 2d sess., 1867, S. Rept.156, serial 1279, pp. 3–4, 5, 6. See also Chaput, "Generals, Indian Agents, Politicians," p. 274.

12. For example, see the memorandum from Charles Houtzky (Horetzky), November 27, 1873, RG 10, NAC, vol. 3605, file 2912, reel C-10105, pp. 3–4, 10; and extract from Reverend George McDougall [to Minister of the Interior David Laird], January 7, 1874, Laird Papers, NAC, MG27 I D 10.

13. "Report by William Spragge," *Sessional Papers*, 1874, no. 17, vol. 6, p. 6.

14. For example, see Sen. Jacob Howard, *Congressional Globe*, 40th Cong., 1st sess., July 17, 1867, vol. 38, p. 684.

15. "Report of the Indian Peace Commission, January 7, 1868," in U.S. Department of the Interior, *Annual Report of the Commissioner of Indian Affairs for the Year 1868*, p. 32.

16. Sen. Reverdy Johnson, *Congressional Globe*, 40th Cong., 1st sess., July 18, 1867, vol. 38, p. 715.

17. See William McDougall, House of Commons, *Debates*, December 6, 1867, p. 203; May 28, 1869, p. 487; and Charles Connell, May 28, 1869, p. 503.

18. Sen. Samuel Pomeroy, *Congressional Globe*, 40th Cong., 1st sess., July 17, 1867, vol. 38, p. 681.

19. *Report of the Commissioner of Indian Affairs for the Year 1868*, p. 11. See also Taylor, "Indian Policy for the Canadian North-West," p. 20; Carter, *Lost Harvests*, p. 23.

20. Samek, *Blackfoot Confederacy*, p. 25.

21. General Pope to General Sherman, August 11, 1866, in U.S. Department of War, *Report of the Secretary of War for 1866*, 39th Cong., 2d sess., 1867, "Appendix," p. 23.

22. Rep. James H. D. Henderson, *Congressional Globe*, 39th Cong., 1st sess., March 28, 1866, vol. 36, p. 1702.

23. Sen. James Harlan, *Congressional Globe*, 41st Cong., 1st sess., April 1, 1869, vol. 41, p. 421.

24. *The Manitoban*, reprinted in Hall, "'A Serene Atmosphere'?" p. 142.

25. Robert Machray, archbishop of Rupert's Land, to Alexander Morris, May 24, 1875, Morris Papers, NAC, vol. 539, reel M-70, p. 4.

26. Morris, *Treaties of Canada with the Indians*, p. 217.

27. Mardock, *Reformers and the American Indian*, p. 25.

28. "Report of the Indian Peace Commission," January 7, 1868, Department of the Interior, *Report of the Commissioner of Indian Affairs for 1868*, p. 42.

29. Mattison, "Indian Missions and Missionaries," p. 141.

30. Jones, *Treaty of Medicine Lodge*, p. 122.

31. Mattison, "Indian Missions and Missionaries," p. 145.

32. "Report of the Great Peace Commission, January 7, 1868," pp. 43–44.

33. Prucha, *American Indian Policy in Crisis*, p. 22.

34. U.S. Department of the Interior, *Annual Report of the Commissioner of Indian Affairs for 1864*, pp. 3–4.

35. For a description of Indian educational philosophy and practices, see Miller, "'The Three Ls': The Traditional Education of the Indigenous Peoples," chap. 1 in *Shingwauk's Vision*, pp. 15–38.

36. Sen. John Henderson quoted in *Proceedings of the Great Peace Commission*, p. 80.

37. "Indian Peace Treaties," *The New York Times*, October 29, 1867, p. 4.

38. Sen. Lot M. Morrill, *Congressional Globe*, 40th Cong., 3d sess., February 15, 1869, vol. 40, p. 1208; and February 18, 1869, p. 1349.

39. David Laird, Minister of the Interior, "Report of the Department of the Interior for 1874," *Sessional Papers*, 1875, no. 8, vol. 7, p. 5.

40. J. A. N. Provencher, "Report of the Indian Commissioner," October 30, 1875, RG 10, NAC, vol. 3830, file 62,509 (pt. 1), reel C-10145, pp. 13–14.

41. See text of the treaties in Morris, *Treaties of Canada with the Indians*, pp. 315, 319, 323, 333, 345–46, 353. The commitment to the Blackfoot appears on p. 371.

42. Joseph Howe to Simpson, Dawson, and Pither, *Sessional Papers*, 1872, no. 22, vol. 7, p. 6.

43. Provencher, "Report of the Indian Commissioner," October 30, 1875, p. 16.

44. For example, see Alexander Morris to Sir John A. Macdonald, October 26, 1872, and February 25, 1873, Macdonald Papers, NAC, vol. 252, reel C-1673; and Alexander Morris to the secretary of state for the provinces, December 13, 1872, RG-10, NAC, vol. 3586, file 1137, reel C-10103.

45. *The Manitoban*, reprinted in Hall, "'A Serene Atmosphere'?" p. 146.

46. Morris, *Treaties of Canada with the Indians*, p. 217.

47. Rep. Benjamin Butler, *Congressional Globe*, 40th Cong., 2d sess., May 28, 1868, vol. 39, p. 2639.

48. M. G. Dickieson to the Minister of the Interior, January 7, 1873, RG 10, NAC, vol. 3609, file 3229, reel C-10106.

49. Carter, *Lost Harvests*, p. 18; Utley, *Last Days of the Sioux*, p. 23.

50. Carter, *Lost Harvests*, p. 17.

51. Trennert, *Alternative to Extinction*, p. 191; Utley, *Indian Frontier*, p. 61. See "Treaty of Fort Laramie with the Sioux, etc.," 1851, Article 5, in Kappler. *Indian Treaties*, pp. 594–95.

52. Sen. William Stewart, *Congressional Globe*, 41st Cong., 3d sess., February 22, 1871, vol. 43, p. 1508. See also Carter, *Lost Harvests*, p. 16.

53. Report by J. A. N. Provencher to the minister of the interior, December 31, 1873, RG-10, NAC, vol. 3608, file 3084, reel C-10105, p. 11 (English translation of original in French).

54. Morris, *Treaties of Canada with the Indians*, p. 205.

55. Hagan, "The Reservation Policy," p. 164.

56. Carter, *Lost Harvests*, p. 69.

57. See remarks by Henry Prince and Wasuskookoon in *The Manitoban*, reprinted in Hall, "'A Serene Atmosphere'?" pp. 146–47. These resulted in the "Outside Promises" memorandum composed on the last day of Treaty 1 negotiations. Memorandum, August 3, 1871, RG 10, NAC, vol. 3571, file 124 (pt. 2), reel C-10101; Alexander Morris to minister of the interior, March 27, 1877, 4–5. NAC, Morris Papers, NAC, reel M-69, pp. 3. See also petitions by Sweetgrass and Kihewin to Adams Archibald, April 1871, in Morris, *Treaties of Canada with the Indians*, pp. 170–71, and scattered references throughout Morris, including pp. 49, 63, 66, 68, 122.

58. Carter, *Lost Harvests*, p. 78.

59. Otis, *Dawes Act and the Allotment of Indian Lands*, p. 9.

60. Rep. Asahel Hubbard, *Congressional Globe*, 39th Cong., 1st sess., March 27, 1866, vol. 36, p. 1684.

61. Gen. John Sanborn quoted in *Proceedings of the Great Peace Commission*, p. 136.

62. See remarks by Sen. Timothy Howe and Sen. William Stewart, *Congressional Globe*, 41st Cong., 3d sess., February 22, 1871, vol. 43, p. 1502.

63. Carter, *Lost Harvests*, pp. 156, 211–13, 218–19; Dyck, "An Opportunity Lost," pp. 121, 125–26, 127, 133.

64. Alexander Campbell, Department of the Interior, August 6, 1873, Minute 983(a), Privy Council Minutes, RG-2, NAC, ser. 1, vol. 83, reel C-3305, pp. 2–3.

65. Remarks by Wemyss Simpson, in Morris, *Treaties of Canada with the Indians*, p. 36.

66. Adams Archibald quoted in *The Manitoban*, reprinted in Hall, "'A Serene Atmosphere'?" p. 128.

67. Memorandum of the Department of the Interior by David Laird, April 27, 1875, Minute 427(a), Privy Council Minutes, RG 2, NAC, ser. 1, vol. 108, reel C-3311, pp. 7–9. See also Hall, "'A Serene Atmosphere'?" p. 119.

68. Alexander Campbell to E. A. Meredith, 21 July 1873, RG 10, NAC, vol. 3603, file 2036, reel C-10104.

69. David Laird (unsigned) to Alexander Morris, July 7, 1875, RG 10, NAC, vol. 3621, file 4767, reel C-10108.

70. "Copy of a Report of a Committee of the Honourable the Privy Council," April 30, 1875, RG 10, NAC, vol. 3621, file 4767, reel C-10108.

71. Beal and Macleod, *Prairie Fire*, p. 53; Carter, *Lost Harvests*, p. 56.

72. Morris, *Treaties of Canada with the Indians*, p. 185.

73. Morris, *Treaties of Canada with the Indians*, pp. 217–18.

74. Alexander Morris to Ministry of the Interior, March 27 1877, MG-10, vol. 3636, file 6694-2, reel C-10111.

75. David Hall argues that the Indians of Treaty 1 compelled the government to make several alterations to its treaty-making plans (Hall, "'A Serene Atmosphere'?" p. 118). Blair Stonechild and Bill Waiser describe the persistent Indian negotiators of Treaty 6 as having "extracted a number of concessions from Morris" (Stonechild and Waiser, *Loyal till Death*, p. 20). John L. Taylor claims that the treaty terms were augmented "in the field" and that they "were made in response to Indian demands" (Taylor, "Indian Policy for the Canadian North-West," p. iii). These authors are all attempting to make a point about an active Indian role in treaty making, and their evidence supports such conclusions. They do not, however, extend the assertion of Indian influence beyond the expansion of treaty terms, a matter that warrants an in-depth examination itself.

76. Grant, *Moon of Wintertime*, p. 164. See also Miller, "Creating a Residential School System," chap. 4 in *Shingwauk's Vision*, pp. 89–120.

8. BUFFALO PRESERVATION

1. On the pervasiveness of the image of the "vanishing Indian," see Dippie, *Vanishing American*.

2. Trennert, *Alternative to Extinction*, pp. 138–39.

3. Carter, *Lost Harvests*, p. 43.

4. Indian Commissioner N. G. Taylor quoted in *Proceedings of the Great Peace Commission*, p. 90.

5. Sen. John Henderson quoted in *Proceedings of the Great Peace Commission*, p. 73.

6. Henderson quoted in *Proceedings of the Great Peace Commission*, p. 41.

7. Grinnell, *The Fighting Cheyennes*, p. 273.

8. Spotted Tail quoted in *Proceedings of the Great Peace Commission*, p. 93.

9. Satanta quoted in *Proceedings of the Great Peace Commission*, p. 74.

10. Spotted Tail quoted in *Proceedings of the Great Peace Commission*, p. 58.

11. Wooster, *The Military and United States Indian Policy*, p. 208.

12. Gen. W. T. Sherman quoted in Waltmann, "The Interior Department, War Department, and Indian Policy," p. 153.

13. Gen. Philip Sheridan quoted in Prucha, *The Great Father*, 1:561.

14. Columbus Delano, secretary of the interior, quoted in Prucha, *The Great Father*, 1:561.

15. Haines, *The Buffalo*, p. 205. Sen. Henry Wilson introduced the bill; *Congressional Globe*, 42nd Cong., 2d sess., February 16, 1872, vol. 45, p. 1063.

16. Buffalo Chief quoted in *Proceedings of the Great Peace Commission*, p. 82.

17. Treaty with the Kiowa and Comanche, Article 11, in Kappler, *Indian Treaties*, p. 980.

18. Jones, *Treaty of Medicine Lodge*, p. 180–82. For the terms of the Little Arkansas treaty, see "Treaty of the Little Arkansas with the Cheyenne and Arapaho," 1865, Articles 2 and 3, in Kappler, *Indian Treaties*, pp. 888–89.

19. Hagan, *United States-Comanche Relations*, p.32; Jones, *Treaty of Medicine Lodge*, pp. 176, 177.

20. "Treaty of the Little Arkansas," 1865, Articles 2 and 3, in Kappler, *Indian Treaties*, p. 888.

21. General Sherman quoted in *Proceedings of the Great Peace Commission*, p. 97.

22. Jones, *Treaty of Medicine Lodge*, p. 181.

23. Prucha, *American Indian Policy in Crisis*, p. 24.

24. *Congressional Globe*, 41st Cong., 2d sess., vol. 42, p. 4046.

25. *Proceedings of the Great Peace Commission*, p. 158.Over the course of its seventeen-month existence, the personnel on the Great Peace Commission fluctuated due to the more pressing commitments of individual members; for instance, General Sherman was recalled at one point to testify at Pres. Andrew Johnson's impeachment hearing. At its final meeting in October 1868, only two of the civilian commissioners—Taylor and Tappan—remained convinced of the humanitarian program. They were outnumbered and outvoted by the military officers present.

26. See remarks by Morris in *Treaties of Canada with the Indians*, pp. 228, 241; and remarks by Laird, pp. 258, 267, 271.

27. Morris, *Treaties of Canada with the Indians*, p. 211.

28. For a few examples among many, see Alexander Morris to the secretary of state, June 7, 1873; Alexander Morris to Alexander Mackenzie, August 20, 1875, vol. 553, reel M-70, pp. 1–2; and Alexander Morris to minister of the interior, October 26, 1876, January 19, 1877, February 19, 1877, Morris Papers, NAC, reel M-69.

29. David Laird (unsigned) to Alexander Morris, July 7, 1875, RG-10, NAC, vol. 3621, file 4767, reel C-10108.

30. This legislation established restrictions on when buffalo could be hunted, how many could be taken, and how old the buffalo had to be before killed. The law passed the Northwest Council in 1877, but either because it was not enthusiastically enforced or because it was impossible to make effective, the measure was repealed the following year. It was also very unpopular with the buffalo-hunting Indians. See remarks by David Laird in Morris, *Treaties of Canada with the Indians*, pp. 267–68; and in Dempsey, *Red Crow*,

pp. 108–9. For the legislation itself, see "An Ordinance for the Protection of the Buffalo," *Sessional Papers*, 1878, no. 45, vol. 11, p. 26.

31. Carter, *Lost Harvests*, pp. 68, 69, 70.

32. Morris, *Treaties of Canada with the Indians*, pp. 210–11.

33. The "famine relief" clause is unique to Treaty 6 and promises "that in the event hereafter of the Indians comprised within this treaty being overtaken by any pestilence, or by a general famine, the Queen, on being satisfied and certified thereof by her Indian Agent or Agents, will grant to the Indians assistance of such character and to such extent as her Chief Superintendent of Indian Affairs shall deem necessary and sufficient to relieve the Indians from the calamity that shall have befallen them." Morris, *Treaties of Canada with the Indians*, p. 354.

34. Alexander Morris to the minister of the interior, March 27, 1877, RG 10, NAC, vol. 3636, file 6694–2, reel C-10111, p. 10.

35. David Mills, minister of the interior, (unsigned) to Alexander Morris, March 1, 1877, RG 10, NAC, vol. 3636, file 6694–2, reel C-10111.

36. David Laird to David Mills, minister of the interior [n.d., missing pp.1–2], RG 10, NAC, vol. 3654, file 8904, reel C-10114, p. 4.

37. For example, see the preservation plans suggested by A. R. C. Selwyn in Selwyn to E. A. Meredith, April 21, 1874, Laird Papers, NAC; and Department of the Interior memorandum "containing suggestions from Colonel French, N.W.M.P., Father Andre, and a Select Committee of the North-West Council," April 15, 1876, RG-10, NAC, vol. 3641, file 7530, reel C-10112.

38. Morris, *Treaties of Canada with the Indians*, pp. 188, 193, 194–95, 228, 241.

39. David Mills, House of Commons, *Debates*, p. 993.

40. Morris, *Treaties of Canada with the Indians*, p. 267. See also "An Ordinance to Repeal the Ordinance for the Protection of the Buffalo," *Sessional Papers*, 1879, no. 86, vol. 9, p. 2.

9. RATIFICATION, INDIAN STATUS, AND TREATY MAKING

1. E. W. Wynkoop, U.S. Indian agent, to Charles E. Mix, Acting Commissioner of Indian Affairs, October 7, 1868, in U.S. Department of the Interior, *Annual Report of the Commissioner of Indian Affairs for the year 1868*, p. 81; "Report of the Secretary of War," November 20, 1868, *Congressional Globe*, 40th Cong., 3d sess., 1869, "Appendix," p. 8.

2. Rep. Aaron Sargent, *Congressional Globe*, 41st Cong., 2d sess., July 14, 1870, vol. 42, p. 5609.

3. Rep. James Beck, *Congressional Globe*, 41st Cong., 2d sess., July 2, 1870, vol. 42, p. 5137. See also Utley, *Lance and the Shield*, p. 82.

4. Rep. Aaron Sargent, *Congressional Globe*, 41st Cong., 2d sess., February 25, 1870, vol. 42, p. 1575.

5. Rep. William Lawrence, *Congressional Globe*, 40th Cong., 2d sess., March 21, 1868, vol. 39, p. 2065; and "Resolution by Mr. [George W.] Julian," 40th Cong., 2d sess., June 27, 1868, vol. 39, p. 3552.

6. Rep. John Kasson, *Congressional Globe*, 39th Cong., 2d sess., January 31, 1866, vol. 37, p. 894.

7. "Report of the Committee of Conference," *Congressional Globe*, 41st Cong., 2d sess., July 15, 1870, vol. 42, p. 5656.

8. Rep. James A. Garfield, *Congressional Globe*, 41st Cong., 2d sess., July 15, 1870, vol. 42, p. 5638.

9. "Copy of a Report of a Committee of the Honourable the Privy Council," November 4, 1874, RG-10, NAC, vol. 3611, file 3690, reel C-10106.

10. Memorandum by David Mills, minister of the interior (unsigned), January 31, 1877, RG-10, NAC, vol. 3636, file 6694–2, reel C-10111. Emphasis in the original.

11. Memorandum by David Mills, January 31, 1877.

12. "Resolutions of the Great Peace Commission, October 8, 1868," *Proceedings of the Great Peace Commission*, p. 158.

13. Bishop H. B. Whipple quoted in *Proceedings of the Great Peace Commission*, pp 149–50.

14. Felix Brunot quoted in Prucha, *American Indian Policy in Crisis*, pp. 65–66.

15. Prucha, *American Indian Policy in Crisis*, p. 66.

16. Rep. William Lawrence, *Congressional Globe*, 41st Cong., 2d sess., February 25, 1870, vol. 42, p. 1579.

17. See remarks by Rep. Horace Maynard, *Congressional Globe*, 41st Cong., 2d sess., March 3, 1870, vol. 42, p. 1671; and Sen. Samuel Pomeroy, 41st Cong., 3d sess., February 10, 1871, vol. 40, p. 1112.

18. Rep. Halbert Paine, *Congressional Globe*, 41st Cong., 2d sess., July 15, 1870, vol. 42, pp. 5642–43.

19. U.S. Senate, Committee on the Judiciary, *Resolution to Inquire into Effect of Fourteenth Amendment to the Constitution on Indian Tribes*, 41st Cong., 3d sess., 1871, S. Rept. 268, serial 1443, p. 9. See also Schmeckebier, *Office of Indian Affairs*, p. 65.

20. "Amendment to Bill 2615," *Congressional Globe*, 41st Cong., 3d sess., March 1, 1871, vol. 43, p. 1821.

21. Morris, *Treaties of Canada with the Indians*, p. 320.

22. Morris to Sir John A. Macdonald, March 5, 1873, Macdonald Papers, NAC, vol. 252, reel C-1673, p. 2.

23. Morris, *Treaties of Canada with the Indians*, pp. 28, 29, 93, 202, 208.

24. Morris, *Treaties of Canada with the Indians*, p. 61.

25. Morris, *Treaties of Canada with the Indians*, pp. 9, 295.

26. For example, see Morris, *Treaties of Canada with the Indians*, p. 355 (Treaty 6).

27. Treaties with the Kiowa and Comanche, Cheyenne and Arapaho, and Sioux, Article 11 (of each), in Kappler, *Indian Treaties*, pp. 980, 988, 1001.

28. Leighton, "Federal Indian Policy in Canada," p. 42.

29. Stonechild and Waiser, *Loyal till Death*, p. 26.

30. Stonechild and Waiser, *Loyal till Death*, p. 28.

31. Edward Lazarus, *Black Hills—White Justice*, pp. 401, 403.

32. See remarks by Father Constantine Scollen in Dempsey, *Crowfoot*, p. 106; Sen. Sherman, *Congressional Globe*, 39th Cong., 1st sess., April 18, 1866, p. 2013; and Sen. Henderson, 39th Cong., 2d sess., February 23, 1867, p. 1798.

33. Canadian sources offering this viewpoint include Buckley, *Wooden Ploughs to Welfare*, p. 33; and Jennings, "North West Mounted Police and Canadian-Indian Policy," p. 94. An American author who supports this view is William Hagan in "The Reservation Policy," p. 159 and *United States-Comanche Relations*, p. 37.

34. John Marshall quoted in Monikowski, "'Actual State of Things,'" p. 201.

10. "HUMANE, JUST, AND CHRISTIAN"

1. William McDougall, House of Commons, *Debates*, December 6, 1867, p. 203.

2. Albert James Smith, House of Commons, *Debates*, March 26, 1877, p. 995.

3. David Mills, Minister of the Interior, "Report of the Department of the Interior for 1877," *Sessional Papers*, 1878, no. 10, vol. 8, p. xvii.

4. Rep. John Pruyn, *Congressional Globe*, 40th Cong., 3d sess., February 4, 1869, vol. 40, p. 882.

5. Rep. Benjamin Butler, *Congressional Globe*, 40th Cong., 3d sess., January, 28, 1869, vol. 40, p. 683.

6. Sen. William Stewart, *Congressional Globe*, 41st Cong., 3d sess., February 23, 1871, vol. 43, p. 1575.

7. Sen. James Harlan, *Congressional Globe*, 41st Cong., 1st sess., April 1, 1869, vol. 41, p. 421.

8. For examples, see newspaper clippings from the *New York World* on Canadian management of the Indians, RG 10, NAC, vol. 3611, file 3676, reel C-10106; and Carl Schurz, "Present Aspects of the Indian Problem," p. 47.

9. Miles, "The Indian Problem," p. 42.

10. Sen. Jacob Howard, *Congressional Globe*, 40th Cong., 1st sess., July 18, 1867, Vol. 38, p. 711.

Bibliography

PRIMARY SOURCES

Manuscript Materials
Department of Indian Affairs. Central Registry Files. Black (Western) Series. Record Group 10. National Archives of Canada, Ottawa, Ontario.
Department of the Interior. North West Territories Branch Correspondence, 1873–83. Record Group 10. National Archives of Canada, Ottawa, Ontario.
Laird, David. Papers. Manuscript Group 27 I D10. National Archives of Canada, Ottawa, Ontario.
Macdonald, Sir John A. Papers. Manuscript Group 26(A). National Archives of Canada, Ottawa, Ontario.
Mackenzie, Alexander. Papers. Manuscript Group 26(B). National Archives of Canada, Ottawa, Ontario.
Morris, Alexander. Papers. General Correspondence, 1857–96, Including Material from Morris's Administration as Lieutenant-Governor of Manitoba and the North West Territories, 1872–77. Provincial Archives of Manitoba, Winnipeg. (Microfilm, National Archives of Canada.)
The Native American Reference Collection: Documents Collected by the Office of Indian Affairs, part 1, 1840–1900. University Publications of America. Canadian Museum of Civilization, Hull, Quebec.
Privy Council Office. Privy Council Minutes. Record Group 2. National Archives of Canada, Ottawa, Ontario.

Government Documents
Canada. House of Commons. *Debates*, 1867–78.
Canada. *Revised Statutes of Canada*, 1970.
Canada. *Sessional Papers*.
U.S. Congress. *Congressional Globe*. 46 vols. Washington DC, 1834–73.
U.S. Congress. Joint Committee on the Conduct of the War. *Massacre of Cheyenne Indians*. 38th Cong., 2d sess., 1865. S. Rept. 142. Serial 1214.
U.S. Congress. Joint Special Committee. *Condition of the Indian Tribes*. 39th Cong., 2d sess., 1867. S. Rept. 156. Serial 1279.

U.S. Department of the Interior. *Annual Report of the Commissioner of Indian Affairs*, 1864–71.

———. *Annual Report of the Secretary of the Interior*, 1864–71.

U.S. Department of War. *Annual Report of the Secretary of War*, 1864–71.

U.S. House of Representatives. *Aid to Civilization of Indians*. 41st Cong., 3d sess., 1871. H. Doc. 65. Serial 1454.

———. *Commissioners to All Indian Tribes*. 39th Cong., 2d sess., 1867. H. Doc. 88. Serial 1293.

———. *Issue of Arms to Kiowas and Other Indians*. 39th Cong., 2d sess., 1867. H. Doc. 41. Serial 1302.

———. *Management of Indians in British North America*. 41st Cong., 2d sess., 1870. H. Doc. 35. Serial 1443.

———. *Report of Colonel Parker on Indian Affairs*. 39th Cong., 2d sess., 1867. H. Doc. 37. Serial 1302.

———. *Report of Indian Peace Commissioners*. 40th Cong., 2d sess., 1868. H. Doc. 97. Serial 1337.

U.S. Senate. *Information Touching the Origin and Progress of Indian Hostilities on Frontier*. 40th Cong., 1st sess., 1868. S. Doc. 13. Serial 1308.

———. *Possessory Titles of Indian Tribes to Public Domain of United States*. 38th Cong., 2d sess., 1865. S. Rept. 138. Serial 1211.

———. *President's Message on Appropriations to Carry Out Indian Treaties Made by Peace Commission*. 41st Cong., 2d sess., 1870. S. Doc. 57. Serial 1406.

———. *Proceedings of a Military Commission convened by Special Orders No. 23 . . . in the case of Colonel J. M. Chivington*. 39th Cong., 2d sess., 1867. S. Doc. 26. Serial 1277.

———. *Reports upon Indian Affairs in Military Division of Missouri*. 40th Cong., 3d Sess., 1869. S. Doc. 40. Serial 1360.

———. *Resolution on Future Policy of the Government towards the Indians*. 40th Cong., 2d sess., 1868. S. Misc. Doc. 1. Serial 1319.

U.S. Senate. Committee on the Judiciary. *Senate Resolution to Inquire into Effect of Fourteenth Amendment to Constitution on Indian Tribes, and Whether by Provisions Thereof Indians Are Not Citizens of the United States, and Whether Thereby Various Treaties Are Not Annulled*. 41st Cong., 3d sess., 1871. S. Rept. 268. Serial 1443.

Books and Articles

Cowie, Isaac. *The Company of Adventurers: A Narrative of Seven Years in the Service of the Hudson's Bay Company during 1867–1874 on the Great Buffalo Plains with Historical and Biographical Notes and Comments*. 1913. Reprint, Lincoln: University of Nebraska Press, 1993.

De Brou, Dave, and Bill Waiser, eds. *Documenting Canada: A History of Modern Canada in Documents*. Saskatoon SK: Fifth House Publishers, 1992.

Erasmus, Peter (with Henry Thomson). *Buffalo Days and Nights*. Calgary AB: Glenbow-Alberta Institute, 1976.

Hawthorn, H. B., ed. *Survey of the Contemporary Indians of Canada: A Report on Economic Political and Education Needs and Policies*. 2 vols. Ottawa ON: Department of Indian Affairs, 1966–67.

Hunt, F. L. "Notes on the Qu'Appelle Treaty." *The Canadian Monthly and National Review* 9, no. 3 (1876): 173–83.

Jefferson, Robert. *Fifty Years on the Saskatchewan*. Battleford SK: Canadian North West Historical Society Publications, 1929.

Kappler, Charles, ed. *Indian Treaties, 1778–1883*. Washington DC: Government Printing Office, 1904. Reprint, Mattituck NY: Amereon House, 1999.

Laird, David. *Our Indian Treaties*. The Historical and Scientific Society of Manitoba, transaction no. 66. Winnipeg: Manitoba Free Press, 1905.

Miles, Gen. Nelson A. "The Indian Problem." *The North American Review* (winter 1973): 304–14. Reprinted from March 12, 1879.

Morris, Alexander. *The Treaties of Canada with the Indians of Manitoba and the North-West Territories including the Negotiations on which they were based*. 1880. Reprint, Saskatoon SK: Fifth House, 1991.

Proceedings of the Great Peace Commission, 1867–1868. With an introduction by Vine Deloria Jr. and Raymond DeMaillie. Washington DC: Institute for the Development of Indian Law, 1975.

Prucha, Francis Paul, ed. *Documents of United States Indian Policy*. 2d ed. Lincoln: University of Nebraska Press, 1990.

Report of the Royal Commission on Aboriginal Peoples. 5 vols. Ottawa ON: Minister of Supply and Services, 1996.

Richardson, James D., ed. *A Compilation of the Messages and Papers of the Presidents, 1789–1897*. Vol. 3. Washington DC: n.p., 1897.

Robinson, Doane. *A History of the Dakota or Sioux Indians: From Their Earliest Traditions and First Contact with White Men to the Final Settlement of the Last of Them upon Reservations and the Consequent Abandonment of the Old Tribal Life*. 1904. Reprint, Minneapolis: Ross & Haines, 1956.

Schurz, Carl. "Present Aspects of the Indian Problem." *The North American Review* (winter 1973): 45–54. Reprinted from July 1881.

Sherman, William T. *Memoirs of William T. Sherman*. Bloomington: University of Indiana Press, 1957.

———. *The Sherman Letters: Correspondence between General and Senator Sherman from 1837 to 1891*, edited by Rachel Sherman Thorndike. London: Sampson Low, Marston, and Company, 1894.

Taylor, Alfred A. "Medicine Lodge Peace Council." *Chronicles of Oklahoma* 2 (June 1924): 98–118.

SECONDARY SOURCES

Books and Articles

Ahearn, Robert G. *William Tecumseh Sherman and the Settlement of the West.* Norman: University of Oklahoma Press, 1956.

Allen, Robert S. *His Majesty's Indian Allies: British Indian Policy in the Defence of Canada, 1774–1815.* Toronto: Dundurn Press, 1992.

Bailey, John W. *Pacifying the Plains: General Alfred Terry and the Decline of the Sioux, 1866–1890.* Westport CT: Greenwood Press, 1979.

Baker, Donald G. "Color, Culture, and Power: Indian-White Relations in Canada and America." *Canadian Review of American Studies* 3, no. 1 (spring 1972): 3–20.

Bargar, B. D. *Lord Dartmouth and the American Revolution.* Columbia: University of South Carolina Press, 1965.

Beal, Bob, and Rod Macleod. *Prairie Fire: The 1885 North-West Rebellion.* Toronto: McClelland and Stewart, 1994.

Beatty, W. W. "The Goal of Indian Assimilation." *Canadian Journal of Economics and Political Science* 12 (1946): 395–404.

Berger, Thomas R. *A Long and Terrible Shadow: White Values, Native Rights in the Americas.* Vancouver BC: Douglas & McIntyre, 1991.

Berkhofer, Robert, Jr. *The White Man's Indian.* New York: Vintage Books, 1978.

Berthrong, Donald J. *The Cheyenne and Arapaho Ordeal: Reservation and Agency Life in the Indian Territory, 1875–1907.* Norman: University of Oklahoma Press, 1976.

——. *The Southern Cheyennes.* Norman: University of Oklahoma Press, 1963.

Black, Norman Fergus. *History of the Saskatchewan and the Old Northwest.* 2d ed. Regina SK: Northwest Historical Company, 1913.

Bolt, Christine. *American Indian Policy and American Reform: Case Studies of the Campaign to Assimilate the American Indians.* London: Allen & Unwin, 1987.

Bond Head, Francis. "Memorandum on the Aborigines of North America." In *The Native Imprint: The Contribution of First Peoples to Canada's Character,* vol. 2, *From 1815,* edited by Olive P. Dickason. Athabasca AB: Athabasca University, 1996.

Buckley, Helen. *From Wooden Ploughs to Welfare: Why Indian Policy Failed in the Prairie Provinces.* Montreal: McGill-Queen's University Press, 1992.

Carter, Sarah. *Lost Harvests: Prairie Indian Reserve Farmers and Government Policy.* Montreal: McGill-Queen's University Press, 1990.

Chalmers, John W. *Laird of the West.* Calgary AB: Detselig Enterprises, 1981.

Chaput, Donald. "Generals, Indian Agents, Politicians: The Doolittle Survey of 1865." *Western Historical Quarterly* 3 (July 1975), 269–82.

Choquette, Robert. *The Oblate Assault on Canada's Northwest.* Ottawa ON: University of Ottawa Press, 1995.

Christie, Ian R., and Benjamin W. Labaree. *Empire or Independence, 1760–1776: A British-American Dialogue on the Coming of the American Revolution.* Oxford: Phaidon Press, 1976.

Connelly, William E. "The Treaty Held at Medicine Lodge." *Kansas State Historical Society* 17 (1926–28): 601–6.

Danziger, Edmund Jefferson, Jr. *Indians and Bureaucrats: Administering the Reservation Policy during the Civil War.* Urbana: University of Illinois Press, 1974.

Dempsey, Hugh. *Big Bear: The End of Freedom.* Toronto: Greystone Books, 1984.

———. *Crowfoot: Chief of the Blackfeet.* Norman: University of Oklahoma Press, 1972.

———. "One Hundred Years of Treaty Seven." In *One Century Later: Western Canadian Reserve Indians since Treaty Seven,* edited by Ian A. L. Getty and Donald B. Smith. Vancouver: University of British Columbia Press, 1978.

———. *Red Crow: Warrior Chief.* 1980. Reprint, Saskatoon SK: Fifth House Publishers, 1995.

Dickason, Olive Patricia. *Canada's First Nations: A History of Founding Peoples from Earliest Times.* Toronto: McClelland and Stewart Publishers, 1994.

Dickason, Olive Patricia, ed. *The Native Imprint: The Contribution of First Peoples to Canada's Character.* Vol. 2, *From 1815.* Athabasca AB: Athabasca University, 1996.

Dictionary of Canadian Biography. Vols. 9–12. Toronto: University of Toronto Press, 1972–90.

Dippie, Brian W. *The Vanishing American: White Attitudes and U.S. Indian Policy.* Middletown CT: Wesleyan University Press, 1982.

Dyck, Noel. "An Opportunity Lost: The Initiative of the Reserve Agricultural Programme in the Prairie West." In *1885 and After: Native Society in Transition,* edited by F. Laurie Barron and James B. Waldram. Regina SK: Canadian Plains Research Centre, 1986.

———. *What is the Indian "Problem": Tutelage and Resistance in Canadian Indian Administration.* St. John's: Institute of Social and Economic Research, Memorial University of Newfoundland, 1991.

Ellis, Richard N. *General Pope and U.S. Indian Policy.* Albuquerque: University of New Mexico Press, 1970.

———. "The Humanitarian Generals." *The Western Historical Quarterly* 3 (April 1972): 169–78.

Ellis, Richard N., ed. *The Western American Indian: Case Studies in Tribal History.* Lincoln: University of Nebraska Press, 1972.

Fisher, Andrew H. "'This I Know from the Old People': Yakama Indian Treaty

Rights as Oral Tradition." *Montana: The Magazine of Western History* 49 (spring 1999): 2–17.

Fowler, Loretta. *Arapahoe Politics, 1851–1978: Symbols in Crises of Authority*. Lincoln: University of Nebraska Press, 1982.

Friesen, Gerald. *The Canadian Prairies: A History*. Toronto: University of Toronto Press, 1987.

Friesen, Jean. "Grant Me Wherewith to Make My Living." In *Aboriginal Resource Use in Canada: Historical and Legal Aspects*, edited by Kerry Abel and Jean Friesen. Winnipeg: University of Manitoba Press, 1991.

———. "Magnificent Gifts: The Treaties of Canada with the Indians of the Northwest, 1869–1876." In *Transactions of the Royal Society of Canada*. Ottawa ON: Royal Society of Canada, 1986.

Fritz, Henry. *The Movement for Indian Assimilation, 1860–1890*. Philadelphia: University of Pennsylvania Press, 1963.

Goodwill, Jean, and Norman Sluman. *John Tootoosis*. Winnipeg MB: Pemmican Publications, 1992.

Graham, Elizabeth. *Medicine Man to Missionary: Missionaries as Agents of Change among the Indians of Southern Ontario, 1784–1867*. Toronto: Peter Martin Associates, 1975.

Grant, John Webster. *Moon of Wintertime: Missionaries and the Indians of Canada in Encounter since 1543*. Toronto: University of Toronto Press, 1984.

Greene, Jack P. *Colonies to Nation, 1763–1789: A Documentary History of the American Revolution*. New York: W.W. Norton, 1975.

Grinnell, George Bird. *The Fighting Cheyennes*. 1915. Reprint, Norman: University of Oklahoma Press, 1971.

Hagan, William. *American Indians*. Chicago: The University of Chicago Press, 1971.

———. "Private Property: The Indian's Door to Civilization." *Ethnohistory* 3 (spring 1956): 126–37.

———. "The Reservation Policy: Too Little and Too Late." In *Indian-White Relations: A Persistent Paradox*, edited by Jane Smith and Robert M. Kvasnicka. Cambridge MA: Harvard University Press, 1972.

———. *United States-Comanche Relations: The Reservation Years*. New Haven CT: Yale University Press, 1976. Reprint, Norman: University of Oklahoma Press, 1990.

Haines, Francis. *The Buffalo*. New York: Thomas Y. Crowell Company, 1970.

Hall, David J. "'A Serene Atmosphere'? Treaty 1 Revisited." In *The Native Imprint: The Contribution of First Peoples to Canada's Character*, vol. 2, *From 1815*, edited by Olive P. Dickason. Athabasca AB: Athabasca University, 1996.

Hassrich, Royal B. *The Sioux: Life and Customs of a Warrior Society*. Norman: University of Oklahoma Press, 1964.

Hedren, Paul L. *Fort Laramie in 1876: Chronicle of a Frontier Post at War.* Lincoln: University of Nebraska Press, 1988.

Heimert, Alan, and Andrew Delbanco, eds. *The Puritans in America: A Narrative Anthology.* Cambridge MA: Harvard University Press, 1985.

Hill, Douglas. *The Opening of the Canadian West: Where Strong Men Gathered.* New York: John Day Company, 1967.

Hyde, George E. *Red Cloud's Folk: A History of the Oglala Sioux Indians.* 1937. Reprint, Norman: University of Oklahoma Press, 1976.

———. *Spotted Tail's Folk: A History of the Brule Sioux.* Norman: University of Oklahoma Press, 1961.

Jennings, John. "The Plains Indians and the Law." In *Men in Scarlet,* edited by Hugh A. Dempsey. Calgary AB: Historical Society of Alberta in association with McClelland and Stewart West, 1974.

Johnson, Allen, and Dumas Malone, eds. *Dictionary of American Biography.* Vol. 3. 1930. Reprint, New York: Charles Scribner's Sons, 1959.

Jones, Douglas. "Medicine Lodge Revisited." *Kansas Historical Society* 35 (summer 1969): 130–42.

———. *The Treaty of Medicine Lodge: The Story of the Great Treaty Council as Told by Eyewitnesses.* Norman: University of Oklahoma Press, 1966.

Kelsey, Harry. "The Doolittle Report of 1867: Its Preparation and Shortcomings." *Arizona and the West* 17 (summer 1975), 107–20.

Larson, Robert W. *Red Cloud: Warrior-Statesman of the Lakota Sioux.* Norman: University of Oklahoma Press, 1997.

Lazarus, Edward. *Black Hills-White Justice: The Sioux Nation versus the United States, 1775 to the Present.* New York: Harper Collins Publishers, 1991.

Leckie, William H. *The Military Conquest of the Southern Plains.* Norman: University of Oklahoma Press, 1963.

Leslie, John F., and Ron Maguide, eds. *The Historical Development of the Indian Act.* 2d ed. Ottawa ON: Treaties and Historical Research Centre, Indian and Northern Affairs, 1978.

Looy, A. J. "Saskatchewan's First Indian Agent: M. G. Dickieson." *Saskatchewan History* 32, no. 3 (autumn 1969): 105–15.

MacInnis, T. R. L. "History of Indian Administration in Canada." *Canadian Journal of Economics and Political Science* 12, no. 3 (1946): 387–94.

Macleod, R. C. *The NWMP and Law Enforcement, 1873–1905.* Toronto: University of Toronto Press, 1976.

Mardock, Robert W. "The Plains Frontier and the Indian Peace Policy, 1865–1880." *Nebraska History* 49 (summer 1968): 187–201.

———. *The Reformers and the American Indian.* Columbia: University of Missouri Press, 1971.

Mattingly, Arthur P. "The Great Plains Peace Commission of 1867." *Journal of the West* 15 (July 1976): 23–37.

Mattison, Ray H. "Indian Missions and Missionaries on the Upper Missouri to 1890." *Nebraska History* 38, no. 2, (June 1957): 127–54.

———. "Indian Reservation System on the Upper Missouri, 1865–1890." *Nebraska History* 36 (September 1955): 141–72.

Mayhall, Mildred P. *The Kiowas*. 2d ed. Norman: University of Oklahoma Press, 1972.

Meyer, Roy W. *History of the Santee Sioux: United States Indian Policy on Trial*. Lincoln: University of Nebraska Press, 1967.

Miller, J. R. *Shingwauk's Vision: A History of Native Residential Schools*. Toronto: University of Toronto Press, 1996.

———. *Skyscrapers Hide the Heavens: A History of Indian-White Relations in Canada*. Rev. ed. University of Toronto Press: Toronto, 1989.

Milloy, John. "The Early Indian Acts: Developmental Strategy and Constitutional Change." In *The Native Imprint: The Contribution of First Peoples to Canada's Character*, vol. 2, *From 1815*. Athabasca AB: Athabasca University, 1996.

———. "'Our Country': The Significance of the Buffalo Resource for a Plains Cree Sense of Territory." In *Aboriginal Resource Use in Canada: Historical and Legal Aspects*, edited by Kerry Abel and Jean Friesen. Winnipeg: University of Manitoba Press, 1991.

Nichols, Roger L. *Indians in the United States and Canada: A Comparative History*. Lincoln: University of Nebraska Press, 1998.

Nix, James Ernest. *Mission among the Buffalo: The Labours of the Reverends George M. and John C. McDougall in the Canadian Northwest, 1860–1876*. Toronto: Ryerson Press, 1960.

Olson, James C. *Red Cloud and the Sioux Problem*. Lincoln: University of Nebraska Press, 1965.

Otis, Delos Sacket. *The Dawes Act and the Allotment of Indian Lands*. Edited by Francis P. Prucha. 1934. Reprint, Norman: University of Oklahoma Press, 1973.

Patterson, E. Palmer. *The Canadian Indian: A History since 1500*. Don Mills ON: Collier-Macmillan Canada, 1972.

———. "The Colonial Parallel: A View of Indian History." *Ethnohistory* 18 (1971): 1–17.

Plummer, Mark. *Frontier Governor: Samuel J. Crawford of Kansas*. Lawrence: University Press of Kansas, 1971.

Price, Richard, ed. *The Spirit of the Alberta Indian Treaties*. Edmonton AB: Pica Pica Press, 1987.

Priest, Loring Benson. *Uncle Sam's Stepchildren: The Reformation of United States Indian Policy, 1865–1887*. 1942. Reprint, New York: Octagon Books, 1972.

Prucha, Francis Paul. *American Indian Policy in Crisis: Christian Reformers and the Indian, 1865–1900*. Norman: University of Oklahoma Press, 1976.

———. *American Indian Treaties: The History of a Political Anomaly.* Berkeley: University of California Press, 1994.

———. *Atlas of American Indian Affairs.* Lincoln: University of Nebraska Press, 1990.

———. *The Great Father: The United States Government and the American Indians.* 2 vols. Lincoln: University of Nebraska Press, 1984.

———. *Indian Policy in the United States: Historical Essays.* Lincoln: University of Nebraska Press, 1981.

———. *The Indians in American Society: From the Revolutionary War to the Present.* Berkeley: University of California Press, 1985.

Roe, F. G. "The Extermination of the Buffalo in Western Canada." *Canadian Historical Review* 15 (1934): 1–23.

Samek, Hana. *The Blackfoot Confederacy 1880–1920: A Comparative Study of Canadian and U.S. Indian Policy.* Albuquerque: University of New Mexico Press, 1987.

Satz, Ronald. *American Indian Policy in the Jacksonian Era.* Lincoln: University of Nebraska Press, 1975.

Schmeckebier, Laurence F. *The Office of Indian Affairs: Its History, Activities, and Organization.* Baltimore: The Johns Hopkins Press, 1927.

Shapiro, Martin, ed. *The Constitution of the United States and Related Documents.* Arlington Heights IL: Harlan Davidson, 1973.

Sharp, Paul F. *Whoop-Up Country: The Canadian-American West, 1865–1885.* Minneapolis: University of Minnesota Press, 1955.

Sosin, Jack M. *The Revolutionary Frontier, 1763–1683.* Toronto: Holt, Rinehart and Winston, 1967.

Stanley, George F. G. *The Birth of Western Canada: A History of the Riel Rebellions.* 1936. Reprint, Toronto: University of Toronto Press, 1992.

Stanley, Henry M. "A British Journalist Reports the Medicine Lodge Councils of 1867." *Kansas Historical Quarterly* 33 (autumn 1967): 253–54.

Stonechild, Blair, and Bill Waiser. *Loyal till Death: Indians and the North-West Rebellion.* Calgary AB: Fifth House, 1997.

Surtees, R. J. "The Development of an Indian Reserve Policy in Canada." *Ontario History* 61 (1969): 87–98.

Taylor, John L. "Canada's North-West Indian Policy in the 1870s: Traditional Premises and Necessary Innovations." In *Approaches to Native History in Canada,* edited by D. A. Muise. Ottawa ON: Museum of Man, 1977.

Thomas, Lewis Herbert. *The Struggle for Responsible Government in the North-West Territories, 1870–97.* 2d ed. Toronto: University of Toronto Press, 1978.

Thrapp, Dan L. *Encyclopedia of Frontier Biography.* 3 vols. Lincoln: University of Nebraska Press, 1988.

Titley, E. Brian. *A Narrow Vision: Duncan Campbell Scott and the Administration of Indian Affairs in Canada.* Vancouver: University of British Columbia Press, 1986.

Tobias, John L. "Canada's Subjugation of the Plains Cree, 1879–1885." In *The Native Imprint: The Contribution of First Peoples to Canada's Character.* vol. 2, *From 1815,* edited by Olive P. Dickason. Athabasca AB: Athabasca University, 1996.

———. "Protection, Civilization, Assimilation: An Outline History of Canada's Indian Policy." In *Sweet Promises: A Reader on Indian-White Relations in Canada,* edited by J. R. Miller. Toronto: University of Toronto Press, 1991.

Tough, Frank. *"As Their Natural Resources Fail": Native Peoples and the Economic History of Northern Manitoba, 1870–1930.* Vancouver: University of British Columbia Press, 1996.

Trennert, Robert A., Jr. *Alternative to Extinction: Federal Indian Policy and the Beginnings of the Reservation System, 1846–1851.* Philadelphia: Temple University Press, 1975.

Trexler, H. A. "The Buffalo Range of the Northwest." *Mississippi Valley Historical Review* 7 (March 1921): 348–62.

Tucker, Robert W., and David C. Hendrickson. *The Fall of the First British Empire: Origins of the War of American Independence.* Baltimore: Johns Hopkins University Press, 1982.

Upton, L. F. S. "The Origins of Canadian Indian Policy." *Journal of Canadian Studies* 8 (1973): 51–61.

Utley, Robert M. *Frontier Regulars: The United States Army and the Indian, 1866–1891.* Lincoln: University of Nebraska Press, 1973.

———. *Frontiersmen in Blue: The United States Army and the Indian, 1848–1865.* Lincoln: University of Nebraska Press, 1967.

———. *The Indian Frontier of the American West, 1846–1890.* Albuquerque: University of New Mexico Press, 1984.

———. *The Lance and the Shield: The Life and Times of Sitting Bull.* New York: Henry Holt and Company, 1993.

———. *The Last Days of the Sioux Nation.* New Haven CT: Yale University Press, 1963.

Vestal, Stanley. *Warpath and Council Fire: The Plains Indians' Struggle for Survival in War and Diplomacy, 1851–1891.* New York: Random House, 1948.

Waite, Peter B. *Canada 1874–1896: Arduous Destiny.* The Canadian Centenary Series. Toronto: McClelland and Stewart, 1971.

Washburn, Wilcomb. "Indian Removal Policy: Administrative, Historical and Moral Criteria for Judging its Success or Failure." *Ethnohistory* 12 (summer 1965): 274–78.

———. *Red Man's Land—White Man's Law: A Study of the Past and Present Status of the American Indian.* New York: Scribner's, 1971.

Weber, David J. *The Spanish Frontier in North America.* New Haven CT: Yale University Press, 1992.

White-Harvey, Robert. "Reservation Geography and the Restoration of Native Self-Government." *Dalhousie Law Journal* 17, no. 2 (fall 1994): 587–611.

Wooster, Robert. *The Military and United States Indian Policy, 1865–1903.* New Haven CT: Yale University Press, 1988.

Dissertations and Theses

Gulig, Anthony G. "In Whose Interest? Government-Indian Relations in Northern Saskatchewan and Wisconsin, 1905–1951." Ph.D. diss., University of Saskatchewan, 1992.

Jennings, John. "The North West Mounted Police and Indian Policy, 1873–1896." Ph.D. diss., University of Toronto, 1979.

Leighton, J. D. "The Development of Federal Indian Policy in Canada, 1840–1890." Ph.D. diss., University of Western Ontario, 1975.

McKay, Raoul. "Fighting for Survival: The Swampy Cree of Treaty No. 5 in an Era of Transition, 1875–1930." Ph.D. diss., University of Toronto, 1991.

Monikowski, Richard A. "'The Actual State of Things': American Indians, Indian Law, and American Courts between 1800 and 1835." Ph.D. diss., University of New Mexico, 1997.

Owram, Doug. "White Savagery: Some Canadian Reaction to American Indian Policy, 1867–1885." Master's thesis, Queen's University, 1971.

Parrish, Cora Hoffman. "The Indian Peace Commission of 1867 and the Western Indians." Master's thesis, University of Oklahoma, 1958.

Ronaghan, A. "The Archibald Administration in Manitoba, 1870–1872." Ph.D. diss., University of Manitoba, 1978.

Sowby, J. K. "Macdonald the Administrator: Department of the Interior and Indian Affairs." Master's thesis, Queen's University, 1980.

Surtees, Robert J. "Indian Land Cessions in Ontario, 1763–1862: The Evolution of a System." Ph.D. diss., Carleton University, 1982.

Taylor, John L. "The Development of an Indian Policy for the Canadian North-West, 1864–1879." Ph.D. diss., Queen's University, 1975.

Waltmann, Henry G. "The Interior Department, War Department, and Indian Policy, 1865–1887." Ph.D. diss., University of Nebraska, 1962.

Index

DATE DUE
